Dress and Ethnicity

Change Across Space and Time

EDITED BY
Joanne B. Eicher

BERG

Oxford • Washington, D.C.

First published in 1995 by
Berg Publishers Limited
Editorial offices:
150 Cowley Road, Oxford, OX4 1JJ, UK
13590 Park Center Road, Herndon, VA 22071, USA

Library of Congress Cataloging-in-Publication Data

A catalogue record for this book is available from the Library of
Congress.

British Library Cataloguing-in-Publication Data

A catalogue record for this book is available from the British Library.

Frontcover Photograph: Carolyn Nqozi Eicher.

ISBN 0 85496 879 2 (Cloth)
1 85973 003 5 (Paper)

Printed in the United Kingdom by WBC Bookbinders, Bridgend,
Mid Glamorgan.

Contents

Acknowledgements

This volume was enhanced by Shirley Ardener's continued networking and suggestions for additional contributors following the original set of papers presented at the Institute of Social Anthropology at the University of Oxford. An Educational Leadership Award from the College of Human Ecology at the University of Minnesota in 1994 provided me with funds to engage the energies and creativity of Bobbie Sumberg in bringing closure to the manuscripts for submission to Berg Publishers. I appreciate the efforts of Dean Mary Heltsley, College of Human Ecology, for her initiative in originating these faculty awards and to Bobbie for her efforts and perseverance. Diana Eicher picked up where Bobbie left off, and I appreciate her following through with the final details.

Many thanks to Rebecca Bailey for the drawings for the Bridgwood, Durham, Griebel and Renne chapters and to Donna Yamashita-Berry for the Bunu Yoruba map. Kimberly Miller, a colleague from the University of Kentucky, read and critiqued selected manuscripts and raised useful questions. Contributors met deadlines and requests for changes most cheerfully, and I thank each of you. Appreciation goes to Diana Eicher, Masami Suga and Donna Yamashita-Berry for indexing.

Finally, I wish to acknowledge the steady support of my father, George C. Bubolz, in his 94th year who was largely responsible for my entering graduate school and who has always been a source of inspiration.

Joanne B. Eicher
Regents' Professor
University of Minnesota

Preface

This volume arose from a seminar on identity and ethnicity sponsored by the Institute of Social Anthropology at the University of Oxford. Organized by Shirley Ardener, Tamara Dragadze, and Jonathan Weber, in 1989 with the subtitle "The Social Construction of Ethnic Identity", the seminar took as its theme the significance of dress. The organizers asked me to edit a volume from the seminar papers along with others to be invited. My purpose as editor has been to bring together scholars doing fieldwork, in as many continents as possible.

The concept of ethnicity as used in the social sciences is relatively recent, usually being dated back in anthropology to the volume edited by Fredrik Barth (1969), followed by Ardener (1972), A. Cohen (1973), DeVos and Romanucci-Ross (1982), and the more recent work of Tonkin, Chapman, and McDonald (1987) as well as overview essays by R. Cohen (1978) and Yinger (1985). The literature on ethnicity continues to grow and controversies over definitions of ethnicity still plentiful; the purpose of this volume is not to present a uniform view of dress as an aspect of ethnic identification, but to contribute to these controversies. The authors of the articles in this book represent a variety of disciplinal orientations including social anthropology, textiles and apparel, art history, and folklore, and consequently take several different stances in their use of the term that illustrate the complexity of the concept of ethnicity.

The definition of dress follows that used by Eicher and Roach-Higgins (1993); and Roach-Higgins and Eicher (1992) which includes modifications and supplements to the body, extending concern beyond apparel to allow appraisal of body and hair conformation, texture and color, scent and sound. Four of the eight papers presented at the seminar were available for this book and the remainder were then commissioned. All are based on the scholars' own field research.

References

Ardener, E. (1972a), "Language, Ethnicity and Population," *Journal of the Anthropological Society* of Oxford, 3 (3), pp. 125–32.

Barth, F. (1969), *Ethnic Groups and Boundaries: The Social Organization of Culture Difference*, London: Allen and Unwin.

Cohen, A. (1973), *Urban Ethnicity*, London: Tavistock Publications.

Cohen, R. (1978), "Ethnicity: Problem and Focus in Anthropology", *Annual Review of Anthropology*, pp. 379–403.

deVos, G., and Romanucci-Ross, L. (1982), *Ethnicity: Cultural Continuities and Change*, Chicago: University of Chicago Press.

Eicher, J.B., and Roach-Higgins, M.E. (1992), "Describing and Classifying Dress: Implications for the Study of Gender", in R. Barnes, and J.B. Eicher (eds), *Dress and Gender: Making and Meaning*, Providence and Oxford: Berg.

Roach-Higgins, M.E., and Eicher, J.B. (1992), "Dress and Identity", *Clothing and Textile Research Journal*, vol. 10, no. 4, pp. 1–8.

Tonkin, E., McDonald, M., and Chapman, M. (1989), *Ethnicity and History*, London and New York: Routledge.

Yinger, J.M. (1985), "Ethnicity", *Annual Review of Sociology*, vol. 11, pp. 151–80.

Notes on Contributors

Rebecca Bailey, illustrator for chapters by Ann Bridgwood, Deborah Durham, Helen Griebel, and Elisha Renne, is head of the art department at Meredith College, Raleigh, North Carolina where she teaches drawing and art education. Her PhD research at Michigan State University focused on changing perspectives of dress for pregnant women in the United States from 1850 to 1980. She drew from that research for a chapter in *Dress and Gender*.

Carolyn Behrman conducted her dissertation research on women's work in the changing atmosphere of Swaziland for her degree in anthropology at the University of Pennsylvania. Her teaching, research and writing explore topics such as health and work which cross the subdisciplinary boundaries between the physical and cultural social sciences. On the cultural side, she is currently co-editing a volume on the issues of identity and transnational process.

Ann Bridgwood has degrees in sociology and social anthropology. She taught social science in further education for a number of years and currently tutors for the UK Open University. In addition to researching Turkish Cypriot marriage, she carried out a number of research projects on education, women's employment, women in science and technology and on health. She is employed at the UK Office of Population, Censuses and Surveys, where she currently leads a study of the physical health of prisoners, having previously worked on the General Household Survey.

Malcolm Chapman studied social anthropology at Oxford University, where he completed his doctorate in 1986. He has carried out several years' fieldwork in Celtic-speaking areas. His publications include *The Gaelic Vision in Scottish Culture* (1978) and *The Celts: the construction of a Myth* (1992). In 1989 he took an MBA at the University of Bradford, and subsequently held various posts in teaching and research in the University of Bradford Management Centre. Since 1989 he has been working on the meeting of social anthropology and business studies. He is currently Lecturer in International Business at the University of Leeds.

Deborah Durham is an Assistant Professor of Anthropology at Sweet Briar College in Virginia. She has conducted research on the dialectic between a minority Herero identity and state citizenship in African liberal democracy (Botswana) and is currently working on a book on the subject. She focuses in particular upon public ceremony, cultural associations, and dress.

Joanne B. Eicher specializes in teaching and research on dressing the body as a system of communication. She lived in Nigeria from 1963–66 and conducted research there, specializing in Kalabari dress and culture since 1980. Compiler of two bibliographies of African dress and author of *Nigerian Handcrafted Textiles*, she co-edited *Dress and Gender* with Ruth Barnes for Berg Publishers in 1992 and *Dress and Identity* with Mary Ellen Roach-Higgins and Kim K.P. Johnson for Fairchild Publications in 1995.

Tonye V. Erekosima, grandson of the Kalabari Amanyanabo (King) Kieni Amachree V and great-grandson of the prominent Kalabari trader, John Bull, specialized in the social sciences for his post-secondary education in the U.S. at University of Rochester (B.A.), University of California, Los Angeles (M.A.), Catholic University of America (Ph.D.). His research interests mainly focus on cultural change and identity using the Kalabari as a case study. He is senior arts fellow at the University of Port Harcourt and was director of the Instructional Resources Center.

Helen Bradley Griebel received her Ph.D. from the Department of Folklore and Folklife, University of Pennsylvania. Her research focus is material culture particularly traditional crafts, dress, and foodways. She divides her fieldwork between the U.S. and Greece and recently did field research in Ghana. Currently, she teaches African American Art and American Folk Art at the University of Minnesota.

Carola Lentz is completing her post-doctoral degree on ethnicity in Northwestern Ghana. Prior to her fieldwork in northern Ghana she was Assistant Professor of Anthropology at the Institut fur Ethnologie Freie Universitat Berlin. She has also carried out extensive field work in Ecuador and her Ph.D dissertation was on labor migration among Indian peasants in the Ecuadorian highlands.

Annette Lynch is Assistant Professor of Textiles and Apparel and Curator of Textiles and Costume at the University of Northern Iowa. Her current research interests include Hmong American textiles and dress, West African textiles and dress, and historic costume of the midwestern United States. In addition to ethnicity and dress, she has published articles on dress and cultural change as well as dress and the cultural construction of gender.

D.P. Martinez did her first degree at the University of Chicago, and her Diploma and DPhil in Social Anthropology at Oxford. She is currently a Lecturer in Anthropology with Reference to Japan at the School of Oriental and African Studies, University of London. Among her recent publications are: 'Women as bosses: perceptions of the *ama* and their work' in *Japanese Women Working* edited by Janet Hunter, and 'Women and ritual' in *Ceremony and Ritual in Japanese Society* edited by Jan van Bremen and D P Martinez. London: Routledge.

Elisha P. Renne is with Office of Population Research, Princeton University. Her M.A. thesis on Kalabari Ijo textiles was followed by research on handweaving in the Bunu and Ekiti Yoruba areas of southwestern Nigeria for her Ph.D. Several of her papers on the Bunu material have been published in journals including *Textile History, African Arts* and *Man*. The book *Cloth That Does Not Die: The Meaning of Cloth in Bunu Social Life* (1995) is published by University of Washington Press.

Yvonne J. Seng is Visiting Lecturer in Islamic History at Wesley Theological Seminary in Washington, D.C. She received her Ph.D. from the University of Chicago in Near Eastern Languages and Civilizations. Her scholarship focuses on everyday life in Middle Eastern societies with special emphasis on ethnography as well as legal strategies of both the community-at-large and of women and non-Muslim minorities.

Masami Suga native of Osaka, Japan, is completing research on the aesthetics of Japanese weddings for her Ph.D. in Design, Housing, and Apparel at the University of Minnesota. Her master's research at the University of Minnesota focused on the life history of a Hmong textile artist who fled Laos and settled in Minnesota. She graduated from Tezukayama Gakuin Junior College with a degree in English Literature and moved to the United States to complete a B.A. degree in anthropology at Macalester College. She has been Assistant to the Gallery Director at the Goldstein Gallery, a design and teaching museum of the Department of Design, Housing, and Apparel.

Barbara Sumberg has her Master's degree from the University of Minnesota. Fieldwork for her thesis, from which this article was taken, was conducted in Nembe in the winter of 1992–93. She conducted fieldwork for the Madras Craft Council in Tamil Nadu and Andra Pradesh in Madras, India in 1993–94 on production of the handwoven cotton textile known as Indian madras which is worn extensively in southeastern Nigeria.

Betty Wass is Associate Director of the African Studies Program at the University of Wisconsin-Madison. Her Ph.D. is from Michigan State University in Human Ecology. She spent five years living in Egypt in the 1980s where she worked at the American University in Cairo. Her publications include articles on the *kabba sloht* of Sierra Leone and Yoruba headdress.

Linda Welters is Professor in the Textiles, Fashion Merchandising, and Design Department at the University of Rhode Island. She is also a Research Associate of the Peloponnesian Folklore Foundation in Nafplion, Greece. She conducted field research in Greece in 1983, 1986, and 1990. In addition to European traditional dress, her research interests include the material culture of New England. Her publications include a book titled *Women's Traditional Costume in Attica, Greece*.

Introduction: Dress as Expression of Ethnic Identity

Joanne B. Eicher

Ethnic Dress Defined

Dress is a coded sensory system of non-verbal communication that aids human interaction in space and time. The codes of dress include visual as well as other sensory modifications (taste, smell, sound, and feel) and supplements (garments, jewelry, and accessories) to the body which set off either or both cognitive and affective processes that result in recognition or lack of recognition by the viewer. As a system, dressing the body by modifications and supplements often does facilitate or hinder consequent verbal or other communication. The body modifications and supplements that mark the ethnic identity of an individual are ethnic dress.

Ethnic dress and ethnicity are linked. Manning Nash observed that although ethnicity and ethnic group seem to have clear references, they are "among the most complicated, volatile and emotionally charged words and ideas in the lexicon of social science" (1989: 1). Similarly, "ethnic dress" seems also to have a clear referent. Yet, when examined closely, its use has varied widely, often becoming a synonym for or encompassing other categories such as religious or occupational dress. Ethnic dress has been noted as an aspect of ethnicity, but it has been neglected analytically. This volume sets out to correct this neglect.

Ethnic Dress Across Space and Time

The concepts of space and time are involved in each chapter. The contents are based on research in five continents (Africa, Asia, Europe, North America, and South America) and cover decades, or even several centuries. The authors demonstrate that ethnic dress is

1

not static; several case histories show significant change in form and detail, calling into question the accuracy of designating ethnic dress as "traditional" when this term is used to indicate lack of change.

Change is a critical aspect of each chapter. Six chapters deal with groups that have moved across geographical space: five involve migration from one continent to another and the sixth covers rural-urban migration within one country. Each involves a discussion of history of contact with other peoples; Deborah Durham outlines the use of the Herero woman's dress in Botswana as a national logo, Ann Bridgwood describes the dress of young women for Cypriot courting parties in London, and Carola Lentz reveals how Indian migrants to the city in Ecuador try to hide their Indian identity. Helen Griebel provides a perspective of the movement of the woman's headwrap from West Africa to America over both space and time, and Annette Lynch gives insight on Hmong-American teenagers' dress for New Year celebrations in St. Paul.

These chapters raise the issue of what can be defined as traditional. Yvonne Seng and Betty Wass argue that what Palestinian brides in America see as traditional has neither the same form nor the same functional purpose as dress from earlier times, as shown in examples from museums in Bethlehem and Hebron. Nevertheless, the dress chosen by Palestinian brides in America evokes feelings of pride in being Palestinian and has a political emphasis. Lynch's analysis of the dress of the young Hmong Americans in St. Paul shows that their ensembles no longer distinguish them as exclusively White Hmong or Blue Hmong as it did in Laos; instead they choose to mix several types of dress that result in a more general designation of Hmong. These examples demonstrate that contact with others, through migration out or by contact with travelers, can provoke change in items and ensembles.

In contrast, Lola Martinez and Masami Suga tackle ethnic dress within the geographic space of Japan where nearly everyone is of the same ethnic heritage. Their articles raise the question of how the Japanese communicate ethnicity through dress. Each provides a different perspective, one scrutinizing the naked divers and the other the royal wedding dress of 1993. The wedding garb of the royal couple came from the past, but it has an impact on the wedding garb of ordinary Japanese who dress in a more cosmopolitan fashion on a daily basis.

Malcolm Chapman and Linda Welters turn their attention to Europe. Chapman sees traditional dress in Brittany and Scotland being manipulated for tourist appeal; the kilt was never the popular dress in Scotland, and the white lace *coiffes* of Brittany have been artificially frozen in time. Welters distinguishes several ethnic groups in Greece, such as the Arvanites, Albanians, and Sarakatsani, and contradicts earlier works which claimed distinctions in dress were geographically, that is regionally, based. Instead, Welters points to ethnic consistency across regions of Greece and to the misuse of the term "Vlach," which is often glossed as "bumpkin" and does not necessarily designate a distinct ethnic group.

Two chapters on West Africa covering two adjoining groups, the Nembe (by Barbara Sumberg) and Kalabari (by Tonye Erekosima and myself) also present historical data. Details of dress become critical points of distinction between the Nembe and Kalabari, just as they are critical differentiators of rank within each group. In addition, the construct of cultural authentication is introduced as a term of analysis when assessing articles of dress that become selected, characterized, incorporated, and transformed by a group that has had contact with others. A third West African example, that of the Bunu Yoruba described by Elish Renne, also provides historical material about the weaving of marriage cloth that distinguishes the Bunu from non-Bunu.

Ethnic Dress and Gender

Several chapters in *Dress and Gender* (Barnes and Eicher 1993) included issues of ethnicity along with gender. Similarly the chapters in this book which discuss ethnicity also involve gender, for the two are interwoven in the world of the 1990s. Gender issues involve modesty and flamboyance, concealment and exposure in dress, concerns which are often related to how members of an ethnic group identify proper dress for men and women within cultural parameters. Frequently the focus is on women's dress for specific ethnic occasions, as is shown in the chapters by Lynch on the Hmong-American New Year in St. Paul and by Seng and Wass on Palestinian brides in America. However, from Welters' research we see that the *foustanella* in Greece now falls into the category of national dress, a rather unusual example of men's ethnic dress remaining virtually unchanged.

Ann Bridgwood's article raises issues about the interface between dress, gender, tradition, and modernity within the Cypriot population in London, and about interpretations of appropriate dress for modest females at wedding parties. Carolyn Behrman's work on Swazi beauty queens analyzes a different dimension of gender; she posits a dual system in which the members of the smaller ethnic group appear in types of dress that seem unacceptable to members of the larger group, but then set up a system of negotiation between the two. Such examples again prompt the question of what the characteristics of ethnic dress may be and whether ethnic and traditional always mean the same thing.

Others have concerned themselves with this query. Baizerman, Eicher, and Cerny (1993) addressed the focus on "Western dress" by many scholars, which is usually analyzed from the historical perspective of western civilization; little or no concern is given to the rest of the world. Such a view implies that dress outside of the boundaries of western civilization has experienced little change and is therefore "traditional". In this volume, Barbara Sumberg and I take the argument one step further; we claim that cosmopolitan dress exists across the globe. "Western" dress represents a style with origins in the tailored garments of Euro-Americans, but now, as a way of dress shared by millions of people, it no longer merits that name.

The authors in this volume point to the many complexities of analyzing ethnic dress. The ideas behind ethnicity connect to the preservation of an identity for individuals that links to a meaningful heritage. The controversies that arise in discussions of ethnicity have focused on self-definition as opposed to definition by others, and on the fluidity of the concept of ethnicity as individuals move in time and space. What can be seen from the research in this volume is that ethnic dress helps to position an individual in time and place relationships. Often the details that distinguish ethnic dress are minute, but they are nevertheless critical to those who claim them as part of their heritage of dress. Sometimes what appears as ethnic dress, as in the case of the *coiffe* and the kilt, may seem quaint and picturesque as they appeal to tourists.

These are examples of outsiders' views, an appeal that may have a payoff to the ethnic group continuing to project them to attract attention of travelers. In these cases, the past is frozen in time for a specific purpose. But although preserving the past through dress is one aspect of ethnic dress, such dress can exhibit various types of change.

According to Nash (1989: 5–6), the building blocks of ethnicity are the body, a language, a shared history and origins, and religion and nationality. Nash cites a trinity of boundary markers, kinship, commensuality, and religious cult, as symbols of the existence of the group and at the same time constituting the group (p. 11). He recognizes this trinity as being the deep or basic structure of ethnic group differentiation, with secondary, surface pointers (dress, language, and culturally denoted physical features) allowing members of the group to recognize each other and to be recognized as a group by others: "Difference in dress, from whole costumes to single items of apparel, serve as surface markers of group differences. These items of apparel best serve when visible and public, but items of dress may reinforce group boundaries even if not visible, like the underwear of the Sikhs, or the undergarment of pious Jews" (p. 12). These secondary surface indices must relate to the basic or core elements of ethnic group affiliation: they "stand for and imply differences in blood, substance, and cult and hence to the building blocks of ethnicity" (p. 13). Barbara Sumberg uses this argument to analyze the similarities among neighboring Ijo ethnic groups in the Niger Delta of Nigeria; because similarities between neighbors are great, the issue of dress shifts from a secondary to primary focus of differentiation among the groups. Linda Welters does not refer to Nash, but her research on Greece demonstrates the same line of reasoning.

In sum, the chapters in this book draw attention to new factors to consider when discussing ethnicity. The central focus is on the study of dress as a sensory system of non-verbal communication.

References

Baizerman, S., Eicher, J.B., and Cerny, C. (1993), "Eurocentrism in the Study of Ethnic Dress", *Dress*, vol. 20, pp. 19–32.

Barnes, R., and Eicher, J.B. (eds), *Dress and Gender: Marking and Meaning in Cultural Contexts*, New York: St. Martin's Press.

Nash, M. (1989), *The Cauldron of Ethnicity in the Modern World*, Chicago: University of Chicago.

1

"Freezing the Frame": Dress and Ethnicity in Brittany and Gaelic Scotland

Malcolm Chapman

The problem addressed in this chapter can be simply stated: in Scotland, Scottish Highland "traditional dress", as it is popularly understood, was developed in the late eighteenth or early nineteenth centuries. In Brittany, Breton "traditional dress" has, by contrast, a late nineteenth century or early twentieth century flavour. Why the difference?

When discussing "traditional dress", the quotation marks are a kind of stylistic necessity. I do not mean, by "traditional dress", the clothing that is and always has been worn by the inhabitants of the areas in question. I mean, rather, the clothing that is worn by people who appear in tourist brochures above the caption "traditional dress". In the case of both Scotland and Brittany, this means that we are dealing with rather artificial forms, and not the everyday dress of everyday people.

The "Traditional Dress" of Highland Scotland

The "traditional dress" of Highland Scotland, in this sense, is a collection of clothing for men: its essential item is the tartan kilt, with the addition of items such as knee-length woolen socks, sgian-du, and sporran. This set of garments has *never* been the popular dress of anyone, outside the Scottish Highland regiments of the British army, and outside self-consciously folkloric circles (dancing groups,

7

choirs, the "White Heather Club", and so on). The central item, however, the kilt, does echo the plaid as popularly worn by Gaelic-speaking Highlanders in the period before the last of the Jacobite risings in 1745. The plaid was a single rectangle of locally woven woolen cloth, variously patterned, which was wrapped around the body in different ways according to the exigencies of the weather; it was versatile, and in typical daytime use it left the knees and calves bare. The kilt and the plaid are in many ways very different, but they do share the common characteristic that they are, in effect, skirts and not trousers: they do not, that is, part the crotch. Within majority British society in the eighteenth century, it was popularly accepted that women wore skirts and men wore trousers. The flagrant failure of the Scottish Highlanders to adhere to this oppositional propriety excited the imagination of those who observed them; it continues to do so today (Chapman 1992: 142).

Highland dress and the carrying of arms were both proscribed in the aftermath of the 1745 Jacobite uprising. They were perceived by the English and Scottish authorities to be markers of shared difference, and of martial mobility, and their proscription was a quite explicit act of identity destruction. The "disclothing act" was passed in 1747 and repealed in 1782; by the time of the repeal, the common man of the Highlands had moved into breeches, where he has stayed. The way was open, however, for what I have called elsewhere "the romantic rehabilitation of Highland dress" (Chapman 1992: 140). Walter Scott played a great part in this, particularly in the carefully stage-managed visit of George IV to Edinburgh in 1822; during this visit, and to a certain amount of ribaldry, by this time rather plump George IV disported himself in "Highland dress", and made the dress a possible fashionable wear for a whole new constituency among the privileged of Scotland.

There are many interesting avenues of discussion opening up from this; the central question that I am posing, however, is why then? Why was it in the late eighteenth and early nineteenth centuries that "Highland dress" was codified, appropriated by outsiders, and frozen in its putative "traditional" form? Before discussing this further, I will introduce the Breton example.

The "Traditional Dress" of Brittany

The tartan kilt is perhaps one of the world's best known 'ethnic dresses'. The Scottish Highland regiments, British imperialism,

Jacobite romanticism throughout the English-speaking world, and the love of Scotch whisky, have between them carried a knowledge of this particular form of ethnic particularism to most corners of the world.

In general, Brittany is less visible on the international stage than Scotland (and we return below to the question of why this should be). Accordingly, Breton dress is much less widely known than Scottish Highland dress. It is not without some notoriety, however. In the *New Yorker* of October 25th, 1982 (p. 42) was a cartoon, in which a middle-aged couple were portrayed sitting facing one another across a dining table. The man was normally dressed; the woman was wearing an elaborate headdress — plainly the artist's idea of a Breton *coiffe* from the famous Bigouden region. The man was saying to the woman: "Forgive me, dear, for asking, but were you as ethnic when we were first married?".

Even on an international stage, therefore, it is possible to exploit Breton elements to suggest extremes of ethnic singularity. Within France, it is very easy to do this; if you are looking for "traditional culture" in France, then Brittany is the place to which you will probably first be sent: its language is "traditional" (note the quotation marks); so too are its religion, poetry, music, dance, food, dress, and so on.

In Brittany, "traditional dress" has both male and female forms, but the minimal item (corresponding in this sense to the kilt in Scotland) is the form of headgear for women known in French as a *coiffe*. Large parts of provincial France regard some kind of *coiffe* for women as part of their "tradition". Brittany tends to get more credit than other regions, however, for being defined by this feature. The *coiffe* as it is typically celebrated today in tourist literature is made of white lace (see, for example, *Bretagne*, 1993: 111–15), although other materials have also been used. The *coiffe* can be regarded as a manifestation of the widespread European and Christian requirement that a woman should cover her head in public; this symbolic *pudeur* was then transformed, by love of ornament, into a fine and detailed local millinery.

The readily available picture of the *coiffe* in Brittany is one in which Brittany is divided up into *pays*; these are commonly considered to be ancient units of local belonging, usually of a taxonomic order subordinate to the *région* (Bretagne) or *département* (Finistère, Morbihan, and so on). The *pays* are then each marked by the possession of a unique and ancient style of *coiffe*. Perhaps the most famous example of such a *pays*, not only in Brittany but throughout France, is the Pays Bigouden (whose striking *coiffe* the New Yorker cartoonist was, knowingly or not, trying to portray). The Pays Bigouden covers, more or less, the two cantons of Pont-l'Abbé and Plogastel St-Germain in southern Finistère. The *coiffe* worn by the women of this *pays* is a cylinder of lace over a foot high, perched on top of the head; it has become an icon of folkloric Brittany, even of folkloric France entire, but its use is limited to its own particular *pays*.

Figure 1.1 A bigouden coiffe, about 1950

Variety, Change and Tradition

The exact nature of the use of "tartan" in the old Highlands (say, from the fifteenth to middle eighteenth centuries) has been much argued. The notion that society was divided into clans, each of which wore its own tartan, and whose male members recognized friend and foe in battle according to the tartan that they wore, is almost certainly a post-hoc romanticism, at once an elaboration and an over-simplification of the earlier state of affairs. An elaboration, because the patterns and colours used seem to have been widespread and rudimentary, and what idiosyncrasies there were to have been local rather than "clan" based. An over-simplification, because the relationship between kinship and locality was probably complex, with clan membership, such as it was, defined at least as much by locality as by blood relationship. The modern "tradition", however, is one of unambiguously defined clans, wearing their own specific clan tartans, in fashions loosely based upon mid-eighteenth-century vernacular dress, codified into their "timeless" and popularly received form sometime in the late eighteenth and early nineteenth centuries.

The history of the *coiffes*, and of Breton dress in general, is rather obscure in the eighteenth century; throughout the nineteenth century, however, it becomes increasingly available. The major secondary source is the compendious and fascinating work of René-Yves Creston (1978). Creston organizes his presentation around *pays* and groups of communes. The picture of fashions in *coiffes* which he documents, however, is one of constant change over time, and constant movement over space. Broadly, Creston argues that Breton traditional dress, as it is popularly remembered, was the dress of a social class – the peasant class. Specifically, it was the dress of this class in the post-revolutionary period (post–1789), when new freedoms of action and self-definition were available. It was, moreover, a phenomenon linked to industrialization elsewhere in Europe, since these new freedoms could now be exercised in the arena of dress, using cheap and readily-available mass-produced fabrics (Creston 1978: 21–40).[1]

1. It should perhaps be noted that in giving precedence to "class" as an analytical device here, rather than looking, say, to "nationality", Creston is entering a complex political and moral domain, where prejudices and partial interpretations abound. Broadly, Breton communist and socialist analysts have preferred "class", while right-wing Breton separatists and nationalists have preferred "nation"; these preferences

If one looks carefully at any particular style or region, it is clear that there is little stability, either in style or location. Styles changed rapidly, and often out of all recognition. Looking at the styles of *coiffe* that have succeeded one another in a particular area, allows one to speak of "evolution", as Creston does, but often the thread of continuity is minimal, at least to outward appearances – reducible, perhaps, to "*coiffes* continued to be worn" (see, for example, Creston's diagrams of the *coiffes* of the region of Pont l'Abbé from 1806 to 1939, p. 45).

The story of these changes needs to be pursued at the very local level for it to be intelligible. My own particular interest is in the region of south-west Finistère, where the regions of Cap-Sizun and the Pays Bigouden meet (see Chapman 1986, ch. 5), and where the rhythms of metropolitan modernization have been slightly behind those of, say, northern Finistère or eastern Brittany. Creston, in his discussion of these areas, shows how local ambitions, local patterns of communication, local occupations (fishing and fish-canning as against peasant farming, for example), combined to create a fast moving picture of regional and stylistic change in the late nineteenth century, and on to about 1940 or 1950 (Creston 1978: 116). The post-war period saw an almost complete end to new recruitment to *coiffe*-wearing (just as it saw a very rapid decline in new recruitment to Breton-language speaking). Many of those who *had* worn *coiffes* continued to do so, at least in south-west Finistère; the *coiffe*-wearing group was aging, however, and as the years went by was quite literally dying out. When I was living in the area between 1978 and 1984, the *coiffe*-wearers who wore the Penn-Sardin of Douarnenez and Plouhinec, or the Bigouden *coiffe* of the Pays Bigouden, seemed to be mostly over 60, many of them widows. Several that I knew died while I was there; their daughters were not *coiffe*-wearers, and did not become so. France, one felt, had finally arrived (Weber 1979).

We have, therefore, a reality in which *coiffe* styles changed rather rapidly, and in which the area of use of any particular *coiffe* changed rather rapidly as well. There was, it seems, a very strong tendency for the women in contiguous areas either to wear the same kind of *coiffe* at any one time, or to define themselves in opposition to an adjacent area by wearing a different kind of *coiffe*. This tendency

---

spill over into virtually any subject which the analysts touch (for detail, see McDonald 1982). Without wishing to engage in this debate here, I can only say that I find Creston's argument broadly convincing.

co-existed, however, with constant search for ever-finer, more modish, or more practical versions of headgear, and with recruitment of individuals from one type to another on ever-moving frontiers.

What is remembered, however, and now celebrated in folkloric festivals, is that each *pays* had its own traditional *coiffe*. Thus the Bigouden *coiffe*, which reached its final extraordinary elaboration as late as 1950, after a century or more of ceaseless innovation, is now regarded as the "traditional" *coiffe* of the Pays Bigouden. Innovation has ceased, and the *coiffe* is now only worn by a small number of old women. There is a certain will, within the complex of tourist literature and folkloric writing, to forget the history of constant change, and to remember the end product of this change as a single and timeless style, tied to a particular and unchanging region – in this case the *pays* of the Pays Bigouden. Evidence for the history of turbulent change is abundant, but is not promulgated. What the world seems to want, in looking at these examples, is timelessness. Because the *coiffes* that *are* worn are unchanging, and because they are now obsolete (in that there are no new recruits to *coiffe*-wearing), it is relatively easy to perceive these features as the end of a period of unchanging traditionality. Nobody writes or tells untruths about these things, precisely: it is rather that the end of the *coiffe* is perceived as the end of a certain kind of "traditional life", and that the move from tradition to modernity is perceived in structurally simple terms, as a move from an unchanging state to one of constant movement. Social anthropologists, who lived inside Malinowskian functionalism for a generation or so, have every reason for understanding how compelling ideas of this kind can be. They seem to have become part of the folk-repertoire of modern historiography; perhaps they are built into inter-generational perception in some kind of ineluctable way.

To get an idea of how lace *coiffes* were perceived in the mid-nineteenth century, we can perhaps profitably cite a Breton broadsheet song, "Ar c'his ancienna hac ar c'his a zo brema" ("Old fashions and new fashions"). The song, in thirteen verses, generally laments the disappearance of good old-fashioned austere peasant ways, and their replacement by dissipation, debauchery, vanity, fashion and modernity. Verse 5 goes:

Goechal en peb guiaden
E doa peb mates e steuen
Cetu eno e zoaleten:
   Honnes voa ar c'his ancienna
Mes brema merc'h eur c'hlasqer boued
A zoug voulous, franch, colinet,
Eur chal, eur c'hoef dantelezet:
   Honnes ar c'his a zo brema

(Before, in any old stuff
a servant girl was dressed,
That was her rig;
That was the old style.
But now a girl is out to attract,
her head in velvet, open, collared,
In shawl, and lace coiffe;
That is the modern style.)[2]

Viewed from this perspective, lace *coiffes* were part of a modernity which also included the breakdown of traditional morality in general (the same song goes on to speak of girls who *drink*, who put themselves forward, who run after boys; these are, by implication, the wearers of lace *coiffes*). It is a strikingly different picture of mid-nineteenth century Brittany from that drawn in the modern tourist literature.

To do full justice to the historiography of the *coiffe*, one would need to look also at the closely associated phenomenon of the *pays*. *Coiffe* and *pays* are often coterminous in a quite literal sense (the *coiffe bigoudenne*, the Pays Bigouden), and the area of distribution of a *coiffe* is given logic by the boundaries of a *pays*. The *pays*, like the *coiffe*, is assumed always to have been there: it is the archetypal unit of 'belonging' in French popular discourse. Like the *coiffe*, however, many (perhaps most) *pays* in Brittany seem to be of relatively recent origin, to have roamed around the map, and to have been, in a sense, born along with the modern styles of *coiffe* with

---

2. This is from the broadsheet "Ar c'his ancienna hac ar c'his a zo brema" (Bibliothèque Municipale, Rennes, 77756, no.19, *Rimou, Gwerziou*, tome II). It is not dated, but it was published by the Imprimerie Lédan, of Morlaix; many of the broadsheets published by this house were the work of Alexandre Ledan (1777–1855). The translation (which may be deficient; one or two features I still find puzzling) is mine.

which their terminology is shared.

In spite of their assumed ancient status, the evidence for *pays* in earlier periods is not compelling. Croix, in his voluminous thesis on Brittany in the sixteenth and seventeenth centuries (Croix 1981: 31–3), observes that Bretons outside Brittany seem to have used few adjectives of a *pays* type in self-description; he remarks that looking for *pays* in the historical record, "poser le problème a surtout valeur de pétition de principe", and this might be regarded as a general solution to the process though which "ancient" *pays* are created by modern inspection. In similar vein, Creston notes that at the time of the *chouan* uprisings, shortly after the Revolution of 1789, the many Breton peasants who found themselves arraigned before republican courts did not use a *pays*-based lexicon to describe themselves (Creston 1978: 31).

Today, however, the *pays* is something whose existence is desired; it is where urban people "really" come from, or dream of returning to: "le pays, dont on sait au moins une chose au départ: c'est que beaucoup souhaitent y vivre" (Laurent and Lemaitre 1979). This desire is an important historiographical feature: people buy books about the ancient *pays*. It is, of course, true that all *pays* have always been there in a geographical sense, and that the region of any modern *pays* has always had people living in it; the physical and demographic continuity is easily read back as the "history of the pays", even if the "pays", in a conceptual sense (with its modern boundaries, modern dress, and modern linguistic diacritica) is a thing of yesterday. Many writers approach the problem in this way, contributing to the sense of ancient definition even while at the same time offering historical material which belies this (see, for example, the excellent work of Cornou and Giot (1977), on the Pays Bigouden).

In both Brittany and Scotland, then, we have histories of turbulent change, both in the styles of dress involved, and in the nature of the self-definition of social groups. It may not be an accident that in both the Breton and Scottish cases, popular historiography has tended to construct a set of discrete and unchanging social units (*pays*, clans), each with its own unchanging traditional dress (*coiffes*, tartans). The two cases are very different, as will be seen below, but they have these rather striking similarities. Is this something to do with troubled modernity seeking ancient securities of definition? Social anthropologists are not typically sympathetic to the sense of "psychological need" which this question seems to invoke, but there does seem to be some relationship between this "freezing of tradition", and the overt discourse of modernity; I return to this point in my concluding remarks (for a related discussion, see McCrone, Morris and Kiely 1995).

The "Construction" of the Celts

Elsewhere, in a more general treatment of the Celts, I have argued that the various peoples known under this title (which embraces the Scots and Bretons, as well as the Welsh, Irish and others) owe their modern identity to four interlocking processes (Chapman 1992: 209). I will briefly repeat the argument here, with a few interpolations relevant to this particular context. The four processes are:

1. The elaboration of an opposition "self/other", with the "Celts" (under whatever title) figuring as the "other", and with oppositions like Greek/Keltoi, Roman/Galli, Anglo-Saxon/Welsh, English/Celtic (or French/Breton) succeeding one another. Geographically and conceptually, the second of each of these pairs is peripheral. The content of the second (or rather, what is noticeable about the second) is primarily determined by the content of the first.
2. The steady progression of fashions from a center to a periphery, with new fashions appearing at the center and steadily moving to the periphery, before being replaced in their turn by the same continuing process. This process is in many respects indifferent to boundaries constructed under the first process: the content of categories constructed under the first process can change continuously, while the categories themselves appear static.
3. A systematic function of the meeting of incongruent category systems, causing the perceiving culture to construct the perceived as inconstant, unreliable, irrational, colourful, or given to excess and inadequacy.
4. Romanticism: this glamourises the "other" that is constructed in processes 1 and 3, and introduces a complicated refraction – an apparent counter-current – into the observation of process 2.

This four-process model has considerable explanatory power when applied to Celtic examples. In the case of dress, we can look at the four processes to see how they apply. In relation to process 1, for example, it is clear that there is a real will, within both France and the United Kingdom, to construct pictures of Celtic singularity, using fairly simple binary oppositions (traditional/modern, for example) which make intelligible the difference between France and Brittany, or England and Highland Scotland. Dress examples are consistently used in this process (kilts or trousers, coiffes or bare heads), and are given a spurious timelessness thereby.

Process 2 is very clearly demonstrated through dress examples. As presented above, the process is of course over-simplified; in the longer version of this argument, I stress that "center" and "periphery" in these terms are conceptual rather than necessarily geographic entities, that the direction of movement is not invariant, that different "centres" compete, and that on a continuum of possibilities "center" and "periphery" are entirely relative concepts. That said, there is a long and strong tendency for London and Edinburgh to perform the "central" role for Highland Scotland, and for Paris to perform this same role for Brittany (for Highland Scotland, see Macintyre 1952: 230–3; for Brittany, Weber 1977: 71, and Creston 1978: 50). When one descends to local social and geographic detail, an extremely complex picture opens up – one in which local and regional capitals, religious centers, areas of temporary prosperity, cosmopolitan sea-ports, the temporary and local availability of certain kinds of cheap fabric, and so on, exert various and changing influences. Local geography, beyond considerations of mere distance, also plays its part; the peninsulas, rivers and infertile ground of Finistère have unquestionably influenced the social aspects of local identity, providing some limited rationale for the pattern of currently accepted *pays*, and the distribution of (for example) styles of *coiffe*. Creston again provides a fascinating description of the relative and changing nature and distribution of the three predominant *coiffes* of south-west Finistère, the "bigouden", the "penn sardin", and the "kapenn", in which all of the influences mentioned above play their part (Creston 1978: 103–29).

Process 3 has its conceptual derivation in structural anthropology, and may not be readily accessible as a notion to those unfamiliar with the background. Dress features, however, illustrate this process also. Many points might be made, at different levels of detail. Perhaps the most conspicuous example in this area has already been referred to: the Highland men who, so it seemed to their observers, wore dresses, in flagrant contravention of established propriety. This classificatory anomaly excited attention, and it did not need much tweaking of structural oppositions (such as male:female, controlled:uncontrolled, pastoral:settled, wild:civilized) to generate the notion of men whose sexuality was ever-accessible, wild, uncontrolled, and exciting (see

Chapman 1992: 141–3, and below). In Brittany, there is no single example with quite this conceptual force. We might, however, look at the *coiffe* as an element which seemed, from outside Brittany, to represent old-fashioned morality and religiosity: where women covered their heads and constrained their bodies and behaviour by pins and laces, there seemed to be an abundance of ancient piety. External views of Brittany invariably express this perception (see, for one of the earliest and most influential of such expressions, Souvestre 1836). For self-consciously modern Parisians, from the early nineteenth century onwards, understanding of such phenomena was built around oppositions such as: modern : traditional, unconstrained : constrained, irreverent : pious, bare heads : tightly laced *coiffes*, immoral : moral.

From *within* the *coiffe*-wearing areas, however, as we have seen, the relevant categories of interpretation were quite different. There, rapidly changing fashions in *coiffes* were themselves seen as manifestations of modernity, with all the implications of vanity, immorality, and loss of control over female sexuality, which might seem to belong to the left-hand side of the oppositions listed above. These interpretations, which were lived by the participants, ran directly counter to those generated by the external view. They could, however, and did, co-exist for long periods. An interesting sense of the tensions involved can be had by comparing, for example, the immensely popular children's books starring Bécassine, the naive and good-hearted "Breton housemaid in Paris", with Youenn Drezen's *Itron Varia Garmez* (1941), or the more recent cartoon series by P. Stephan (1983). In these works there are, among other things, some entertainingly various graphical renderings of *coiffe*-wearing women, which illustrate the disparate experiences and interpretations referred to above.

In the original version of this argument, I wrote:

> Processes 2 and 3 provide constantly renewed material for process 1. It is not always easy to sort the effects of these different processes out, for they overlie one another; the observations resulting from them are in many respects incompatible, and so are the object of a good deal of creative forgetfulness and fudging (in order, for example, that process 2 should always seem to provide support for process 1. (Chapman 1992: 209)

We can see that both the Breton and the Scottish cases are rich in process 2 examples, and I have tried to give some hint of the kind of "creative forgetfulness and fudging" through which they appear to give support to a constantly sustained (and would-be timeless) version of process 1.[3] I have also tried to suggest some process 3 examples which are relevant to the interpretation of dress.

The Freezing of the Frame

The problem posed at the beginning of this paper was one of timing. Scottish Highland traditional dress is a version of styles from the late eighteenth and early nineteenth centuries, which in its popularly received form has not changed radically since that time. Breton traditional dress is a version of styles from the late nineteenth and early twentieth centuries (even, as in the case of the Bigouden *coiffe* in its "final" form, as late as 1950). Why was the final photographic image, the "freezing of the frame", enacted at different times in the two different countries?

To answer this question we need to look at process 4, "romanticism". This is a gross attempt to try to capture a great deal in one word; there are, of course, multiple problems of definition and interpretation. By "romanticism", in this context, I mean something like this: process 2 is characteristically a one-directional phenomenon; outwards from London, outwards from Paris. In the process of nation-state formation over the last century or so, however, there seems to come a period, in any particular nation, when internal ethnic variety becomes an object of interest, of celebration. One outcome of this is that the fashions of the fringe, which previously had been definitionally unfashionable in central terms, become objects of interest at the center; the fringe is revalued, by the center, and what I have called an "apparent counter-current" appears in process 2: George IV starts to wear "Highland dress", Parisian salon society starts to take an interest in ancient Breton verse, and so on.

The timing of this, however, the timing of the intervention of process 4 into process 2, varies from one country to another. In

3. One fine example of this concerns an interpretation of the history of the Bigouden *coiffe*. Remember that the Bigouden *coiffe* was constantly changing, and that its most conspicuous recent change was towards ever-increasing height; remember also that the folkloric gaze requires changelessness in its "traditions". Marion Deschamps (1980), in her *Portrait of Brittany* brings these two irreconcilable features together in a masterly manner: "in certain districts the height used to be increased every generation" (or, as we might paraphrase it, "they had an unbroken historical tradition of continual change").

particular, and in the Celtic context, the United Kingdom and France displayed marked differences. This can be illustrated in many different ways, but I find it useful to discuss the problem under three different headings: political, demographic and literary.

Political Differences

After the defeat of the last Jacobite uprising in 1746, Georgian Britain was an increasingly secure political and geographical unit. The source of revolt, in the Highlands, had been far from other enemies, and after Culloden the military and social "pacification" of the Highlands was thorough. In subsequent decades, Britain prospered in war and trade. By 1815 it was the unchallenged leading world power, in both military and economic terms. Highland dress was, as we have seen, proscribed in 1747, but even during its proscription intellectuals in Britain began to take an interest in the Scottish Highlands. Once the Highlanders were no longer a threat, they were apt to become an object of romantic interest: in some ways, they were the *first* object of romantic interest. The plaid and the kilt had symbolic value as markers of these changes:

> Before 1745, the bareness of the Highland knee was regarded as a sign of primitive savagery, and the freedom of movement of the Scottish Highlander was something that could only be deplored, from the point of view of the law-abiding Lowlands. After 1745, the bare Highland knee became a piece of noble savagery and the freedom of movement of the Scottish Highlander became a laudable escape from the unnatural constraints of urban industrial civilization. The kilt suggested an apparently ready access to Highland masculine sexuality, and so to passion and violence; these also changed from being deplorable to being desirable features. (Chapman 1992: 142–3)

France, during the same period, was undergoing relentless internal upheaval. Its internal minorities, large as they were, overlapped in unsettling ways into other polities; in wartime, Brittany was a constant object of interest to the omnipresent British navy. In this context, France was more inclined to ignore its internal variety, even to wish to *suppress* it, than to celebrate it; at least in ethnic terms, "the stakes remained too high for the romantic risk to be taken" (Chapman 1992: 136).

Demographic Differences

England and southern Scotland were the first countries in the world to achieve rapid population growth, on the back of industrialization. During the period from about 1780 to 1850, unprecedented rates of population growth were achieved, and it was not until the 1920s that any real slow-down became apparent. During this same period, the population of the Scottish Highlands grew much more slowly, held down by emigration, famine, and family limitation (see Flinn et al 1970). The relative demographic preponderance of industrial Britain to the Scottish Highlands was moving very heavily in favour of Britain. In France, by contrast, demographic growth throughout the nineteenth century was sluggish; the French authorities, indeed, became increasingly worried about this, and about its effect upon productive and military capacity. To make matters worse, Brittany was experiencing relatively rapid population growth, especially in the western and Breton-speaking (that is, more alien) areas (see Aries 1971). The rhythms of this were complex, based in the early part of the nineteenth century upon increasingly intensive exploitation of land, and towards the end of the century on semi-industrialization in fishing and agro-industry. Nevertheless, the fact was there. There are several points that can be made here. The first and perhaps most important in the context is that these demographic trends only confirmed Britain in its centralized security (there was no threat in celebrating Highland identity), while they conversely confirmed France in its deepening insecurity. The second is that "ethnic identities" do not exist in and of themselves; they require a meeting of at least two "identities", so that a difference can be noticed. When a large group meets a small group, one possible consequence is mute assimilation. Something of the sort was happening in the Highlands in the period immediately after 1745. Under process 4, however, the large group celebrates the small group, and draws it into its symbolism. The larger the large group, and the more the small group assimilates into the larger in order to convey information about itself, the more convincing will be the assertion of the identity of the small group: in spite of the fact that these features actually relate to an objective reduction in the personnel and differentiating criteria of the small group. Industrial Britain elaborated an internationally famous "identity" for the Scottish Highlanders, while the "real" Scottish Highland identity dwindled in important senses, not least demographically.

In France, by contrast, Brittany was *growing* in relation to France; in these circumstances there was, so to speak, a lot of Breton identity, but few people in France wanted to know about it: it was a threat, not a delight. Or to put it another way, when we look at the relative international celebrity of the Scottish Highlands and of Brittany, we might say that the more there seems to be of it, the less there is: a study of the rise and fall of the numbers of speakers of the Breton and Scottish Gaelic languages provides a keen illustration of this (the Scottish Gaelic speaking population probably reached its maximum, both in relative and absolute terms, sometime in the eighteenth century; the Breton speaking population reached its maximum, both in relative and absolute terms, over a century later, probably just before the Great War of 1914–18). Statistics relating to emigration bear out the same points; emigration from Highland Scotland was a normal feature of life, forced or unforced, by the late eighteenth century; emigration from Brittany was never so far-flung nor so numerous, and it was not until the late nineteenth century that it began to be perceived as a social or moral threat to the Breton population (Treogat 1900; Le Bail 1913).

Literary Differences

Scottish Highland life erupts onto the world literary scene with the publication in 1760 of James Macpherson's purported translations of the ancient Gaelic bard *Ossian* (Macpherson 1760, 1761). Macpherson's *Ossian* became the centre of the world's most notorious and enduring literary controversy; it also, fitfully but surely, brought the Scottish Highlands into the forefront of the British and European imagination. There is not space to discuss this here (for detail, see Chapman 1978); what is important is that this was the first European example of a minority literature attracting fame, notoriety and interest. It was followed by many other examples, with an uncannily similar structure of creative forgery. The Breton example came nearly a century later, in the form of Villemarque's *Barzaz Breiz* (Villemarque 1846; for an exhaustive discussion, see Gourvil 1959). Influential Scots, worried about the controversy over *Ossian*, set up an inquiry into their provenance, which reported its findings in 1805 (see Mackenzie 1805). Influential Bretons, worried about the controversy over the *Barzaz Breiz*, set up their own folkloric investigation, which published its results eighty years later, in 1885 (Bourgault-Ducoudray 1885). The enthusiasm for the "folk" and for "folklore" were first elaborated in Great Britain (see Dorson 1968), and rather belatedly imported into France. "Folklore", moreover, had been closely tied to the "Celts" in its British elaboration, and this continued in France (see the predominance of Breton material in the *Revue des Traditions populaires*, edited by Paul Sebillot in the first decade of the twentieth century). This "insular Celtic" interpretation of the Breton "folk" was itself influenced by a particular resolution of the debate over whether the Bretons had been originally "British" Celtic invaders or surviving indigenous Gauls (Tanguy 1977; McDonald 1982, 1989; Guiomar 1987).

The above discussion, under its three headings, is intended to summarise a general argument: France came later, and with less enthusiasm, to recognition of its internal minorities, than did Great Britain. That is why "Breton traditional dress" is frozen in a relatively recent form, and why "Scottish Highland traditional dress" is so much "older".

Final Comments

The difference in timing between "Scottish Gaelic" and "Breton" traditional dress is an important marker of many other differences between the two greater contexts, those of Great Britain and France. The difference of timing highlights some important objective differences between the two examples. There is about a hundred years between the two, and this period (wherever we place its beginning and end, sometime between the late eighteenth and early twentieth centuries) was one of quite remarkably rapid change. "Freezing the frame" is (at least as I understand it) a metaphor from motion-picture photography, built upon still photography, using an image (the "frame") from a much older tradition of two-dimensional artistic representation. The technology for creating and holding the "frame", however conceived, changed greatly over the period that we are considering.

The last Scottish Highlanders to wear the plaid as an item of normal dress did so sometime in the late 1740s. For a generation Highland traditional dress was actually forbidden, and never re-emerged as a truly popular dress of the native inhabitants of the Highlands. Towards the end of the eighteenth century, the "frame" was frozen in memory and recollection, in oils and watercolours, and in the kind of creative intervention to which Trevor-Roper (1983) has drawn attention; it was a frame into which the Highland regiments, the Scottish aristocracy, and the British royal family, all stepped. If there had been no 1745, no Culloden, no fear of Jacobitism, no Clearances, no emigration (if . . .), then it is not impossible that, at the end of the eighteenth century in the Scottish Highlands, something rather like a system of "clans", living each in their own *pays*, each with their own "tartan", might have emerged out of the interaction of central influence and local ambition – a confirmation of the Romantic gaze, but with a strong element of local participation and authenticity nevertheless (rather analogous to the situation in Brittany a century later, as described above). This never happened, however. As a result, "Highland dress" has always subsequently had a feel either of central interference (alien upper middle classes, special occasions, choirs, ceilidhs and tourists), or of the Scottish diaspora (where ready access to symbols of unEnglishness was far more important than any consideration of the genuine authenticity of such symbols).

In Brittany the position was rather different. "Traditional dress", as I have defined it, was present in most of western Brittany until the first decade of the twentieth century, and in some areas until much later (even, in some exiguous senses, until today). The frame was frozen on photographic, and even cinematographic, media. The most compelling and frequently published images are those of black and white photography, suggesting the period of the early part of this century when, at least in many areas, "traditional dress" lost its local vitality (the photography of Jos le Doaré, produced for the emerging tourist market, and used by Creston and many others, is exemplary here). I have argued above that "traditional dress" in Brittany was not timeless and archaic, but that it was instead part of a local rhetoric of finery and fashionability, ambitious wealth, and modernity. The tourists, however, saw things otherwise: what they saw was ancient folklore, comical archaism, traditional piety, the old order of things. This would have been true in Scotland as well, but that the traditionally clad natives left the field after Culloden in 1746, and the tourists did not start to arrive until after Walter Scott's *Lady of the Lake*, published in 1810. In Brittany, the locals were still wearing "traditional dress" while the tourists were milling around them with cameras. Even in distant corners of Finistère, the desires of the tourist had come to have an imperative, reality-determining character as early as the first decade of this century: when the Municipal Council of Plouhinec, a seaside commune in south-west Finistère, was asked to express an opinion in 1910 of a proposed railway through the area, it replied: "Le Conseil Municipal de Plouhinec estime que cette ligne doit avant tout servir les intérets des contribuables et non celui des touristes étrangères" (Plouhinec Council Archives, March 20, 1910). Creston puts it like this:

> Il faut ajouter . . . la gêne qu'éprouvent les porteurs de costumes bretons, comme l'éprouvent d'ailleurs les femmes, de se voir regardés comme des pièces de musée par le tourist en mal de photographies. Combien de fois n'avons-nous pas vu, dans les pardons et les fêtes, des touristes armés de kodaks prendre des photos de famille en costumes bretons! Ils ne pensaient certainement pas qu'en prenant ces photos, ils incitaient les paysans bretons qui portaient leur costumes régionaux à les abandonner, pour ne plus être, pour les touristes, un object de curiosité. (Creston 1978: 51)

If you were a Breton wearing "traditional dress" in, say, 1930, you were individually in two quite contradictory positions: you were, in your own eyes, wearing modish, elegant dress, expressive of wealth and taste; you were, in the eyes of those taking photographs, a timeless and quaint folkloric ornament. In this example, as in so many others over the centuries, the central definition prevailed over the native definition; I do not think it was so much that people disliked being an "object of curiosity", as Creston puts it, but that the awareness of the two contradictory definitions could not readily co-exist in the same person. And so the peasants of Brittany took off their "traditional" clothes. As they did, so the increasingly large urban population of post–1945 France, and indeed post–1945 Brittany, conceived an increasing enthusiasm for folk habits, and began to form societies for their preservation and use. Some of the most successful and visible of these societies attend to matters of dress; they are highly visible at the (by now "traditional") "Fêtes de Cornouaille", held in Quimper every summer. Giot provides a pleasing cameo, from life: a grandmother from the Pays Bigouden, wearing the *coiffe* of her normal daily life, is standing in Quimper with her grandson, waiting for a bus; they are watching the parties of folklore enthusiasts dressed in "traditional dress", as they leave the "Fêtes de Cornouaille". The grandmother says to the grandson: "regarde ces hommes déguisés en Bretons" (Giot 1978: 17–18).

Giot goes on, "mon histoire s'arrête la, avec ce cri du coeur du peuple" (p. 18). And yet, what harm are they doing, "ces hommes déguisés en Bretons" (not to mention "ces femmes")? The people of Brittany took their own course through the fashionabilities of the last hundred years, after all; they were not *made* to wear "traditional dress", nor made to abandon it. To be sure, they had various influences coming at them from outside the confines of Brittany, but wishing those away is wishing away the world. Those involved in autonomy-seeking Breton politics commonly regard activity concerning political independence, or Breton language use, as the serious hard edge of the "struggle"; by contrast, they regard attention to dress as a dangerous distraction, a feeble capitulation to the folkloric demands of alien tourists. One can see their point, and I do not have space to argue this issue here. I have, however, come to the view that the makers, wearers and celebrators of "traditional dress" are largely to be admired: they add color and loveliness to their own lives and to those of others, and they do not mind being laughed at from time to time. Their view of their own activity is no doubt full of "illusions" (Giot 1978: 16); the illusions have no ill-will in them, however, and are generally less dangerous, and less seriously self-deceptive, than those which drive a good deal of politico-linguistic activism in such a context. And they are illusions which, although not precisely *shared* by the "real" Breton population, are at least tolerated: the careful attention to the crafting of costume, to lace and embroidery, on the part of those involved in the making of "traditional dress", is undoubtedly admired by the women of those areas where "traditional dress" used to be worn. I have spent several years in south-west Finistère, where the biggest Breton festival in this genre, the above-mentioned "Fêtes de Cornouaille" in Quimper, takes place. I was often told to go and see it; "déguisés" or not, the people involved were doing something which, in the villages around, was broadly approved of, particularly among the women (or at least, such is my impression: I am minded of a church that one no longer attends; one does not want the bother of going oneself, but one is glad that somebody is keeping it up). And because the move from "tradition" to "modernity" in Brittany has been so rapid, so recent, there are still old people among the observers of folklore festivals who can feel genuinely nostalgic: here, acted out before them, is their own youth; strange, even laughable, but enchanting as well.

The dress example carries one quickly into other areas, as the above discussion shows perhaps to excess. One area which is immediately suggested, and which I have scarcely touched on, is that of dance. In both Scotland and Brittany the self-conscious wearing of "traditional dress" is often associated with the dancing of "traditional dances". Folkloric festivals like the "Fêtes de

Cornouaille", or any one of the many tartan festivals in Scotland, are as much festivals of dance as of dress.

In some ways, one might regard "traditional dress", in both Scotland and Brittany, as part of a popular and vernacular discourse about "modernity". "Traditional dress", frozen in its frame, is a repeated statement about the modern condition, as it is popularly conceived: it is the symbolic inversion, on high days and holidays, which tells people what it is that they are in their ordinary daily lives. In their ordinary daily lives, they are, in their own eyes, "modern", which is something to do with being French- (or English-) speaking, with being part of a more or less homogeneous nation-state, with working in towns and offices, and so on. The study of dress gives us some clues as to the structure of "modernity", in the only sense in which the concept is valuable – as it is lived and understood.

References

Ariès, P. (1971), *Histoire des populations françaises*, Paris: Seuil.

Bourgault-Ducoudray, L. (1885), *Trente mélodies populaires de Basse-Bretagne*, Paris (collected in Brittany in 1881 at the instance of the Ministry of Public Instruction and Fine Arts of the French Government).

Bretagne (1993), St. Malo: Brittany Ferries.

Chapman, M. (1978), *The Gaelic Vision in Scottish Culture*, London: Croom Helm.

Chapman, M. (1986), "A Social Anthropological Study of a Breton Village, with Celtic Comparisons", unpublished D. Phil thesis, Oxford University.

Chapman, M. (1992), *The Celts: the Construction of a Myth*, London: Macmillan.

Cornou, J., and Giot, P. (1977), *Histoire et origines des bigoudens*, Le Guilvinec: Le Signor.

Creston, R.Y. (1978), *Le Costume Breton*, Paris: Tchou.

Croix, A. (1981), *La Bretagne aux 16e et 17e siècles: la vie – la mort – la foi*, Paris: Maloine S.A. Editeur (2 vols).

Deschamps, M. (1980), *Portrait of Brittany*, London.

Dorson, R. (1968), *The British Folklorists*, London: Routledge and Kegan Paul.

Drezen, Y. (1977), *Itron Varia Garmez* (with illustrations by R.Y. Creston), Al Liamm (first published 1941 by Skrid ha Skeudenn).

Flinn, M. et al. (1970), *Scottish Population History from the Seventeenth Century to the 1930s*, Cambridge: Cambridge University Press.

Giot, P.-R. (1978), "Préface" to Creston, *Le Costume Breton*.

Gourvil, F. (1959), *Théodore Hersart de la Villemarqué (1815–1895) et le*

"Barzaz Breiz" (1839–1845–1867) – Origines, Editions, Sources, Critique, Influences, Rennes: Oberthur.

Guiomar, J.-Y. (1987), *Le Bretonisme: les historiens bretons au XIXe siècle*, Rennes: Société d'Histoire et d'Archéologie de Bretagne.

Laurent, L. and Lemaitre, T. (1979), "Defense et Illustration du 'Pays'", *Economie et Statistique*, vol. 110, INSEE.

Le Bail, G. (1913), *L'émigration rural et les migrations temporaires dans le Finistère*, Paris: Giard et Brière.

McCrone, D., Morris, A., and Kiely, R. (1995), *Scotland – the Brand: the Making of Scottish Heritage*, Edinburgh: Edinburgh University Press.

McDonald, M. (1982), "Social Aspects of Language and Education in Brittany", unpublished D.Phil thesis, Oxford University.

McDonald, M. (1989), "We are not French!" in *Language, Culture and Identity in Brittany*, London: Routledge.

Macintyre, D. (1952), *The songs of Duncan Ban Macintyre* (ed. and trans. A. Macleod), Edinburgh: Oliver and Boyd.

Mackenzie, H. (1805), *Report of the Committee of the Highland Society of Scotland appointed to inquire into the Nature and Authenticity of the Poems of Ossian*, Edinburgh: Archibald Constable.

Macpherson, J. (1760), *Fragments of Ancient Poetry collected in the Highlands and Islands of Scotland and translated from the Gaelic or Erse language*, Edinburgh.

Macpherson, J. (1761), *Fingal, an Ancient Epic*, Dublin.

Souvestre, E. (1836), *Les Derniers Bretons*, Paris.

Stephan, P. (1983), *Superbigou Attaque*, Spezet: Breizh.

Tanguy, B. (1977), *Aux Origines du Nationalisme breton*, Paris: 10/18.

Tréogat, A. (1900), *L'immigration bretonne à Paris*, Paris: Maloine.

Trevor-Roper, H. (1983), "The Invention of Tradition: the Highland Tradition of Scotland", in J. Hobsbawm and T. Ranger (eds), *The Invention of Tradition*, Cambridge: Cambridge University Press.

Villemarqué, Th. H. (1846), *Barzaz Breiz: Chants Populaires de la Basse Bretagne*, Paris: Franck.

Weber, E. (1979), *Peasants into Frenchmen*, London: Chatto and Windus.

2

Dancing the Jar: Girls' Dress at Turkish Cypriot Weddings

Ann Bridgwood

Introduction

Dress, particularly fashion, has attracted the attention of writers from a variety of disciplines and perspectives including psychoanalysis, psychology, semiotics, anthropology, and feminism (Wilson 1985). Within semiotics, it has been analysed as a sign system; Barthes (1972), for example, argues that fashion is an enclosed system of signs. As with any sign, fashions are arbitrary, and only have meaning in relation to each other. Hebdige (1979) draws on the work of Barthes, and brings together semiotics, Althusser's theory of the levels of the social formation, Gramsci's theory of hegemony and Levi-Strauss' concept of "bricolage" to furnish an explanation of style. Although he agrees with Barthes that the objects of style are arbitrarily chosen, Hebdige believes that they have a meaning outside the sign system; they are homologous with the focal concerns, activities, group structure and collective image of the subculture, and hold and reflect the central values of the group which adopts them.

Differences between male and female dress are frequently decoded as an expression of gender relations (Sharma 1978). In the Mediterranean and in Islamic societies (often denoted as "honor-shame" societies), anthropologists have interpreted cultural insistence on modest female dress as part of the "shame" syndrome (Campbell 1964; Jeffery 1979; Sabbah 1984). In these societies, it has been argued, male sexual desire, once aroused, is uncontrollable. Women are expected to carry the burden of avoiding such an eventuality by, among other things, dressing modestly; failure to do so may result in the loss of their reputation. Modest dress enhances the reputation of a woman's father, brothers or husband because it can be seen that she is under the control of the menfolk of her household. Control over female dress can also be part of a male strategy for achieving upward social mobility; Saifullah Khan (1976) and Chapkis (1988) have argued that the veil is most often worn in Islamic societies by the wives and daughters of those who have, or who seek to raise their status.

Dress is also used as a marker of ethnicity. The distinctive dress worn by some members of ethnic minorities in Britain and elsewhere has been variously interpreted as expressing an aspiration to succeed (Hebdige 1979; Lurie 1981), ethnic pride (Hebdige 1979; Wilson 1985), or a challenge to hegemony (Hebdige 1979). It can also be a symbol of relations between different ethnic groups (Lees 1986). Women's dress often takes on a particular significance in the iconography of ethnic minority cultures. Chapkis (1988) says that women's bodies are often the repository for "tradition"; when "traditional" dress is worn by women, it can be seen as an attempt to preserve or recreate a real or imagined past.

The interface between dress, gender, tradition and modernity is, however, complex and ambiguous. Ballard and Ballard (1977) and Saifullah Khan (1976) note that Sikh and Pakistani men who migrated to Britain in the 1950s usually adopted western dress, but women who traveled to join their husbands in the 1960s wore the same costume as in the homeland, making only minor modifications to allow for differences in climate. Wilson (1985) believes that women who adhere to or re-adopt "traditional" dress can symbolize authenticity in the face of imperialism, but at the price of being excluded from modernity, which is negotiated by men. MacLeod (1993) shows, in contrast, that participation in modernity in the form of working in office jobs has led many lower middle class women in Cairo to re-adopt covering dress and the veil. She interprets this as a symbolic resolution of the economic and ideological conflicts generated by the difficulty of reconciling paid employment, marriage and motherhood, and as an expression of a sense of loss for the status and power of a Muslim wife and mother.

Yet, as both MacLeod and Sabbah (1984) argue, the contradictions are not truly resolved. Wearing the veil at work asserts the primacy of wifehood and motherhood in Islamic societies, denies the economic dimension of women, and emphasizes that they only enter the workplace by special exemption. The adoption of western dress is equally loaded with ambiguities. Crawford (1984) believes that women who adopt western styles are attempting to find a definition of themselves in terms of the modern, western world. In so doing, they are withdrawing from participation in the kind of specifically female cultural power described by MacLeod, but before they have negotiated a re-definition of themselves and of their power in the modern world.

In this chapter I examine the styles of dress worn by Turkish Cypriots living in London, focussing particularly on the dress worn by single teenage girls[1] on ritual occasions such as weddings. Starting from Hebdige's (1979) assertion that styles hold and reflect the central values of the group which adopts them, I argue that girls' dress symbolizes attempts to explore alternative interpretations of respectable femininity appropriate to London in the late 1980s. I further argue that this dress can be decoded as an expression of the ambiguous interface between gender, tradition and modernity. The fashionable dress worn by Turkish Cypriot girls and young women in London acts both as a medium through which traditional practices – in this case, making marriages – persist, and as a means of reflecting and facilitating social change. This chapter is based on research conducted in London and in northern Cyprus between 1982 and 1989.

Dress and Respectability

There were approximately 45,000 Turkish Cypriots living in Britain in the late 1980s, the majority in London and the surrounding counties (Bridgwood 1985). The peak period for migration was in the 1950s and 1960s, which means that a whole generation has been born and brought up in Britain. Many migrants left Cyprus for economic reasons, and traveled to Britain in the hope of improving their standard of living (Berk 1972). In contrast to their female kin in Cyprus, the majority of women in London have paid employment.

---

1. The focus of the chapter is on the dress of teenage girls aged between 15 and 21, an age-group which would normally be designated as "young women". There is no term for "young woman" in Turkish. A female is a girl (*kız*, also a maiden), until her marriage, when she becomes a woman (*kadın*). After the menopause she is an old woman (*koca-karı*, literally a "husband-wife"). A male passes through four stages; he is successively a boy (*oğlan*), a young man (*genç*), a man (*adam*, a status which he gains on marriage) and an old man (*ihtihar*). In keeping with Turkish Cypriot usage, I use the term "girl" to designate an unmarried female except when she is in her mid-twenties, in which case I use the term "young woman".

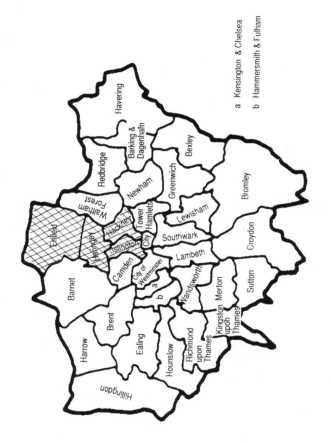

Map 2.1 London

a Kensington & Chelsea
b Hammersmith & Fulham

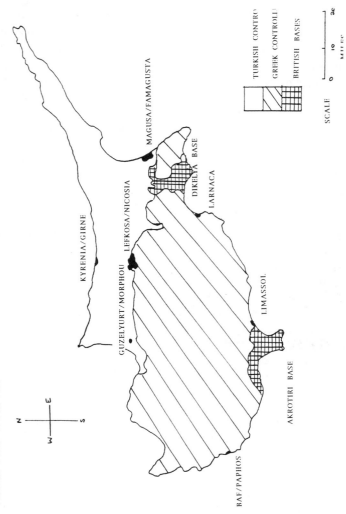

Map 2.2 Cyprus

TURKISH TOWN NAMES ARE GIVEN FIRST

Many early migrants, both men and women, worked in the clothing industry on arrival in London (Oakley 1971; Ladbury 1979), following the example of previous groups of migrants (Wilson 1985). It was estimated in 1979 that 60 percent of Cypriot women (Greek as well as Turkish) worked in this industry (Leeuwenberg 1979), many of them doing piecework at home (a practice known in the UK as outworking). At that time, up to half of London's fashion trade was produced by women working at home (Campbell 1979). Young Cypriot women are increasingly entering white collar and professional work, and training as hairdressers and beauticians, but middle-aged women continue to work in Cypriot-owned clothing factories or as outworkers, and mothers of young children take in sewing to do at home, which enables them to combine wage-earning with childcare. Dress therefore has more than the usual significance for Turkish Cypriots in London.

One of the principles illustrated by the styles of dress favored by Turkish Cypriots is the importance of respectability. Respectability is a key constituent of both male and female reputation, but its parameters differ for men and women. Female respectability depends on a modest demeanour, moderation in speech and dress, the satisfactory performance of domestic roles, and controlled sexuality – a constellation of attributes which is often labeled shame (Campbell 1964; Schneider 1971; Herzfeld 1980). Shame, however, has negative connotations, whereas *namus*, the term used by Turkish Cypriots, has a more positive meaning; it has been translated as sexual honor by Meeker (1976), while Turkish Cypriots use the term respectability when speaking in English. Respectability is of crucial importance to a single girl because it is the main criterion by which her marriageability is assessed, and loss of reputation can make it difficult for her to marry.[2] Young men must also be respectable if they are to make a good marriage, but modesty and purity are not expected from them; more important is evidence that a young man can apply

2. It is assumed by the majority of Turkish Cypriots that all young people will eventually marry, although a small minority choose to remain single or to cohabit. Unless their daughter is still in full-time education, parents start looking for a husband for her at any time after her sixteenth birthday. A young woman who has reached her twenties and shows a reluctance to marry will be subjected to a great deal of persuasion from her parents and other relatives to meet some suitable young men. A young man will be subjected to similar pressure once he reaches his mid-twenties. Turkish Cypriot parents do not speak of their daughters as "burdens", and there is no obligation to provide a large dowry. Most make a substantial contribution to a couple's wedding expenses, but the cost is usually shared with the groom's parents.

himself to his work, provide for a family, and desist from anti-social behavior such as drug-taking, excessive drinking or gambling. Ambitions to become self-employed or to start his own business also count in his favor. Respectable men are only occasionally described in Turkish as *namuslu* (respectable). They are more likely to be referred to as quiet (*yavaş*) or as a good man (*iyi bir adam*). The term "respectable" is used for both sexes in English.

In the past, respectability and modesty in dress were assured by concealing the body and, in the case of women, the face. In the early twentieth century, women in Cyprus wore an outfit consisting of baggy trousers (*şalwar*), a loose tunic, a veil covering the head and shoulders (*çarşaf*), and a thin gauze veil covering the face (*yaşmak*). Outside their immediate family, they only went unveiled in the presence of other women, and a young man was not supposed to see his fiancée's face before their wedding. The act of covering or concealing the hair has frequently been interpreted as a sign of self-restraint, control, and a denial of sexuality (Campbell-Jones 1979; Jeffery 1979; Lurie 1981). Men wore baggy, knee-length breeches, knee-high boots, white shirts, a waistcoat and a form of turban (Salvator 1983). A photograph taken by Thomson (1985) in 1878, just after Cyprus passed under British rule, shows a high-class (Greek) Cypriot woman wearing western dress, but informants' accounts suggest that Turkish Cypriot villagers only began to discard elements of their previous costume in the 1920s and 1930s. First to go for women was the *yaşmak*, then the loose trousers were replaced by ankle-length pantalettes worn under a long dress. Although it is occasionally possible to see elderly villagers wearing a modified form of this costume, the majority of men and women adopted western styles of dress during the 1930s and 1940s, before the main period of migration to Britain. Only very elderly village women now wear a veil. As the majority of migrants were in their twenties and thirties when they moved to Britain (Oakley 1971), most wore clothes which did not differ substantially from those worn by other Londoners at the time. Men were virtually indistinguishable by their dress. Only elderly women, moving to Britain to join their sons and daughters, wore remnants of the former costume, such as a headscarf.

In striving to decide what constituted respectable dress in London in the late 1980s, Turkish Cypriots had access to several, occasionally competing definitions of respectable femininity. The British, usually referred to as the "English," who ruled Cyprus for just under a century, have undoubtedly influenced styles of dress both in Cyprus

Figure 2.1 Older woman in Cyprus wearing a light veil (drawn by Rebecca Bailey© from a field photograph by Ann Bridgwood).

and, more recently, in London. A whole generation of girls has attended school and college in England and worked with English women, and up to one-quarter of Turkish Cypriot men in Britain marry English women (Bridgwood 1985). Girls and women are therefore well aware that definitions of respectability vary, and that dress which is not acceptable to some Turkish Cypriots would be considered respectable by many English people. Western dress is associated with modernity, a value to which many Turkish Cypriots in London subscribe. Cypriot women like to be fashionable and are in fact often ahead of fashion, as their involvement in the clothing industry means that they have access to new styles before they appear in the shops.

Turkey, which is seen by many Turkish Cypriots as their motherland, offers another standard of comparison. Educated and prosperous Mainland Turks living in large cities are admired by Turkish Cypriots for their stylish dress, but village women are often labeled as backward (*geri*) for continuing to wear *şalwar* and a veil. Mainland Turkish women who settled in Northern Cyprus after the 1974 war and who wear a *şalwar* and veil are similarly designated. This type of costume is only worn in London on special occasions such as festivals or holidays, when young people dress up to perform Turkish dances. Women wear a prayer scarf (*yemeni*) for *mevlits* – prayer readings for the dead – but there is very little evidence of Islamic fundamentalism or of moves to re-adopt the veil among Turkish Cypriots.

In summary, there has been a striking, although gradual, change in the norms of respectable dress for women. Although they have come from a situation where women were expected to conceal their bodies and faces from men's eyes, the majority of Turkish Cypriot women in London do not dress significantly differently from most English women, and men are virtually indistinguishable. This does not mean, however, that dress carries the same meaning for both groups, or that the norms are exactly the same. Women and girls are still expected to observe certain norms of modesty, and older people abhor what they see as the worst excesses of fashion, particularly if they transgress the requirements of female respectability. They argue that skirts should not be too short, nor necklines too low, although girls and young women do not always agree with them. Transparent and clinging fabrics are not approved of, and tight jeans which emphasize the buttocks are frowned on. Immodest dress is described as open (*açık*), a term which is also used to refer to a woman who is not considered respectable. Some parents forbid their daughters – and occasionally their sons – from wearing styles which they consider unacceptable, which can cause resentment among young people.

In addition to the almost universal adoption of western dress, there has been a shift in cultural conceptions of the ideal body shape. In Cyprus, a full, but not fat, figure is favored for single people, but bulk is admired in the married; women usually wear a (British) size 16 by their mid-twenties and may need a size 20 by their mid-thirties. Skinniness is thought ugly, and was formerly considered a sign of ill-health. In London, in contrast, there is a trend towards a slimmer figure, among married as well as single people; this is particularly true of women. Women in their twenties and thirties bemoan the "loss of their figure" which is seen as an inevitable consequence of maternity, and, like many English women, they occasionally diet, go to keep-fit classes, do workouts at home, and use fitness or exercise videos.

Bulk is a sign of prosperity and success in agricultural societies, while thinness indicates failure (Lurie 1981; Chapkis 1988). Bulk on women has the additional connotation of maternity, and of the status and respectability of being a wife and mother (Hirschon 1978; Crawford 1984; Chapkis 1988). A slim figure, on the other hand, is considered by some commentators to be boyish and pre-pubertal, and to connote powerlessness (Coward 1983; Wilson 1985). I will return to these arguments later.

Dancing the Jar: Girls' Dress at Turkish Cypriot Weddings

Weddings and engagement parties are the major life cycle rituals celebrated by Turkish Cypriots in London. In the mid-1980s, circumcision parties became more popular than formerly, and a few families hold large parties to mark six-month day (*altı aylık kına*), a thanksgiving for a child's surviving the first six months of life. Between 600 and 1,000 guests are invited to these parties, which are held in hotels, dance halls and town halls. Guests are provided with a full meal, plentiful drink and live entertainment. The hospitality is "repaid" by pinning banknotes onto a bride and groom at a wedding, or by placing money in the soldier's cap worn by boys at their circumcision parties. For the majority of families, parties of this kind form the center of their social life. During any given weekend, between one-third and one-quarter of Turkish Cypriots living in

London are likely to be at a wedding.

Weddings offer an excellent forum for display and conspicuous consumption, and people usually take care to look their best. A failure to dress well always suggests laziness, and is thought to indicate moral, as well as sartorial, slovenliness. On social occasions, it is in addition taken as an insult to the host. Both men and women like to present themselves well, and devote a good deal of time and money to their appearance. The majority of men wear a suit, shirt and tie for special or formal occasions, in contrast to the jeans, open-necked shirts, sweatshirts or sweaters favored for everyday wear.

Women's dress on ritual occasions is more marked than men's by age differences. Single girls are expected to make the most of their looks, and they spend a lot of time thinking about and perfecting their appearance. They choose attractive and flamboyant clothes in bright colors, made from silky, shiny materials, with lots of frills and flounces. Make-up is applied to achieve noticeable effects; lipsticks and eye make-up are of bright and striking colors. Both girls and women wear their best jewellery, usually gold. In contrast to the previous practice of covering the head, girls and young women now grow their hair to shoulder length and longer, and arrange it in a way which emphasizes "body", thus making an erotic feature of it (Leach 1958; Firth 1973; Savage-King 1988).

It has become increasingly common for young married women to dress and make-up in a similar fashion to single girls, although this is not really approved of by older people who feel that they should dress more soberly. Strapless dresses, figure-hugging clothes, short skirts and lots of frills and flounces, for example, are not always thought suitable for married women, especially if they have children. It can, however, be difficult to distinguish between single and young married women at weddings – the wedding rings of the latter often provide the only clue. Whereas middle-aged women normally favor a skirt with a blouse or sweater for daily wear, they will wear a suit or a skirt or dress of simple style with a jacket for more formal occasions. Their aim is elegance rather than flamboyance, and most prefer rich to bright colors, plum rather than cherry red, for example. Influenced to some extent by English women of their own age who continue to make the most of their looks – both Joan Collins and Margaret Thatcher are admired as women who look good for their age – Cypriot women in London continue to use make-up into their late forties and early fifties, whereas their kin in Cyprus tend to cease using it in their late thirties or early forties. Older women wear dresses and skirts with a headscarf at home, and suits, thick stockings and a headscarf for social events.

Most weddings include a short ritual known as "dancing the jar".[3] The jar (*testi*) is a water pitcher made of unglazed clay (which can be bought at most Cypriot grocery stores), filled with small change and covered with a red cloth. The money is said to symbolize the bride's treasure — her virginity — and the red cloth the blood which will be shed on her wedding night. Ideally, it should be danced by seven virgins, seven being a particularly auspicious number.[4] The girls, who are usually sisters or cousins of the bride and groom, dance in turn, each one holding the jar high in the air as she twists and turns in the dance. While they are dancing, relatives stuff banknotes into their clothes, which are later used to pay the band. When they have all danced, the jar is smashed and children scramble for the money. The breaking of the jar symbolizes the breaking of the bride's hymen. One of the dancers may try to retrieve the red cloth, as it is believed by some that the successful girl will be the next to marry. Girls who know that they are going to participate in this dance dress in their most glamorous outfit, the fit and cut of which often show off their figure and emphasize erotic features such as breasts and buttocks. Off-the-shoulder or strapless dresses, hairstyles which emphasize "body", and noticeable make-up, are all designed to draw attention to a girl's looks.

It comes as something of a surprise, given the cultural emphasis on respectable femininity, to see girls dancing thus in front of an audience of several hundred, being not only watched by men but also recorded on video. Their behavior is in part rendered respectable by the environment. Lurie (1981) believes that the meaning of any costume depends on the circumstances in which it is worn, and dress

3. The ritual is almost certainly a transformation of a feature of village weddings in Cyprus in the 1920s and 1930s. In some villages, prior to consummation of the marriage, the bridegroom placed a water pitcher on the roof of the marital home. The following morning, assured of his wife's virginity, he climbed up onto the roof and smashed the pitcher, thus proclaiming his wife's honor to the whole village. A smaller and more private version of "dancing the jar" features in quilt parties held by some brides in Cyprus a few days before their wedding, when their trousseau is displayed to female kin. Informants say that the ritual is fairly recent, and it is likely that it was copied from London weddings, video recordings of which are sent to relatives in Cyprus.
4. Seven is also considered to be the most auspicious age for boys to be circumcized. Many parents now prefer the operation to be performed at an earlier age, in which case it should ideally be done in an "odd" year; that is, at the age of one, three or five. Weddings and circumcision rituals share several common features.

Figure 2.2 Dancing the jar in London (drawn by Rebecca Bailey©
from a field photograph by Ann Bridgwood).

worn on ritual occasions is often characterized by a degree of licence. The girls are under parental supervision throughout the evening, their costume has been vetted by their parents and everyone present is aware that the rules governing the choice of dress on ritual occasions are different from those operating in everyday life. Display, if properly managed, can be modest. Jeffery (1979) describes how a new bride among the Pirzade (who observe strict *purdah*) is permitted to indulge in display and decoration for a few years after marriage. She wears fine materials and bright colors, and is shown off to visitors. Hers is a silent display, however; she says little and observes a modest demeanour. Indeed, she is a caricature of modesty. Although Turkish Cypriot girls dance in public, any attempt by a young man to start a conversation would be quickly warded off by a father or brother. This type of dress is only acceptable, in parents' minds, because it is linked to marriageability.

Turkish Cypriot marriage can be broadly described as "arranged" (in Turkish, people speak of "making" rather than of "arranging" marriages), in that parents often play an active role in choosing their children's spouses. The young people have the final say over whether or not a proposed match goes ahead, and girls and young men living in London increasingly find their own partners. Even in the latter cases, however, the couple ask their parents to arrange a *dünürcülük*, the occasion on which a young man and his family ask a girl's father for her hand in marriage. Although there are pockets of dense Turkish Cypriot settlement in London, the Turkish Cypriot population as a whole is dispersed over a wide geographical area. Parents can let it be known among their friends and acquaintances that they are looking for a husband for their daughter, but weddings provide an ideal opportunity to signal this to a wider audience. The ritual of dancing the jar is an accepted way of "announcing" publicly that a girl is on the marriage market, and parents may urge their daughters to take part. A young man who finds one of the dancers attractive can ask his parents to arrange a meeting with her family. Looks alone are not a sufficient basis for a marriage, as the standing of the girl's family and her own reputation are also of crucial importance, but catching a young man's eye is often the first step in initiating the process. Some girls resent the "cattle market" atmosphere of the dance, which young men often jestingly refer to as "for sales" (the verb *satmak*, "to sell", was formerly used to describe the act of giving a girl in marriage), and avoid participating in the ritual as they find the whole procedure highly embarrassing.

Why are young men not displayed in the same way? Girls and young men are not in an equivalent position in the marriage market. The cultural norms of female modesty prevent girls from taking an active role in seeking a husband, but it is acceptable for a young man to look around for a suitable girl, and to suggest to his parents that they should arrange a meeting with the family of a girl to whom he is attracted. It may also be easier for young men to find a wife. As noted earlier, up to one-quarter of Turkish Cypriot men in London marry foreign (mostly English) women. The number of women marrying foreign men is much smaller, amounting to only a handful a year. This is largely because girls have far fewer opportunities to meet men socially, whereas young men usually have a number of foreign girlfriends before they marry. These pre-marital relationships sometimes become serious and result in marriage. Although I do not have the data to make a definitive statement, there may be a "shortage" of eligible young men, a possibility which appears to be confirmed by evidence that more young women than young men turn to Cyprus to find a spouse (Bridgwood 1985).

Exploring Respectable Femininity

Mulvey (1981) argues that, in a world ordered by sexual imbalance, pleasure in looking has been split between active/male and passive/female. The determining male gaze projects its fantasy on to the female figure, which is styled accordingly. Coward (1983) believes that women's bodies and the messages which dress adds are the repository of social meanings of sexuality. A woman's dress is often decoded as an indicator of her sexual respectability; women are compelled to make themselves attractive in ways which involve submitting to cultural beliefs about appropriate sexual behavior and ways of dress. Berger (1972) writes movingly of the way in which a woman's self-being is split in two; into the surveyor and the surveyed. She must constantly survey herself, doing so through male eyes, because what is normally thought of as her success depends on her appearance. Knowing that she is the object of the male gaze, she turns herself into an object of vision. Men's bodies and dress convey different messages; again according to Berger, a man's presence is dependent on the promise of power, whether moral, physical, temperamental, economic, social or sexual, which he embodies.

At first sight, it would appear that Turkish Cypriot girls turn themselves into objects of vision to be displayed in order to be "sold".

Although parents deny vehemently that they are selling their daughters, the young men who call the dances "for sales" are not so far wrong, as they provide parents with an opportunity to display their offering on the marriage market. The dress worn by the girls and the money donated by their kin for the band are evidence of their family's financial standing. The messages which are communicated by girls' bodies and dress are, however, ambivalent.

On the one hand, by wearing glamorous outfits and making themselves up, they appear to presenting themselves to the gaze of young men. On the other, some girls try to subvert the dance to their own ends, in an attempt to exercise a degree of control over the process of marriage-making. Many would like to meet their own husband rather than have a marriage arranged for them, but few have the opportunity to do so. Couples sometimes meet at school, college or work, but girls tend to be closely supervised in their free time, and it can be difficult for them in the course of normal social life to get to know suitable young men well enough for a friendship to develop into marriage.[5] Some girls therefore welcome the opportunity to try and attract a suitor by dancing because they feel that they can at least present a self-image which is of their own choosing.

Looking,[6] for Turkish Cypriots, is closely linked to the idea of romance. Older couples who eloped after failing to win their parents' approval for their marriage say that, even when they had little opportunity to speak to each other prior to their marriage, they knew that they loved each other because they "saw it in the eyes." This has an added resonance when it is remembered that a woman's eyes were the only exposed part of her face in the days of the *yaşmak*. Although girls have little opportunity actively to search for a husband, they can at least put themselves into a position where they can be chosen for their looks. This has much more romantic appeal for most girls than having a marriage arranged for them by their parents. At the same time, it is a reflection of their disadvantage in the marriage market; unable openly to seek a husband, and possibly

5. It is not uncommon for second and third cousins living in London to marry each other. The majority of matches of this type on which I collected data were of the couple's own choosing. Wedding parties and other family gatherings provide an opportunity for girls to get to know distantly-related young men from other branches of their family reasonably well. First cousins, one of whom lives in Cyprus and one in London, occasionally marry — again by choice.
6. I use the term "looking" rather than "gazing" here to indicate that looking was a mutual process, distinct from the one-way male gaze.

in competition with other girls for eligible young men, a girl can only present herself for the scrutiny for others. She is not supposed to speak to unknown young men, and can therefore do little more than project an ideal image of herself.

The gaze is also fraught with danger. Although beliefs about the evil eye are dismissed as nonsense by some young people, many Turkish Cypriots still believe that illness and misfortune can come to those who have an "eye" on them. Babies are protected from such an eventuality by having a *maşallah* brooch, which invokes God to watch over them, pinned on their clothing. Newly-circumcized boys, brides and newly-delivered mothers are similarly surrounded by protective ritual. "Eyes" are often associated with jealousy and envy, and ostentatious display is sometimes avoided to ward off misfortune. Participation in the dance therefore generates anxiety, although this is usually discussed in terms of the likely effect on a girl's reputation rather than on the possibility of her becoming a victim of the evil eye.

Girls who take part in the ritual of dancing the jar are caught in a series of contradictions. They have to compromize between dressing attractively enough to bring themselves to the attention of young men, and remaining sufficiently modest to avoid being thought fast or "open." Those who err on the side of modesty run the risk of being thought "ugly." There is a very thin dividing line between the two, and it is extremely difficult to get the balance exactly right.

Turkish Cypriot girls are well aware of these risks. It is hardly surprising that they devote so much time to getting ready for weddings and carefully assess the impression that different outfits and hairstyles will make on observers. How much control can a girl exercise over the gaze of others? She knows that she cannot determine how other people decode her dress, and has to try and reach an acceptable balance between appearing attractive and remaining respectable. Her family's reputation is an important variable in that those with wealth and standing are less likely to suffer a loss of reputation than others. Even so, there are always some individuals who will judge a girl to be "ugly" or "open", particularly if they know nothing about her character or family background. In trying to find a husband for their daughter, parents run the risk of damaging her reputation and of provoking envy and accusations that they are flaunting their wealth.

Some girls, albeit unwittingly, challenge their parents' view that attractive dress is bound up with marriageability. Not all of those who

Figure 2.3 A modern Cypriot birthday party in London (drawn by Rebecca Bailey© from a field photograph by Ann Bridgwood).

take part in the dance do so with thoughts of attracting a suitor. Some girls welcome the opportunity to be the center of attention, given that they are normally supposed to be self-effacing in the presence of people other than their kin. Most derive a great deal of pleasure from choosing, buying and wearing attractive clothes, and some try to have a different outfit for each wedding. Getting ready for a wedding, although sometimes fraught with anxiety in case an outfit, hairstyle or make-up should appear unattractive or "open", is also intensely pleasurable and exciting, and girls look forward to making a good impression.

This separation between dressing up and marriage-making is even more evident in the case of young married women who, it has been argued, do not look significantly different from their single sisters. Rather than forming part of a strategy to attract a husband, their dress and slim figures are symbolic of an ambivalence which many young women feel towards maternity (Bridgwood 1985). Their parents are, at least partially, aware of this, and complain that their daughters are too thin and do not eat enough. Far from suggesting an aesthetic of powerlessness (Coward 1983; Wilson 1985; Chapkis 1988), a slim figure can be seen as an indication that Turkish Cypriot women in London are valued as much by their husbands for their earning power as for their reproductive capacity, as women's earnings make an essential contribution to achieving culturally-desired standards of living.

Some girls and young women go further and separate attractive dress from the controlled environment which renders it respectable. A few young women organize their own parties, to celebrate a birthday or a similar occasion, for which they pay themselves; older people are rarely present at these parties. The young women who host these events are usually in their twenties, and employed in white collar or professional jobs which accord them a degree of autonomy and confer respectability. This to some extent protects them from criticism, although not everyone would condone their behavior. Many parents refuse to allow their daughters to attend such parties because they are unsupervised. Nevertheless, they represent a challenge by young women to parental views of how they should dress, and in what circumstances.

Conclusion

When reading the literature on dress, one sometimes gets the impression that women cannot win. If they wear concealing outfits or are veiled, they are seen as icons of tradition; if on the other hand they adopt western dress, they are described as trapped in an image of powerlessness (Crawford 1984; Chapkis 1988). Dress is never value-free; there is no style which does not carry some connotation of, for example, imperialism, oppression or liberation. Turkish Cypriot women who adopt elements of British costume are not necessarily slavishly copying western dress and abandoning their own cultural values. The dress worn by Turkish Cypriots in London is as much a reflection of their own culture as of British culture.

It is important to look not only at dress, but at the meanings surrounding it and the environment in which it is worn. Western dress can be simultaneously a sign of change, an agent of change and a preserver of tradition; it can symbolize the complex relationships between gender, tradition and modernity. From being veiled in the presence of non-related men, Turkish Cypriot girls are now allowed to expose themselves to the gaze of dozens of young men. In a controlled environment, this helps to maintain parental involvement in making marriages. Dress can act as a vehicle for exploring new ideas; as Wilson (1985) says, it can be used to express and explore our more daring aspirations. Some girls subvert the dance to their own ends in the hope of attracting their own husband, thus diminishing their parents' role and undermining tradition. Young married women go further by separating attractive dress and marriage-making. The increased financial independence of young women allows them to experiment with dress, and alternative sources of respectability such as work make modesty in dress less critical in the assessment of their reputation. The parties which young people organize for themselves represent a further step, in that they suggest that an environment free from parental supervision can nevertheless be respectable.

These changes potentially threaten the very basis of Turkish Cypriot society in London. Many parents argue that, should they become less involved in marriage-making, rates of out-marriage would increase and Turkish Cypriot identity would be diluted. Interestingly, young people who reject this argument when single sometimes ruefully admit that they agree with their parents once they have children of their own. Competing interpretations of female respectability – one of the main criteria by which Turkish Cypriots distinguish themselves from the English – also potentially undermine cultural distinctiveness. The contradictions which the girls experience during the dance are symptomatic of the wider contradictions experienced by Turkish Cypriots in attempting to retain a distinctive identity appropriate to London in the late 1980s.

Finally, it is interesting to ask to what extent Turkish Cypriot girls and women have been influenced by feminism. There are, of course, some young women who consider themselves to be feminists; others would say that they are not feminists, but would like to have a marriage based on partnership. Few are completely untouched by feminism, in that most want to work, to choose their own jobs, to have a say in the choice of their husband, and to have children when they want. Very few would say that respectability was of no importance, but their understanding of the term differs from that of their parents.[7] Rather than labelling themselves as feminists, many young Turkish Cypriot women are exploring different interpretations of respectable femininity, which means that the parameters of respectability are gradually changing.

Acknowledgements

I am grateful to the Central Research Fund of the University of London, which made grants available for fieldtrips to northern Cyprus, and to the Radcliffe-Brown Memorial Fund, which gave financial support towards the cost of writing up the research on which the chapter is based. Thanks are due to David McKnight of the London School of Economics, who supervised the research. Peter Loizos, although having no formal supervisory role, has nevertheless given generously of his time and offered continuing encouragement and support. Patricia Melville, Lesley Saunders, Malcolm Rigg and Roger Blackmore read and commented on earlier drafts of the chapter, and made many interesting and valuable suggestions.

7. Parents' definitions of respectability have also changed. Middle-aged women who were brought up in Cyprus with the idea that married women did not work outside the home soon accepted this as normal, respectable and even desirable behavior after migrating to England.

References

Ballard, R., and Ballard, C. (1977), "The Sikhs: The Development of South Asian Settlements in Britain," in J. Watson (ed.), *Between Two Cultures*, Oxford: Blackwell.

Barthes, R. (1972), *Mythologies*, London: Jonathan Cape.

Berger, J. (1972), *Ways of Seeing*, London: BBC and Penguin Books.

Berk, F. (1972), "A study of the Turkish Cypriot community in North London, with particular reference to its background, its structure and the changes taking place within it", unpublished M. Phil. thesis, University of York.

Bridgwood, A. (1985), "Marriage, Honour and Property: Turkish Cypriots in North London", unpublished Ph. D. thesis, University of London.

Campbell, B. (1979), "Lining their pockets," *Time Out*, July 13–19.

Campbell, J. (1964), *Honour, Family and Patronage: A Study of Institutions and Moral Values in a Greek Mountain Community*, Oxford: Oxford University Press.

Campbell-Jones, S. (1979), *In Habit*, London: Faber.

Chapkis, W. (1988), *Beauty Secrets: Women and the Politics of Appearance*, London: Women's Press.

Coward, R. (1983), *Female Desire: Women's Sexuality Today*, London: Paladin.

Crawford, S. (1984), "Person and Place in Kalavassos: Perspectives on Change in a Greek Cypriot Village," unpublished Ph. D. thesis, University of Cambridge.

Firth, R. (1973), *Symbols: Public and Private*, London: Allen and Unwin.

Hebdige, D. (1979), *Subculture: The Meaning of Style*, London: Methuen.

Herzfeld, M. (1980), "Honour and Shame: Problems in the Comparative Analysis of Moral Systems," *Man NS*, vol. 15, pp. 339–51.

Hirschon, R. (1978), "Open Body/Closed Space: The Transformation of Female Sexuality," in S. Ardener (ed.), *Defining Females: The Nature of Women in Society*, London: Croom Helm.

Jeffery, P. (1979), *Frogs in a Well: Indian Women in Purdah*, London: Zed Press.

Ladbury, S. (1979), *Cypriots in Britain: A Report on the Social and Working Lives of the Greek and Turkish Cypriot Communities in London*, London: National Centre for Industrial Language Training.

Leach, E. (1958), "Magical Hair," *Journal of the RAI*, vol. 88, pp. 147–64.

Lees, S. (1986), *Losing Out: Sexuality and Adolescent Girls*, London: Hutchinson.

Leeuwenberg, J. (1979), *The Cypriots in Haringey*, London: The Polytechnic of North London School of Librarianship, Research Report No. 1.

Lurie, A. (1981), *The Language of Clothes*, London: Heinemann.

MacLeod, A.E. (1993), *Accommodating Protest: Working Women, the New*

Veiling and Change in Cairo, New York: Columbia University Press.

Meeker, M. (1976), "Meaning and Society in the Near East: Examples from the Black Sea Turks and the Levantine Arabs," *International Journal of Middle East Studies*, vol. 7, pp. 243–70, 383–422.

Mulvey, L. (1981), "Visual Pleasure and Narrative Cinema," in T. Bennett, S. Boyd-Bowman, C. Mercer and J. Woollacott (eds), *Popular Television and Film*, London: British Film Institute.

Oakley, R. (1971), "Cypriot Migration and Settlement in Britain," unpublished Ph. D. thesis, University of Oxford.

Sabbah, F. (1984), *Woman in the Muslim Unconscious*, London: Pergamon.

Saifullah Khan, V. (1976), "Purdah in the British Situation," in D.L. Barker and S. Allen (eds), *Dependence and Exploitation in Work and Marriage*, London: Longman.

Salvator, Archduke Louis (1983), *Levkosia: The Capital of Cyprus*, London: Trigraph (first published in 1881).

Savage-King, C. (1988), "Short Back and Sides," *New Statesman and Society*, 4th Nov. 1988.

Schneider, J. (1971), "On Vigilance and Virgins: Honour, Shame and Access to Resources in Mediterranean Societies," *Ethnology*, vol. 10, pp. 1–24.

Sharma, U. (1978), "Women and Their Affines: The Veil as a Symbol of Separation," *Man NS*, vol. 13, pp. 218–33.

Thomson, J. (1985), *Through Cyprus with the Camera in the Autumn of 1878*, Trigraph: London (first published in 1879).

Wilson, E. (1985), *Adorned in Dreams: Fashion and Modernity*, London: Virago.

3

Ethnicity in Greek Dress

Linda Welters

Traditional Greek dress of the late nineteenth and early twentieth centuries displays an unusual variety in both form and decoration. Writers on the subject struggle to explain this sartorial jumble by prefacing their interpretations with such phrases as "inexhaustible multiplicity" (Benaki 1948: 21) and "virtually impossible to classify" (Desses 1962: 54). Angeliki Hatzimichali, the pioneer in the study of Greek folk art, made distinctions between clothing styles based on geography (plains, mountains, islands, towns and cities) in her early work. She also pointed out differences between everyday clothing and bridal and festival wear, as well as variations based on the age of the wearer. Later in her career she began to think in terms of the forms of the garments themselves and organized them into groups based on the presence of a particular component, such as the *sigouni*, a sleeveless coat, the *kavadi*, an open coat with sleeves, or the *foustani*, an outer dress with full skirt (Hatzimichali 1977: 15). Papantoniou refined and expanded the scholarship on Greek dress by presenting regional types in terms of their stylistic influence – Byzantine, Renaissance, or Turkish – as well as their chronological development (Papantoniou 1976, 1978, 1981).

I propose that dress sometimes functioned to identify individuals as members of specific ethnic groups[1] living within Greece, especially in areas on the Greek mainland with a mixed population. Peoples of diverse ethnic backgrounds lived in these regions for centuries. Important for this study are Greek-Albanians, Sarakatsani and Vlachs.

---

1. Ethnic group is defined here as "any group of people who set themselves apart and are set apart from other groups with whom they interact or coexist in terms of some distinctive criterion or criteria which may be linguistic, racial or cultural" (C. Seymour-Smith (1986), *Macmillan Dictionary of Anthropology*, London: Macmillan Press).

The dress of these peoples, rooted in their own traditions, often served to differentiate them from their neighbors at a glance.

The concept of ethnicity in Greek dress is not new. Non-Greek scholars who studied specific cultural groups in Greece recognized the communicative power of dress. Wace (1914) included a chapter on dress in his account of life and customs among the Vlachs of the northern Pindus, whereas Leigh Fermor (1962) discussed the garb of the Sarakatsani he met in his travels in northern Greece.

Greek scholars recognize the ethnic influence on traditional dress in their country, although they do not emphasize it. Instead Hatzimichali and others of her generation presented Greece's dress traditions as part of national heritage. A re-examination of the roots of modern Greek culture, including popular art, began during the period between the two world wars and continued after the Second World War (Clogg 1985: 317). Major works published by leading Greek museums, which bear titles such as *Hellenic National Costumes* (Benaki 1948 & 1954) and *Embroideries and Jewellery of Greek National Costumes* (Zora 1981), underscore the nationalistic tendencies of this period. In the introduction to *Hellenic National Costumes*, Hatzimichali wrote "Greek costume is the living and aesthetic expression of a single large national group, and particular local types are but the various manifestations of this group" (Benaki 1948: 21).

But was Greek dress really "national"? The label "national costume" implies that special clothing was worn to affiliate the wearer with a particular nation. The only true "national" dress in Greece was the folksy romantic ensembles adopted by Greece's King Otto and Queen Amalia in the late 1830s and worn by diplomats and aristocrats in the main towns (Papantoniou 1981: 11, 47). The creation of "national dress" in Greece was part of an international trend in the western world, which idealized rural life and its down-to-earth values in the aftermath of social changes brought on by the Industrial Revolution. It also had political meaning; as in other European countries, identification of what is more accurately described as ethnic or regional dress as "national dress" helped to unify diverse populations and define national boundaries. Even after most of Greece abandoned traditional dress in favor of styles inspired by western European fashion, Greeks donned their traditional attire on national holidays to celebrate their independence, thus reinforcing the association of Greek dress with Greece as a nation.

Understandably, the concept of ethnicity in Greek dress was not a popular stance to take in early publications on the subject. Greeks have endeavored since their independence from Ottoman rule to define who they are. Haunted by the glory that was ancient Greece, modern Greeks have resisted acknowledging their country's mixed ethnic heritage. The dress of the country's various ethnic groups has been downplayed, as have other aspects of ethnicity such as customs, folklore and language. Instead, Greek writers have emphasized the uniquely "Greek" characteristics of the clothing which varied from region to region.

Most Greek dress of the nineteenth and early twentieth centuries has been described as "regional dress." Like rural dress from other areas of Europe, one of its functions was to identify the wearer as coming from a group of villages within a certain district. Regional variations in Greek dress have been fairly well documented, particularly women's dress which changed considerably from one group of villages to the next. Still, attributing all variations in Greek dress to regionalism based on geographic, stylistic and historic influences is misleading. It is necessary to consider the concept of dressing to represent ethnic identity within a community of mixed heritage in order to understand the role of dress in signifying cultural affiliation. We shall see in the following discussion that this occurred at both the micro and macro levels on the Greek mainland.

This chapter is based on four field research projects conducted in Greece between 1983 and 1990. The methodological approach was ethno-historical. Tape-recorded interviews with nearly four hundred villagers in Attica, the Peloponnesian provinces of Argolida and Corinthia, in Boeotia and western Fokida on the mainland and throughout the island of Euboea form the basis of my sources. Extant garments in the villagers' dowries and in museum collections aided in understanding stylistic differences between the various clothing types, and written and pictorial observations by travelers from the seventeenth to the twentieth centuries also provided information.

Ethnic Groups in Greece

Greece is home to numerous ethnic groups including Albanians, Vlachs, Koutsovlachs, Arvanito-Vlachs, Karaghounides, Sarakatsani, Bulgarian Muslims, Turks, Sephardic Jews, and Serbs. Nineteenth-century travelers in search of the descendants of the ancient Greeks were disappointed to find so little of what they considered pure Greek blood in the towns and villages surrounding the famous ancient sites, yet exhilarated at the colorful human landscape created by this ethnic mix. One traveler wrote of Albanians who had "overrun the whole province" of Attica and of the few towns which had remained "free from contamination" of the Slavic races (Rodd 1892: 5), while another exclaimed enthusiastically: "I saw the 'Albanian' costume for the first time in Athens" (Harrison 1878: 82). Almost all the authors of the many travelogs from this period described local garb whenever they encountered it. Such descriptions provide benchmark data about the dress of specific ethnic groups and the context in which they were found.

The people I interviewed resided in a geographical area of mainland Greece which extends in a circle around Athens and encompasses a ring of provinces or regions (see map). This area is diverse in that it includes historically important cities such as Athens, Nafplion, Thebes and Delphi, old port towns famous in the heyday of sailing ships, agricultural markets such as the one at Argos, rugged mountains such as the Killini range in the Peloponnese, fertile plains such as Messoghia in Attica and Livadia in Boeotia, and islands adjacent to the mainland, such as Euboea.

In this large area several ethnic groups existed more or less as neighbors. Peasants of Albanian ancestry and nomadic shepherds of Sarakatsani origin lived among the settled Greeks, and the appellation of "Vlach" was applied to some groups in this area as well. Language, livelihood, physical traits, housing forms and clothing styles differed between the groups. Each group retained its own customs and manners through a social structure that discouraged intermingling with other groups except for commerce. Marriages were arranged by the families of the bride and groom to ensure that alliances outside the ethnic community did not occur.

Today these groups consider themselves Greeks first and members of an ethnic group second. It must be remembered that these groups have lived in the land that is now called Greece for centuries. Some migrated there during the Byzantine era; others came while Greece was under Turkish rule. Greece's present political boundaries were determined only in this century. The collapse of the Ottoman Empire and the subsequent exchange of populations between Greece and Turkey in 1922–23 re-located thousands of refugee families to various parts of the "new" Greece (Clogg 1985: 313). Thus, while political and cultural leaders tried to assimilate the various ethnic traditions of the many groups living in Greece under the rubric of "national," the groups themselves functioned as distinct cultural units, as they had

Map 3.1 Greece

done for hundreds of years under foreign rule, until mass communication and economic development finally blurred their individual identities.

Greek-Albanians

Greeks of Albanian ancestry inhabit villages throughout central Greece, calling themselves *Arvanites*. The movement of Albanians into Attica and the Peloponnese began in the fourteenth century. The Albanian settlement of Attica began at the official invitation of Catalan rulers who were attempting to repopulate the region after devastation by Navarrese soldiers of fortune. Settlement extended into the mountainous parts of Boeotia and to the southern section of Euboea, and finally to the islands of Salamis, Aegina and Anghistri in the Saronic Gulf and Andros in the Aegean Sea. Much later, during the Turkish occupation, Albanians appeared on the islands of Hydra, Spetsae and Poros. In the Peloponnese, Albanian immigration increased in the late fourteenth century; records indicate that 10,000 Albanian men, women and children appeared at the Isthmus with their animals in 1394, probably in flight from the Turks (Vacalopoulos 1970: 10). By the nineteenth century, Albanians were unofficially estimated to constitute between one-fourth (About 1857: 49) and one-half (*Handbook* 1884: 58–64) of the population of mainland Greece.

Albanians who settled in Attica, the Peloponnese and other parts of central Greece were from southern Albania. They were Orthodox Christians, just like the Greeks. The Albanians lived on excellent terms with their Greek neighbors, but resisted efforts to be completely Hellenized; they very seldom intermarried with Greeks (*Handbook* 1884: 59). They preserved their own Albanian dialect known as *Arvanitika* well into the twentieth century in some areas; this is particularly true of the Messoghia villages of Attica, which were almost entirely Albanian. Elderly Greek-Albanian women I interviewed sometimes considered *Arvanitika* their first language and apologized for their poor speaking ability in Greek.

In Messoghia during the Turkish occupation, even non-Albanians, observing the favorable treatment the Moslem Albanian mercenaries of the Turks accorded the Albanians, adopted Albanian identity. One author noted that in this area, "it may be presumed that whole Greek villages were assimilated by the Albanians" (Vacalopoulos 1970: 12).

Albanians living in the mountainous parts of the central Peloponnese were shepherds who practiced a nomadic lifestyle.

Randolph, who visited Turkish-occupied Greece from 1671 to 1679, described those he saw in Arcadia: "the Albaneses (who are shepherds, and 3 times the Number, as the Turks, and Greeks which are in these parts) live most in Tents, removing their tents and herds according to the season of the year . . ." He remarked that they "kept themselves up in the mountains" (Randolph 1687: 12).

In other regions the Albanians were more rapidly Hellenized, notably on Aegina and Hydra, where the development of a successful merchant fleet made the Albanians the aristocrats of the islands. Here, Hellenization was accelerated due to contact with the outside world gained through travel and to the necessity of speaking Greek rather than Albanian for commercial purposes (Arnaoutoglou 1986: 9–12).

According to old travel books, the nineteenth-century traveler could readily identify Greek-Albanian peasants by their dress. The people and their garb, labeled as "Albanian," were frequently described in contemporary written accounts or depicted in watercolors and engravings. The main components of dress associated with Greek-Albanian women were a distinctively embroidered chemise or shift and a thick white woolen sleeveless coat called *sigouni* and for men an outfit with a short full skirt known as the *foustanella*. Some names for the components of women's garments were Albanian rather than Greek (Welters 1988: 93–4). For instance, bridal and festival chemises with hems embroidered in silk were termed *foundi*, meaning "the end" in Albanian.

Edmund About, a French traveler, described female clothing as it was in the mid-nineteenth century:

> The Albanian women wear a long shift of cotton cloth, embroidered, at the skirt, the collar, and the sleeves, with silks of all colours – this is the principal part of their clothing; to this is added an apron, and a paletot of thick woollen, a broad sash of black wool; and for the head-dress, a cotton scarf embroidered like the shift. One constantly meets women with this elementary clothing. (1857: 31–2)

A half-century later not much had changed when Baedecker observed: "The Albanian peasant women still adhere to their national dress, consisting of a long shirt, embroidered at the sleeves and kept in place by a leather girdle; above this is a short white woolen jacket. In their hair and round their necks they wear strings of coins" (1909: xlviii–xlix).

Identifying the Greek-Albanian man by his clothing was more difficult after the War of Independence, for the so-called "Albanian

Figure 3.1 Bridal couple from Spata, 1870s. The groom eventually became the mayor of Spata, a prosperous village of Attica inhabited by Greek-Albanians. He wears a *foustanella* of the type made popular after the War of Independence. The bride wears an elaborately embroidered chemise called *foundi* with a *griza*, a local variant of the *sigouni*. Photograph: Privately owned. Copied by Linda Welters with permission during field research.

costume" became what has been identified as a "true" national dress on the mainland of Greece. In admiration for the heroic deeds of the Independence fighters, many of whom were *Arvanites*, a fancy version of the *foustanella* was adopted by diplomats and philhellenes for town wear. Otto, the Bavarian prince invited by the newly independent Greeks to be their king in 1833, made the *foustanella* official court dress. Lord Byron, the most famous philhellene of the time, was painted wearing a *foustanella*. As the nineteenth century wore on, European-style frock coats and sack suits gradually replaced the *foustanella* among urban dwellers, while the peasants more or less continued to wear it into the twentieth century. In the Peloponnese especially, the men continued to wear the *foustanella* even after the women had given up traditional dress for European-style clothing.

The *foustanella* has been described as a development of the medieval tunic, worn like a long shirt belted at the waist (Rodd 1892: 73). In the nineteenth century the *foustanella* consisted of a wide-sleeved shirt and a multi-gored skirt made from many yards of linen or cotton. A short vest or jacket, wide belt, leggings and fez cap completed the outfit. Versions worn by the wealthier townspeople after the war had voluminous knee-length skirts, velvet jackets and gaiters couched with gold thread. The poorer peasants wore a one-piece version of this garment which used less fabric. It was called *poukamiso* (Greek for shirt) rather than *foustanella* (*fousta* is an Italian word meaning skirt). Often the *poukamiso* was made from checked cotton handwoven at home rather than white machine-woven muslin purchased in a nearby town. The peasants omitted the fancy vests and gaiters and wore instead simple vests or capes and white woolen leggings.

To this day the *foustanella* is inextricably tied to the idea of the modern Greek state. When school boys dress up to celebrate national holidays such as Greek Independence Day (March 25) they wear *foustanellas* made by their mothers on home sewing machines or bought at the local costume shop. Cartoons depicting Greeks with other nationalities illustrate the Greek in his *foustanella*. Tourists can still see versions of this outfit in Athens on the Evzones who guard the tomb of the Unknown Soldier in front of the Old Palace building at Syntagma Square.

Sarakatsani

Another ethnic group easily identified in the past by their clothing
were the Sarakatsani. The Sarakatsani were transhumant shepherds
who roamed all over Greece, from Thrace through Macedonia, Epirus,
Thessaly, Central Greece, northern Euboea, Attica and the northern
Peloponnese. They were reputed to have gone as far as Asia Minor in
previous centuries (Benaki 1948: 53). Their flocks were their
livelihood and determined their social organization.
Until recently these shepherds moved seasonally with their sheep
and goats. Every year on October 26, St. Demetrius Day, they
transported themselves from their summer pastures high in the
mountain ranges of mainland Greece to the winter grazing lands in
the lower valleys. In spring a reverse migration began on April 23,
St. George's Day (Hatzimichali 1977: 298). Although the Sarakatsani
considered their summer pastures in the mountains to be their home,
they had no permanent settlements (Leigh Fermor 1962: 29). In the
mountains they lived in black goats' hair tents. On the plains they
constructed temporary housing of bent saplings thatched with twigs
and grass which were semi-spherical in shape (Allen 1985: 5). Only
in the last few decades have most Sarakatsani settled permanently in
villages near their summer or winter pastures. Socially, the Sarakatsani
were organized in clans based on male kinship. Each group of families
was led by a *tsellingas* (clan leader) who maintained order within the
group and represented the shepherds to the outside world, particularly
in the negotiation of winter grazing rights (Koster and Koster 1976:
280; Allen 1985: 5).
The origins of the Sarakatsani are unknown. They are not
mentioned by name in the ancient historical accounts, but some
authors suggest that they have lived in Greece for centuries, even
millenia, following their nomadic way of life (Leigh Fermor 1965:
32; Hatzimichali 1977: 298). Linguistically, the Sarakatsani can be
identified by their spoken language, which is an archaic form of
Greek that did not vary from one group to another (Allen 1985: 6).
Their other manners and customs also were similar from area to area
which strengthens the argument for a common origin.
Sarakatsani women's clothing was made almost entirely by
themselves and shared basic characteristics all across Greece. These
features make it an excellent example of ethnic dress. It was
distinguished from the regional dress of peasants and townspeople by
its components, fabrication and decoration. Although some garments,

such as the chemise, were common to all female Greek dress, other garments, such as the indigo-dyed *foustani*, were distinctly Sarakatsani. This skirt was spun, woven and embroidered from sheep's wool, then permanently pleated by stitching the folds into place and wetting them. Embroidery motifs unique to the Sarakatsani were cross-stitched in wool on chemises, skirts and aprons. In technique and motif, Sarakatsani embroidery varied little across Greece. Leggings and undersleeves were knitted in stark geometric patterns. On top was worn a *segouna*, different from the Albanian garment of similar name in that it was dark blue, almost black, and decorated with geometric motifs. These garments were finished off with large buckles worn at the waist or silver chains draped across the chest. The only clothing items purchased were jewelry, shoes and cotton fiber for making the chemises; otherwise, the Sarakatsani were self-sufficient (Hatzimichali 1977: 298–341).

While the form of the clothing worn by Sarakatsani women varied little from one geographic location to another, use of accessories and surface decoration sometimes differed. In Thrace the women wore a wide cloth belt with triangular motifs which encircled the body. In Attica, aprons were cross-stitched with floral designs. In central Greece the Sarakatsani women added purchased laces and ribbons to their aprons and skirts (Hatzimichali 1977: 298–341).

Sarakatsani men were not as uniform in their attire as Sarakatsani women. The men wore outfits made from handwoven wool with either trousers (*panovraki*) or *foustanella* skirts, depending on the local tradition (Papantoniou 1981: 11). In terms of clothing, women rather than men were the visible carriers of culture within the Sarakatsani communities because they were consistent in their use of black *segouna* and stitched, pleated skirts.

Vlachs

A third ethnic group were the Vlachs, who were concentrated in the heart of the Pindus mountains, particularly in the provinces of Epirus, Macedonia and Thessaly. Many conflicting theories have been advanced concerning the origins of the Vlachs (Vacalopoulos 1970: 12–15). Regardless of whether they were Roman colonists, Wallachians, Roumanians or latinized Greeks, it is agreed that they have occupied territory in Greece for nearly a thousand years. The most distinguishing characteristic about the Vlachs is their language, which is a dialect of Latin (Wace 1914: 2; Leigh Fermor 1962: 27;

Figure 3.2 Spyros and Vangelis Koutlas and their wives. Both the men and the women wear the Thracian version of Sarakatsani attire. Photograph: Courtesy of the Benaki Museum.

Allen 1985: 6). Because of this, it is postulated that they first inhabited the area in the Dark or early Middle Ages when Latin was a spoken language in Greece (Vacalopoulos 1970: 14).

Wace, who studied the Vlachs and their customs in detail, defined their territory as ranging from the peninsula of Acarnania in the south to Bulgaria and Serbia in the north (1914: 1). Although there was no exclusive Vlach town, their home was in the northern Pindus mountains where their flocks grazed in summer. When winter approached, they descended to the plains of Thessaly and Macedonia. The group studied by Wace in 1910–11 called themselves *Romai* (Romans) rather than Vlachs. He explained that the Vlachs earned a bad name for themselves among the Greeks during the latter nineteenth century by agitating for the right to form their own schools (1914: 7–9); this developed into a full-scale political movement for a separate Vlach state in Turkish-occupied northern Greece. The Turks finally recognized them as a separate nationality in 1905.

Vlachs were frequently singled out as a distinct population in mid-nineteenth century travelogs (*Handbook* 1884: 58–64). Baedecker described their nomadic life on Mt. Olympus (1909: xlvi–xlix). Rodd stated that the Vlachs enjoyed a reputation for management and breeding of sheep and goats (1892: 37); About (1857: 50) noted that "the Wallachs" slept in the open air on the hillsides among their flocks. However, since the Vlachs were also nomadic shepherds, western travelers frequently labeled all tent and hut dwellers as Vlachs (Leigh Fermor 1962: 27–8); shepherds of Greek or Albanian heritage, as well as the Sarakatsani, were mistaken for Vlachs. This fact creates confusion in identifying the authentic Vlach in primary sources. For example, a lithograph by Theodore Leblanc entitled "Vlach Women, Moréa" (Moréa being the old name for the Peloponnese) probably depicts a Greek or Albanian shepherdess in Arcadia.

To complicate the identification of Vlachs even further, the word *vlach* in Greek has other meanings. Vlach can denote simply a shepherd, but it also is used in a derogatory manner by Greeks when referring to the rough, unpolished behavior associated with villagers or peasants: "[country] bumpkin, clodhopper, boor" (Stavropoulos 1988).

Assigning a prototypical ethnic dress to the Vlachs of Greece is therefore difficult. Various writers have provided descriptions of Vlach clothing which, when compared, reveal that Vlach attire either was not distinctive or was associated with the Vlachs of a particular geographic region. Black hooded cloaks of homespun goat's hair were

Figure 3.3 "Vlach Women, Moréa". Two women and a baby are portrayed as tent-dwellers high in the mountains of the Peloponnese. The term *vlach* was applied to shepherds throughout the Peloponnese even if they were Greek or Albanian.

Tinted lithograph by Theodore Leblanc. From the album *Croquis d'aprés nature faits pendant trois ans de séjour en Gréce et dans le Levant.* (1833–34) Paris.

Photograph: Courtesy of the Peloponnesian Folklore Foundation.

mentioned as being worn by the Vlachs, although other shepherds wore them also (Rodd 1892: 38; Leigh Fermor 1962: 28). Wace stated that "it may be said that the Vlachs of Samarina in Epirus have a national costume" although it was "'subject to changes of fashion" (1914: 60). He described men's apparel as consisting of a shirt, homespun woolen leggings, a vest, and a black sleeveless woolen coat called a *tsipune*. For women, the basic garment was a one-piece dress of machine-made fabric, an Amalia-type jacket, and a sleeveless dark woolen coat called *duluma*. Papantoniou (1981) illustrated Vlach attire from Macedonia which differed substantially from the Epirote styles in Wace's photographs; in the text, she associates two types of male garments with the Vlachs, the white trousers (of the type seen in Fig. 3.4) and the homemade *foustanella* (Papantoniou 1981: 11, 41). It should be remembered that both trousers and *foustanella* were also worn by Sarakatsani men.

This muddled picture should not be interpreted as meaning that Vlachs did not communicate their ethnicity through dress. Rather, the communication took place on a micro level. If we consider that clans of shepherds traveled relatively short distances when moving between seasonal pastures, then the need to communicate ethnicity through dress was local at best. In the Pindus, where Vlach territory overlapped with that of the Sarakatsani, the clothing of each group was only one of many cultural traits which differentiated them. Language was another; a Sarakatsani shepherd told Leigh Fermor that, "If you hear a shepherd use the word *lapte* [the Vlach word for milk] hit him over the head" (1962: 30).

In regions where Vlach and Sarakatsani territory overlapped, it was chiefly the women who communicated ethnicity through dress. Vlach women, by wearing clothing unlike that of Sarakatsani women, signified that they belonged to the Vlachs rather than to the Sarakatsani. Comparing female Sarakatsani dress to female Vlach dress, Leigh Fermor stated: "Costumes in Greece, especially those of the women (and, most notably those of the Vlach women), change, even more frequently than accents, from village to village; yet the garb of the Sarakatsánissas, with the barest minimum of variation, is the same all over Greece" (1962: 30). Observing both Vlachs and Sarakatsani in northern Greece, he stated further: "Everything – manners, customs, clothes, folklore, beliefs, appearance, feeling and, above all, language – thrusts them further apart" (1962: 28–9).

Ethnic Identity Through Dress: Problems and Caveats

As we have seen, certain components of dress were associated with particular ethnic groups in Greece. In Attica, the white woolen *sigouni* was worn by Greek-Albanian peasant women over garments with identifiable embroidery motifs. Dark blue pleated wool skirts, distinctively embroidered chemises and patterned leggings signified a Sarakatsánissas. In the Pindus, Vlachs could be identified by such garments as the *duluma* and *tsipune* of the Samarina shepherds. But does this allow us to make the sartorial generalization that all Greek-Albanian women wore the white *sigouni*? The answer is a definite "no."

Ethnicity in Greek dress is complex. It is important to remember that using dress to signify ethnic identity happened at both the macro and micro level in mainland Greece. Whereas the *foustanella* represented Greek nationalism to Greeks and non-Greeks alike, the lesser-known *foundi* of the peasant woman of Attica communicated that the wearer was Greek-Albanian to the inhabitants of a much smaller geographical area. Greek dress could also have more than one meaning. For example, within Attica, the colors and patterns of the embroidered *foundi* indicated both ethnicity (Greek-Albanian) and geographical origin (Messoghia villages of Attica). Thus, Greek dress can be simultaneously both ethnic dress and regional dress.

Three of the complexities I encountered in field research can be analyzed in light of the previous discussion. These are the association of Greek-Albanians with the white *sigouni* in some localities only; the confusion over ethnic groups from the geographic region known as Roumeli; and the linking of the word *Vlach* with a particular style of festival dress.

The White *Sigouni*

One hypothesis generated by the field research projects in Attica and Argolida-Corinthia was that the white *sigouni* was associated with Greek-Albanians. In villages throughout Attica Greek-Albanian villagers identified this garment as theirs. Other ethnic groups in Attica knew that the outfit with the white *sigouni* was worn by the *Arvanites*. In Argolida and Corinthia, where the population was of mixed ethnic background, I was told again that only the *Arvanites* wore the *sigouni*. However, I had to modify the hypothesis when I encountered the white *sigouni*, stylistically related to those of Attica, Argolida and Corinthia, in the non-Albanian villages of northern Euboea.

How can we explain why the peasants of northern Euboea, particularly those of Aghia Anna, wore the *sigouni* associated with inhabitants of Albanian extraction in Attica and Argolida-Corinthia even though they were not of Albanian extraction? A plausible explanation lies in the widespread use of variants of the *gouna*, a sleeveless overgarment inherited from the near-Eastern clothing repertoire. At one point in time all peasants in the Balkans may have worn a garment like the *sigouni*. Many similar garments survive in the traditional dress of other countries which were part of the old Ottoman empire, all the way to Hungary (Gervers 1975: 64). In Greece, the *sigouni* was preserved in regions which were populated by tradition-bound peasants – whether the peasants were Greek or Greek-Albanian – while peasants in other regions abandoned the *sigouni* in favor of more recent modes of dress.

On the micro level the *sigouni* took on the ethnic identity of the group that was wearing it only when outsiders migrated to the community, thereby making it necessary to distinguish ethnic affiliation based on appearance. In this sense it signified that the wearer came from a specific locality as well as from a certain ethnic group. Thus, the *sigouni*, embellished in the local tradition, was both a regional garment and an ethnic signifier. On the island of Euboea, the *sigouni*-wearers of the northern villages never interacted with the Greek-Albanians who lived many miles away in the southern part of the island; thus, the *sigouni* did not signify ethnic affiliation for those living in the Aghia Anna villages. It was simply a type of regional dress.

Similarly, not all areas of Albanian settlement in Greece have traditional clothing which includes the *sigouni*. Traditional attire attributed to the wealthy islands of Hydra and Aegina was of a type associated with the seafaring Greeks, baggy breeches for men and Turkish-inspired silk gowns for women. In the southern Argolid, elderly Greek-Albanians whose villages are situated close to the sea, such as Didima and Fourni, have only the dimmest memories of the *sigouni* and the old embroidered chemise. Probably these villagers gave up the medieval-type garments generations ago, as evidenced by photographs circa 1900 showing fashionable dress for men, women and children (Welters 1989: 26–7). These *Arvanites* kept their language, but lost other aspects of their ethnicity early due to their commercial ties to the outside world, whereas those living in the agriculturally-based villages of the plains were more conservative in their customs. For the Greek-Albanians, their association with the embroidered chemise and the white *sigouni* occurred on a micro level.

Roumeliotisses and Vlachs

Another source of confusion were the names affiliated with the Sarakatsani. I encountered Sarakatsani on all four research projects. On October 31, 1986, my car was stuck behind hundreds of sheep and goats led by Sarakatsani shepherds moving from their summer plateau to winter grazing lands above Nemea in Corinthia. In Boeotia, I photographed a trio of occupied Sarakatsani huts on the road to Pavlos. I interviewed Sarakatsani who had settled in the villages of Daou Penteli and Pikermi in Attica, Malandreni in Corinthia, Adami in Argolida, Dionysos on the line between Boeotia and Fthiotida, and Mandoudi in Euboea. None of these people referred to themselves as Sarakatsani and neither did their neighbors; instead they called themselves *Roumeliotes* (people from Roumeli) or *vlachoi* (shepherds).

In the Peloponnese, we showed photographs of the old Albanian-type outfits from Argolida to interviewees, who repeatedly identified them as those worn by *Roumeliotisses* (women from Roumeli). According to the interviewees, these people were *skinites* (tent-dwellers) who came down every year from Ziria in the Killini mountains. No modern map shows a village or district by the name of Roumeli. Finally, a family showed us a set of garments of the type the interviewees were describing. It revealed the tell-tale signs of the Sarakatsani: pleated indigo wool *foustani*, distinctively embroidered chemise and geometrically patterned leggings. Our interviewees were remembering the unusual-looking clothing of the Sarakatsani women who annually migrated to their district during the winter season to graze their sheep. To their eyes, the 3" x 5" pictures of the old Argolida dress resembled the clothing of the Sarakatsani women.

The name *Roumeliotes* was applied to the Sarakatsani because centuries ago they returned to mainland Greece to pasture their sheep every summer (Koster and Koster 1976: 280). That part of mainland Greece was known during Roman times as Roumeli (Leigh Fermor 1962: 1). Hence, the name *Roumeliotisses* was applied to Sarakatsani women from mainland Greece who wore their characteristic garb in Argolida.

In Attica, Boeotia and Euboea, whole villages were founded and

Figure 3.4 Bride with husband and father, Daou Penteli, Attica, 1925. The men wear the white trousers similar to that found in Epirus and other Vlach/Sarakatsani regions. The bride wears a mix of components, some of which are Sarakatsani. Both male and female garments communicate that the wearers are not members of the dominant ethnic group in the region, the Greek-Albanians.
Photograph: Privately owned. Copied by Margaret Hodder with permission during field research.

settled by the Sarakatsani. Here the Sarakatsani I interviewed described themselves as *vlach*, meaning shepherds. Often they would say that their ancestors had come from Roumeli, in northern Greece. They also spoke of their sheep and their clan leader, the *tsellingas*. When both men and women described female clothing, however, it was clear that they were of Sarakatsani rather than Vlach origin.

The wedding photograph in Figure 3.4 illustrates the complexities of differentiating a Vlach from a Sarakatsani. The wedding took place in Daou Penteli, a village close to Spata, where the couple in Figure 3.1 were married. Daou Penteli is a Sarakatsani settlement, whereas Spata is an Albanian village. The shepherds of Attica distinguished themselves from the dominant ethnic group in the area, the *Arvanites*, through clothing. The bride wears an outfit which differs from the so-called Albanian dress of the Messoghia region in which she lived. From the front it also differs from the Sarakatsani outfit from Thrace illustrated in Figure 3.2 with its wide cloth belt. Her husband and father, both shepherds, wear the white trousers associated with Vlach and Sarakatsani men from Epirus. She called herself a *vlacha* when interviewed in 1983, but we know that the territory of the Vlachs did not extend down this far. The Sarakatsani, however, were known to graze their flocks in Attica. Her clothing tells us that she is not Greek-Albanian, but does it have Sarakatsani characteristics? The chest jewelry and headscarf are similar to those worn by the Sarakatsani of Attica (Hatzimichali 1977: 303). Confirmation of Sarakatsani origin came in her description of the indigo-blue pleated *foustani* common to all Sarakatsani female clothing (the *foustani* is hidden from view by the apron in the photograph).

The *Vlachika*

A third problem concerns the double meaning of the word *vlach*. As noted earlier, *vlach* can mean the rough unsophisticated behavior associated with peasants as well as the people known as the Vlach. By association, the village-style clothing worn by peasant women was sometimes called the *vlachika*.

Peasant women in Attica, Argolida, Corinthia and Boeotia who married in the first forty years of the twentieth century consistently referred to their bridal and festival dresses by the name *vlachika*. At that time, the traditional white *sigouni* and embroidered chemise were being abandoned by the younger generation for a bridal and festival dress that bridged the transition to European fashion. Instead of the

Figure 3.5 Wedding photograph, Vasileos and Maria Dritsa, Moulki, Corinthia, 1926. The Greek-Albanian bride is wearing the Argolida-Corinthia version of the *vlachika* outfit. Her *sigouni* was made by Kondoyiannis of Moulki.

Photograph: Privately owned. Copied by Linda Welters with permission during field research.

hand-embroidered chemises of their mothers, these young women wore lace-trimmed white dresses and pastel *crêpe-de-chine* frocks not unlike those of their fashionable counterparts in Britain and the United States.

Over the dresses were worn updated versions of the *sigouni*. These were made professionally and soon regional variations developed. Fancy aprons and silk veils completed the ensembles. The overall effect of these ensembles was considered very attractive by the generations who married between the world wars; this contributed to the pride felt by peasant communities when their young women appeared on festival days in such finery. One elderly woman from Corinthia recalled that young women who were not wearing the *vlachika* were discouraged from participating in the group dances characteristic of village festivals: "'You are shaming them' the old women would shout from behind; 'you are destroying the beauty of the dance!'"[2]

The *vlachika* outfit was worn by women in Greek-Albanian villages, but sometimes it was worn in non-Albanian villages also. Its association with the negative meaning of the term *vlach*, rather than the ethnic group Vlach, was revealed in the interviews. Some young women who considered themselves "modern" resisted wearing any sort of traditional dress. Due to increased communication with the world beyond the village, these women were aware of the negative view city-dwellers took of peasant life; not wishing to look like country bumpkins, one by one they abandoned traditional dress in favor of fashionable dress. Often the incentive came from their husbands, who did not want to marry brides wearing the *vlachika* when they themselves were attired in European-style suits.

In this case the *vlachika* did not mean that the wearer was a Vlach, or even a shepherdess, but neither did it mean that she was necessarily Greek-Albanian, although more often than not, she was an *Arvanitissa*. Rather, it associated the wearer with traditional village life in a country whose ethnic divisions were eroding as it modernized.

Conclusion

My research indicates that dress functioned to identify at least three of the many ethnic groups in Greece, Greek-Albanians, Sarakatsani

---

2. Georgia Oikonomou, tape-recorded interview by Linda Welters and Katerina Kalamitsi, Athikia, Corinthia, November 6, 1986.

and Vlachs. Each of these groups utilized clothing on a micro level to communicate their ethnicity to non-group members inhabiting the same geographical area. This also happened on a macro level as is seen in the example of the blue pleated *foustani*, which was the unmistakable sign of the Sarakatsani wherever they moved with their flocks on the Greek mainland, even if they called themselves by another name. Sometimes a garment served as an indicator of an ethnic group on a micro level, that is to say, only used by that group within a specific geographical area. Vlach women, by wearing garment forms that differed from the Sarakatsani in their region, indicated ethnicity through dress. In Attica, the *sigouni* signified that the wearer had come from one of the Greek-Albanian villages. The same garment had no such connotation in northern Euboea, where the inhabitants were all indigenous Greeks and ethnic identity was not an issue.

We also observed that the study of dress as related to ethnicity in Greece is not without problems. Chief among them for my work was the use of the word *vlach*. Vlach could mean the Latin-speaking shepherds of the northern Pindus, who had a recognizable traditional dress. *Vlach* also could mean "shepherd," a term which often was applied to any nomadic group in Greece, including the Sarakatsani. Lastly, *vlach* carried a pejorative meaning as Greece was modernizing. The many derivatives of the word *vlach* − *vlachos*, *vlachi*, *vlacheia* and *vlachika* − connotated the backwardness of village life. The women who wore the *vlachika* outfit were neither Vlachs nor shepherdesses, although some were Greek-Albanian. Here the *vlachika* outfit associated the wearer with village life rather than a specific ethnic group.

The study of dress as related to ethnicity in Greece solves some of the puzzles inherent to the "regional" or "national" approach. In Greece, the many varieties of traditional dress cannot simply be attributed to regional differences because they differ so much in form. The concept of dressing to affiliate with an ethnic group helps to explain the multiplicity of dress types within the regions of the Greek mainland. Both clothing form and details of form determine whether a particular garment communicates nationality, signifies affiliation with a group of villages, or identifies the wearer as a member of a particular ethnic group.

The townspeople who gave up their Turkish-style clothing after Greece attained its independence communicated solidarity with the new Greek democracy by wearing *foustanella*. This is a clear example of national dress. At the same time, those who dwelled in villages and on the mountainsides kept their traditional clothing forms, specifically the *sigouni* and the chemise. If all other cultural factors were the same, only the decoration of the traditional clothing forms varied from one group of villages to the next. In this sense Greek dress is regional dress. But if within a region more than one ethnic group was competing for resources, such as land or grazing rights, clothing was used to signified ethnicity. Thus, the *sigouni* of the Greek-Albanian peasants of Attica and Argolida-Corinthia became ethnic dress as well as regional dress. Finally, the distinctive clothing forms of Sarakatsani women were similar wherever these shepherdesses roamed with their clans. Therefore the attire of the Sarakatsani functions as ethnic dress, not as regional or national dress.

References

About, E. (1857), *Greece and the Greeks of the Present Day*, New York: Dix, Edwards & Co.

Allen, P. (1985), "The Sarakatsani: Ethnographic Notes," in *Female Costume of the Sarakatsani*, Providence: Brown University and Haffenreffer Museum of Anthropology, pp. 4–11.

Arnaoutoglou, C.K. (1986), *Hydra*, Athens: Melissa Publishing House.

Baedecker, K. (1909), *Greece: Handbook for Travellers*, 4th edn, Leipzig: Karl Baedecker.

Benaki, A.E. (ed.) (1948–54), *Hellenic National Costumes* (text by A. Hatzimichali), 2 vols, Athens: Benaki Museum.

Clogg, R. (1985), "Eclipse and Rebirth: From the Ottoman Period to Modern Greece," in R. Browning (ed.), *The Greeks: Classical, Byzantine and Modern*, New York: Portland House, pp. 301–20.

Desses, J. (1962), "Greek Dress Through the Ages," *Connoisseur*, vol. 150, (May 1962), pp. 54–6.

Gervers, V. (1975), "The Historical Components of Regional Costume in South-eastern Europe," *Textile Museum Journal*, vol. 4, no. 2, pp. 61–78.

(1884) *Handbook for Travellers in Greece*, 5th edn, London: John Murray.

Harrison, J.A. (1878), *Greek Vignettes*, Boston: Houghton Osgood.

Hatzimichali, A. (1977), *The Greek Folk Costume*, vol. I (T. Ioannou-Yiannara and A. Delivorias, eds), Athens: Benaki Museum and Melissa Publishing House.

Koster, H.A., and Koster, J.B. (1976), "Competition or Symbiosis?: Pastoral Adaptive Strategies in the Southern Argolid, Greece," *Annals of the New York Academy of Sciences*, vol. 268, Feb. 10, pp. 275–85.

Leigh Fermor, P. (1962), *Roumeli: Travels in Northern Greece*, New York: Harper and Row.

Papantoniou, I. (1978), "Συμβολή στη Μελέτη της Γυναικείας Ελληνικής Παραδοσιακής Φορεσιάς" [A First Attempt at an Introduction to Greek Traditional Costume (Women's)], *Εθνογραφικά*, vol. 1, pp. 5–92.

—— (1976), "Οι Χωρικές Φορεσιές της Αργολιδοκορινθίας, *Πρακτικά Α Διεθνούς Συνεδρου Πελοποννησιακών Σπουδών*, pp. 419–467.

—— (1981), *Greek Costumes*, Nafplion: Peloponnesian Folklore Foundation.

Randolph, B. (1687), *The Present State of the Island of the Archipelago (or Arches), Sea of Constantinople and Gulph of Smyrna with the Islands of Candia and Rhodes*, Oxford.

Rodd, R. (1892), *The Customs and Lore of Modern Greece*, London: David Stott.

Stavropoulos, D.N. (1988), *Oxford Greek-English Learner's Dictionary*, Oxford: Oxford University Press.

Vacalopoulos, A.E. (1970), *Origins of the Greek Nation*, New Brunswick, N.J.: Rutgers University Press.

Wace, A.J.B., and Thompson, M.S. (1914), *The Nomads of the Balkans*, London: Methuen & Co.

Welters, L. (1988), *Women's Traditional Costume in Attica, Greece*, Nafplion: Peloponnesian Folklore Foundation.

—— (1989), "Women's Traditional Dress in the Provinces of Argolida and Corinthia," *Εθνογραφικά*, vol. 7, pp. 17–30.

Zora, P. (1981), *Embroideries and Jewellery of Greek National Costume*, 2nd edn, Athens: Museum of Greek Folk Art.

4

Naked Divers: A Case of Identity and Dress in Japan

D.P. Martinez

Introduction

The title of this chapter is meant to be provocative, just as Japanese female divers (*ama*) are perceived to be provocative. I intend to explore the idea of dress and undress as markers of identity in a society where total nakedness (save in the bath) is taboo and where the wearing of clothing appropriate to one's status in life is important. Naked divers, it must be made clear, were not truly naked by western standards: a loincloth (*koshimaki*) had to be worn at all times. Now that the few remaining divers in Japan dive wearing thick black wetsuits, almost-naked divers exist only in woodblock prints, poetry, novels, and films. Yet, through these media, the image of the female diver has become pervasive throughout Japan.

However, as will be discussed, divers have also long been an object of Japanese academic research, and in this context they seem to exist in a mythic realm of their own: they have been variously described by physiologists as physically and therefore potentially racially different; by folklorists and anthropologists as the remnants of an ancient Japanese matriarchy; or, linked to the notion of a different race, as descendants of Koreans. This last position is an interesting one, premised on a Japanese notion of race (*minzoku*), a term which can also be translated from the Japanese as "tribe" or "ethnos". This approach[1] sees culture and race as somehow mutually determining categories. Thus, such studies talk of Japanese genetic traits in comparison to American genetic traits – conflating *minzoku* with the

---

1. For a brief overview of this position and its leading academic adherents, see Dale 1986: 188–200.

more proper *jinshu* (literally, division of mankind) and making the cultural biological.[2]

So, despite the fact that Koreans and Japanese can be said to belong to the same race (*jinshu*), for most Japanese they are actually perceived to be different races (*minzoku*) and one's blood could be contaminated by intermarriage. It is probably no small coincidence that the *zoku* of *minzoku* is a homonym for a Chinese ideogram which means, among other things, customs and manners.[3] I would argue that while the term *minzoku* makes race an important aspect of ethnicity – therefore implying that ethnicity is an objective fact – its emphasis on culture makes it permissible, with some qualifications, to translate *minzoku* as a term referring to social rather than distinct racial categories.[4] In order to make clear the qualifications that have to be made when using *minzoku*, I would like to turn to another definition of ethnicity.

Abner Cohen has defined an ethnic group as:

> a collectivity of people who (a) share some patterns of normative behaviour and (b) form part of a larger population, interacting with people from other collectivities within the framework of a social system. The term ethnicity refers to the degree of conformity by members of the collectivity to these shared norms in the course of social interaction. (1974:ix–x)

As we shall see, it would be easy to argue that the *ama* fit this definition and could therefore be labeled an ethnic group. Yet, as Cohen (1974: xxi) himself points out, his definition allows for the fact that ethnicity is not sociological, but social and political. What this means is that where there are no biologically differing features such as race, a group of people would have to feel that their shared norms constituted a difference large enough to allow for them to identify themselves as an ethnic group. In short, there is an element of subjectivity in assuming an ethnic identity, and the *ama* are a good example of this: they could easily make a case for being a distinct group, but they have not.

2. This is not a uniquely Japanese approach, as Nash (1989: 125) notes: "the concepts of 'ethnic,' 'nation,' 'class,' 'race,' and 'state' are closely linked in content, sometimes in fact, and sometimes historically fused."

3. It is this *zoku* that makes up the word for folklore, which confusingly for non-Japanese is also read as *minzoku*.

4. In fact, despite the adoption of the English term *esunishiti* (ethnicity) in Japanese to refer to situations outside Japan, it has been noted that ethnicity "has the meaning of *minzoku*" (Miyaji 1987: 4, my translation).

Thus, when Japanese scholars trace *ama* origins back to Korea, they are raising the issue of these communities as being objectively, and therefore ethnically, different. This approach is actually rather subjective because it ignores the fact "[t]hat early Japan was multiracial, that Korean élites operated at the highest levels and that even the Imperial house had foreign blood connections" (Dale 1986: 43). In having Korean connections, then, the *ama* are no more or less Japanese than any other Japanese; so why is it that outsiders find the *ama* so unusual?

What should be clear from the outset is that the all the *ama* (women who dive *and* men who fish)[5] have long been marginal to Japanese society. As marginals, they have become the romanticized "other" in contrast to the group of people most often identified as *the* marginals or outcasts (the *burakumin*) who, far from being romanticized, are still struggling for equal rights in Japanese society.[6] As marginals who are now being incorporated into a mainstream Japanese identity, the *ama* are no different than other groups of marginals such as charcoal makers, metal workers, and hunters. All these groups have lost their outcast identity in the last hundred years (Ohnuki-Tierney 1987).

Thus, it would appear that divers are an interesting case of the ethnicity that could have been but never was. Although fully aware that they are considered different from other Japanese and conscious of the theories on their origins which would brand them as not Japanese, the *ama* have not made any attempt to band together as a group with nationwide interests or demands, and continue to become an ever-decreasing statistic in Japanese census figures.[7] In contrast to the Ainu who claim to be the original inhabitants of the island, and for whom biologists have worked hard in order to find genetic differences (Watanabe et al. 1975: 207–337), the *ama* have not chosen

5. The phonetic term *ama* can be written with three different set of Chinese ideograms: one set literally means "ocean woman", another means "ocean man" and the third means "ocean people".
6. Debate continues on whether the *burakumin* are still a caste-like group or whether they have evolved into a class in modern Japan. These people, considered polluted and polluting because their ancestors worked with leather and the corpses of the dead, are still ostracized. Outwardly no different from any other Japanese (although some scholars have argued that they were originally brought over from Korea), family records are still researched to identify *burakumin* when marriages are being arranged.
7. Since Japan is supposed to be a racially homogenous society, *ama* do not appear in census data as a separate group, but are classed under the general category of people employed in fisheries. In 1985 this group constituted 0.7 percent of the Japanese population (Nippon 1990).

to declare themselves an ethnic group. In order to understand why this has been so, we need first to look to the past.

Divers: Images and Reality

The *ama* dive for seaweed and shellfish, particularly abalone (*awabi*), but not for pearls. They have a long history in Japan: the presence of large shell mounds from the Neolithic indicates that they have been on the islands for at least 2,000 years (Nukada 1965: 27). There is also clear evidence that divers in northern Kyushu migrated from Cheju Island in Korea "a long time ago" while the "Ama of Shima in Mie Prefecture and those of Kada, Wakayama Prefecture, both on the Pacific side are presumed to be of different origin" (Birukawa 1965: 63).

This sort of fuzziness in the material on the *ama* is important: that some, if not all, divers have clearly migrated from Korea cannot be denied, but this is rather problematic given that they have also been described as the last of the ancient true Japanese whose women had higher status than men (Maraini 1962: 17).[8] What is at stake here is an issue mentioned above that is beyond the scope of this paper: that the source of much of ancient Japanese culture was Korea is an awkward fact that cannot be made to fit with modern Japanese perceptions of their own unique identity. For Japanese folklorists, the solution to the problem of the *ama* being representative both of ancient Japan and of migration from Korea has been to posit different origins for different groups of divers.

The divers of Mie Prefecture (where I happened to do my fieldwork) feel free to offer their own theory on the origins of divers through the folk etymology they give for the word *ama*. The term, they say, is derived from Amaterasu, the sun goddess who is also the official ancestress of the Imperial family; this implies, then, that they also descend from the main Japanese deity. This mythic connection to Amaterasu links Mie *ama* closely to the Imperial line. This, as I shall show later, is a rather conscious attempt to describe themselves as truly Japanese.

Whatever their origins, at one time it seems that all the people on the islands we now call Japan did dive; the Chinese dynastic histories during the Wei Dynasty (A.D. 220–265) noted of the place they called

---

8. There is no space here for a discussion of the *ama* and issues of women's status in Japan. I have discussed this in detail elsewhere (Martinez 1993).

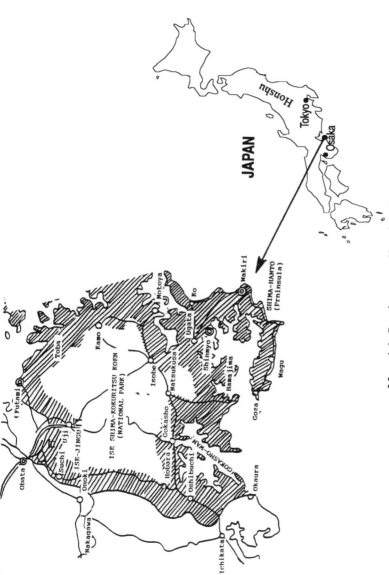

Map 4.1 Southeastern Honshu, Japan.

Queen Country: "The people are fond of fishing; regardless of the depth of the water, they dive to capture fish" (Tsunoda 1951: 10). As time went on, and rice cultivation was introduced from China, diving (and fishing) became specialized skills, with the people who practised them becoming more marginalized from mainstream culture. While fishing remained an important source of food, the fact that the social structure, in imitation of China, was based on settled agricultural communities meant that divers and fishermen were rarely mentioned in historical documents (Sansom 1931: 45).

Divers do appear in other sorts of documents from the eighth through the thirteenth centuries (Christian era), that is, as the subjects of evocative poems written by courtiers. In these poems, the female divers appear to hold many associations for the ancient noblemen and women: they represent melancholy, solitude, nature, and freedom. Their nakedness is not shocking (farming women worked bare-breasted in the summer), but romantic and picturesque. Later, in the eighteenth-century woodblock prints of Utamaro Kitagawa, this image of the *ama* is reinforced by placing them next to fully-clothed female onlookers: often it is these observers who seem to be rather rakish. That Utamaro may have intended some visual pun is possible: the beautiful onlookers appear to be courtesans, workers in the "floating world" or "water business" (*mizu shōbai*), while the divers literally are in a water business. The contrast then is between the innocent almost-naked women and the fully dressed but less-than-innocent courtesans.[9]

Until the 1980s, this contrast between divers and other women was a theme one could find in literature as well as in art. Mishima's first novel, *The Sound of Waves* (1957), pits an innocent, pure, and ultimately Japanese diver against a rival who is westernized and city-educated. However, in the 1980s, domestic tourism seems to have picked up on the latent sexuality of the naked divers and they have since become icons of the desirable female. Throughout the 1980s they were on tourist posters inviting Japanese to come and sample the pleasures of the coastal villages where life remained pure and traditional (Martinez 1990). In the film *Tampopo* (1986), which mixes images of food and sex, they appear briefly as the very sexy seductresses who dive for oysters in, of all places, Tokyo Bay! Thus, in this modern society where a woman's age and marital status is

9. Professor David Plath pointed out this interesting relationship between geisha and divers to me in 1985.

Figure 4.1 Dressed in their *amagi*, Kuzaki divers rest after a morning dive (1985, Photograph by D.P. Martinez).

Figure 4.2 A Kuzaki boat diver (*funado*) dons her face mask (1984, Photograph by D.P. Martinez).

generally identifiable by the style of her dress, the idea of naked divers, or divers dressed in old-fashioned white diving costumes (*amagi*)[10] which cling wetly to their bodies, has become eroticized. What can be said of the lives of divers both traditionally and in modern Japan? The tenth century noblewoman Sei Shônagon gave a very accurate description of them in her travel diaries:

> The sea is a frightening thing at the best of times. How much more terrifying it must be for those poor women divers who have to plunge into its depths for their livelihood. One wonders what would happen to them if the cord round their waist were to break . . . it must take remarkable courage. After the woman has been lowered into the water, the men sit comfortably in their boats, heartily singing songs as they keep an eye on the mulberry-bark cord that floats on the surface . . . When finally she wants to come up, she gives a tug on her cord and the men haul her out of the water with a speed that I can well understand. Soon she is clinging to the side of the boat, her breath coming in painful gasps. The sight is enough to make even an outsider feel the brine dripping. I can hardly imagine this is a job that anyone would covet. (Morris 1967: 247–8)

The seventeenth-century English Captain John Saris also noted coming across "women divers, that lived with their household and family upon the water . . ." as a result of diving "eight fathom deep . . . their eyes . . . do grow as red as blood" (Tames 1981: 56).

The picture we get is one of hard physical work, but also of a lifestyle increasingly at odds with wider society. As Japan became more settled and politically regimented, particularly during the Tokugawa era (1603–1867) when the country was closed to outsiders, the *ama* lived on boats, and traveled up and down both coasts, as well as over to Korea, doing the migrant labour of diving and fishing. The Tokugawa era was also a time when laws governed the types of clothing which could be worn by the four classes. In this context, naked divers were in some ways even more unusual than the outcasts who were so poor that they wore the meanest of clothes.[11]

10. *Amagi* was (and in some areas still is) the clothing worn in between diving sessions when sitting around the fire. It consists of a simple cotton white blouse and a white cotton wrap-around skirt which, in the winter, might be replaced by a quilted dark cotton skirt. Some older women will wear an *amagi* while diving, a habit adopted in twentieth century Mie Prefecture in response to worries about what visiting foreigners might think of naked divers.
11. During the Tokugawa era, no one was allowed to dress above their status. In 1984 some of the oldest women in Kuzaki village (where I did fieldwork) still wore what is considered to be the traditional peasant clothing of the Tokugawa and Meiji

88   **D.P. Martinez**

During the Meiji era (1868–1912) when the patrilineal household and primogeniture inheritance became the legal norms, *ama* communities continued to practice temporary uxorilocal marriages, continued to require husband-service of grooms, and continued to adopt sons-in-law into the household rather than allowing daughters to marry out. These practices, once widespread throughout rural Japan, became so rare after 1868 that the folklorists of the twentieth century upon turning to do research on the *ama*, became convinced that here were the last of the ancient true Japanese.[12] Ironically, now that the patrilineal multi-generation household is no longer a legal unit in Japan, the *ama* communities continue to practise this "old" tradition, thus still branding them as unusual.

The hard physical labor required by diving had other interesting repercussions. In the 1930s physiologists discovered that the women in *ama* communities tended to be taller and heavier than the norm for Japanese women. They also could tolerate long hours in very cold water, something non-divers could not do. Thus, for some researchers this raised a question about their origins and whether they might not be Japanese at all. Physiological studies of the *ama* tended then to group Korean and Japanese divers together, using the same term for both, since physically they were alike.[13] However in the 1980s, the loss of divers' ability to withstand low water temperatures because they had taken to wearing wetsuits meant that for some physiologists the *ama* were no longer interesting (Hong 1983, private communication). The differences between divers and the main population are now seen to be ones of diet and of adaptation which anyone could develop if they begin diving young enough, rather than actual racial differences due to a different gene pool.

Yet, at least in the mid–1980s when I did research in Kuzaki, divers were still a marginal group for most Japanese. The women were seen

---

eras (Takabashi and Goto 1980: 213–26). The non-diving clothing consisted of a dark cotton kimono reaching to mid-calf; a simple belt to tie the kimono; leggings; *zori* for footwear; a long apron held at the waist with braided string; a headscarf and/or straw hat. In the past, this was the clothing worn throughout Japan, with some variations, by all women who did manual labor.

12. Also interesting to note is that another class of individuals in Japan continued practices of adoption and variations on marriage patterns long after the Meiji Restoration: the disempowered aristocratic elite. See Lebra (1993) for a fascinating discussion of this.

13. See, for example, Birukawa (1965), Honda et al. (1981), Hong et al. (1963) and (1965) (on Korean divers), Kang et al. (1963), Kita (1965), Masuda (1981), Miyamura et al. (1981), Nukada (1965), Rennie et al. (1962), and Tatai (1965).

to be totally different from the ideal of modern womanhood: they were often described to me as loud, big, brash, and bossy women. In contrast, I perceived them to be very competent hard workers whose status in relation to their men was no different than other Japanese women. My perception tallied with how the *ama* saw themselves: they were just as Japanese as anyone else and if there were any Koreans around it certainly was not in their village but in the village next door. Or so they claimed; yet ties to Korea did exist. One sixty year-old woman in the village could still count in Korean, claiming to have learned the language while a child traveling to and from Cheju with her parents on the family boat, and at least one family in the village had a Korean ancestress to whom they would not now admit: she had been interviewed by an ethnographer sometime in the 1930s (Segawa 1956: 19). Villagers were adamant in their Japaneseness: they were loyal to the Emperor and practised customs seen as "more traditional than anywhere else" by Japanese folklorists.

The *Ama* as Distinct but not an Ethnic Group

It should be clear by now that although the *ama* are perceived as different by outsiders and while some researchers have emphasized their foreign origins, the *ama* themselves have rejected these depictions. Aware of their otherness, they have used this to some advantage in tourism, but not for other ends. The question is how this is possible, since in a complex modern and industrial society like Japan one would expect ethnicity to develop in response to political and economic demands as it has in other parts of the world.[14] In fact, in the cases where a distinct group identity has become politicized in Japan – the *burakumin* or second-generation Korean immigrants – it has been the issue of foreign origins (hypothetical foreign origins in the *burakumin* case) which has been seen to be the "objective" fact of a fundamental difference. But, somehow, this has not been the case for the *ama*.

The simple reason for this is that when divers put on clothes, they dress just as do other Japanese women and are in fact no different.

14. That is, ethnicity defined as a very modern phenomenon more likely to occur in complex societies where political and economic interests divide rather than join various groups of people. Thus Nash (1989: 127) warns that ". . . ethnicity as forged in the crucible of modern and modernizing nations may be political, economic, or cultural in its struggles and conflicts, or all of them at one time."

However, the simple answer tells us very little. There are several other points to be considered which might help answer the query. First, for more than one hundred years, Japan has laid such emphasis on the ideology of the homogeneity of its race and culture that there is no advantage in claiming to be different. In fact, the disadvantages as evidenced by the continued plight of the *burakumin* are great. Second, since the economic growth of Japan in the 1970s, divers and fishermen have benefited from government grants and other forms of help available to rural areas; consequently rural dwellers have long been the backbone of the Liberal Democratic Party and wield great power.

The third, and I think most pertinent reason, lies in the fact that with increased contact with the outside world, the Japanese have become more and more obsessed with their past and traditions and have gone looking for them in the countryside. This domestic tourist boom was just what fishing villages needed when their resources grew scarce. Not every diving village has become a tourist resort, but those which have, maintain the image of belonging to a *real* Japan which is lost to urban dwellers. The theme is an old one in Japan and hinges, of course, on being able to ignore any niggling doubts about non-Japanese origins.

The case of villages which no longer practise diving as a way of life is another clue to why the *ama* have not become an ethnic group: even in the past, diving families married off their less-skilled daughters to farmers, and in the twentieth century this out-migration of divers grew to that point that the aim of the daughters of divers was to marry out of the fishing community. This points to a crucial fact, which is that the groups of *ama* always have differentiated among themselves: by clothing worn in between dives, by the way they bound up their hair whilst diving, and through regional dialects which gave them more in common with close neighbors — even farmers — than distant diving communities.   Thus, the boundaries between diving communities and non-diving communities in the same area could be crossed, while there was competition and some rather rigid boundaries between diving communities.[15]

Also, as villages in coastal Japan have become incorporated into large conurbations, it is easy for women who do remain in the

15. For example, in Kuzaki there existed a pattern of intermarriage with two other diving communities and some daughters had married into non-diving families in large cities, but no one, I was told, would marry into the diving village just three kilometers down the road.

Figure 4.3 "Diving for abalone" by Kitagawa Utamaro (1753–1806). Print from author's collection, photograph by Paul Fox, 1994. Copies of sections of this print are sold as postcards in Japan. While some details of this print are historically correct (i.e. feeding a child between dives, the baskets used to store abalone in), there is a rather incongruous servant on the right.

community to give up diving, since it is easier to earn money from other sorts of work. For those who want to fit into mainstream society, it is a matter of putting on ordinary clothes, not going near the water, and not marrying a fisherman; a very simple way to erase one's past identity.

Still more important, perhaps, is the fact that this potential ethnic group's identity was premised on how different the *women* were; the only thing written about the men was the possibly disgracing fact that they were dominated by their wives. Clearly, being henpecked is not enough of a reason to band together and demand special treatment; for if nothing else, it is the secret belief of all Japanese men that their wives have the real power in the household. Symbolically it would have been very difficult for the men of diving villages to convince outsiders that *they* were different from anyone else.

Thus, like the emperor to whom some divers claim kinship, the *ama* remain both marginal to the wider society and yet reassuringly Japanese.[16] Again, like the emperor, they no longer need to wear (or rather not wear) any special clothing to identify them. For the time-being, their place in the images used to represent traditional Japan is guaranteed.

Notes

The fieldwork on which this chapter is based was conducted in 1984–86 with return visits in 1987 and 1991. Support for the first two years of fieldwork came from the Japanese Education Ministry (Monbusho) and the Philip Bagby Studentship, Oxford University. I must also thank members of the Oxford Ethnicity Seminar in 1989 and of the SOAS Japan Research Centre Seminar in 1990 for their comments. Special thanks go to Professor Itoh Abitoh, Dr. Roger Goodman, and D.N. Gellner.

16. Yamaguchi (1977) convincingly argues that we can only understand the post-war importance of the emperor if we accept that he is a marginal figure who manages to symbolize all things Japanese. Thus, he is both central to and outside mainstream society. In linking *ama* and the Imperial House together, I want to remind readers of the Korean links both groups had in the past, as well as to point to certain similarities in the way modern society has mythologized them.

References

Birukawa, S. (1965), "Geographic Distribution of Ama in Japan", in H. Rahn and T. Yokoyama (eds), *Physiology of Breath-hold Diving and the Ama of Japan*, Washington, D.C.: Publication 1341, National Academy of Sciences National Research Council.

Cohen, A. (1974), "The Lesson of Ethnicity", in his *Urban Ethnicity*, Tavistock: London.

Dale, P.N. (1986), *The Myth of Japanese Uniqueness*, London & Sydney: Croom Helm and Nissan Institute for Japanese Studies, University of Oxford.

Honda, Y. et al. (1981), "Relative Contributions of Chemical and Non-chemical Drives to the Breath-holding Time in Breath-hold Divers (*Ama*)," *Japanese Journal of Physiology*, vol. 31, pp. 181–6.

Hong, S.K. et al. (1963), "Diving Pattern, Lung Volumes and Alveolar Gas of the Korean Diving Woman (*Ama*)," *Journal of Applied Physiology*, vol. 18, no. 3. pp. 457–65.

—— (1965), "*Hae-Nyo*, the Diving Women of Korea", in H. Rahn and T. Yokoyama (eds), *Physiology of Breath-hold Diving and the Ama of Japan*.

Kang, B.S. et al. (1963), "Changes in Body Temperature and Basic Metabolic Rate of the *Ama*," *Journal of Applied Physiology*, vol. 18, no. 3, pp. 483–8.

Kita, H. (1965), "Review of Activities: Harvest, Seasons and Diving Patterns," in H. Rahn and T. Yokoyama (eds), *Physiology of Breath-hold Diving and the Ama of Japan*.

Lebra, T.S. (1993), *Above the Clouds: Status Culture of the Modern Japanese Nobility*, Berkeley: University of California Press.

Maraini, F. (1962), *Hekura: the Diving Girls' Island*, trans. E. Mosbacher, London: Hamish Hamilton.

Martinez, D.P. (1990), "Tourism and the *Ama*: the Search for a Real Japan", in E. Ben-Ari, B. Moeran and J. Valentine (eds), *Unwrapping Japan*, Manchester: Manchester University Press.

—— (1993), "Women as Bosses: Perceptions of the *Ama* and Their Work," in J. Hunter (ed.), *Japanese Women Working*, London: Routledge.

Masuda, Y. et al. (1981), "The Ventilatory Responses to Hypoxia and Hypercapnia in the *Ama*", in *Japanese Journal of Physiology*, vol. 31, pp. 187–97.

Mishima, Y. (1957), *The Sound of Waves*, trans. M. Weatherby, London: Secker & Warbury.

Miyaji, H. (1987), *Chûtô no esunishiti: funsô to tôgô (Middle Eastern Ethnicity: Conflict and Unity)*, Tokyo: Asia Keizai Kenkyûjo.

Miyamura, M. et al. (1981), "Ventilatory Response to CO_2 Rebreathing at Rest in the *Ama*", *Japanese Journal of Physiology*, vol. 31, pp. 423–6.

Morris, I. (trans. and ed.) (1967), *The Pillow Book of Sei Shônagon*, Harmondsworth: Penguin Books.

Nash, M. (1989), *The Cauldron of Ethnicity in the Modern World*, Chicago and London: The University of Chicago Press.

Nippon: a Charted Survey of Japan (1990), Tokyo: The Kokusei-sha Corporation.

Nukada, M. (1965), "Historical Development of the *Ama*'s Diving Activities," in H. Rahn and T. Yokoyama (eds), *Physiology of Breath-hold Diving and the Ama of Japan*.

Ohnuki-Tierney, E. (1987), *The Monkey as Mirror, Symbolic Transformations in Japanese History and Ritual*, Princeton: Princeton University Press.

Rennie, D.W. et al. (1962), "Physical Insulation of Korean Diving Women," *Journal of Applied Physiology*, vol. 17, no. 6, pp. 961–6.

Sansom, G.B. (1931), *Japan, a Short Cultural History*, Stanford, California: Stanford University Press.

Segawa, K. (1956), *Ama*, Tokyo: Koken Shorin.

Takabashi, H., and M. Goto (1980), *Kinu no minzoku sôsho: rôdôsha (Folk Clothing Series: working people)*, Nagoya: Meigen Shobôkan.

Tames, R. (1981), *Servant of the Shogun, being the True Story of William Adams, Pilot and Samurai, the First Englishman in Japan*, Tenterden: Paul Norbury Publications Limited.

Tatai, K. (1965), "Anthropometric Studies on the Japanese," in H. Rahn and T. Yokoyama (eds), *Physiology of Breath-hold Diving and the Ama of Japan*.

Tsunoda, R. (1951), *Japan in the Chinese Dynastic Histories: Later Han through Ming Dynasties*, L.C. Goodrich (ed.), South Pasadena: P.D. and Ione Perkins.

Watanabe, S., Kondo S., and E. Matsunaga (1975), *Anthropological and Genetic Studies on the Japanese*, vol. 2 of the JIBP Synthesis, Tokyo: University of Tokyo Press.

Yamaguchi, M. (1977), "Kingship, Theatricality and Marginal Reality in Japan", in R. Jain (ed.), *Text and Context: the Social Anthropology of Tradition*, Philadelphia: ISHI.

5

Exotic West to Exotic Japan: Revival of Japanese Tradition in Modern Japan

Masami Suga

n this chapter, I explore recent interest among the Japanese in the revival of Japanese tradition in a society where western ideas, material goods, and practice, once seeming so exotic, are "domesticated" and now fully permeate its consumer market. Based on a set of criteria that make up and determine the degree of one's Japanese-ness, I analyze the modern Japanese perceptions of the past and the Japanese tradition. The royal wedding of June 1993 between the Crown Prince Naruhito and Masako Owada provides a case study. The wedding ritual illustrates how the modern Japanese transform the symbol of the wedding *kimono* of the past into a piece of "new" ethnicity, made available for sale.

The Japanese approach the revival of Japanese tradition from a consumer's orientation. They buy goods and services that represent nostalgia and provide modern convenience at the same time. Through those purchases, they give new meanings to the past, modify the past for modern life, and identify with the newly re-discovered Japanese ethnicity. My knowledge and experience as a native of Japan and the data collected from my fieldwork in Japan supplies the primary description and a tool for analyses on Japan and the royal family.

Westernization of Japan: Before and After

During the Edo period (1603–1868), Japanese government officials pursued a strict *sakoku*[1] policy and cut all communication ties with the rest of the world. No trading or exchange of scholars or artists occurred, with the exception of a limited business relationship with Chinese and Dutch merchants through the port of Nagasaki in Kyushu (Nakagawa and Rosovsky 1965: 313; Yamanaka 1982: 38). For the tiny, island nation[2] surrounded by several bodies of water[3] the *sakoku* meant a total isolation not only from neighboring nations in the East and Southeast Asia, but the whole world as well.

Japan experienced a cultural "cocoon-hood" until 1868 when it made a decision to end the *sakoku* and opened its ports to re-entry of foreign products, technologies, and ideas. Marking the installation of a new emperor,[4] Emperor Meiji, and the end of *sakoku* policy, the new period following Edo was named Meiji, literally meaning "new government" or "new political system." As the literal translation of the name indicates, Meiji symbolized the beginning of the contemporary, centralized Japanese government that emphasized the achievement of foreign missions both in and outside of the country.[5]

The Meiji period (1868–1912) brought rapid transition to Japan's centuries-old tradition, culture, and history. Western technology was introduced, resulting in a drastic shift from manual to mechanized operation in the manufacturing industry. A large-scale silk industry evolved. Many daughters of poor, rural farmers were recruited to work in the industry in the name of *bun'mei kaika* (civilization and enlightenment) (Sims 1973: 54).[6] Western custom influenced Japanese

---

1. *Sakoku* literally means isolation (*sa*) and nation (*koku*).
2. About the size of California.
3. The Pacific Ocean, The Sea of Japan, and the East China Sea.
4. Each era in contemporary Japanese history is marked by the death of an emperor and the installation of a new emperor taking over his father's imperial post. At his installation, a name for *his* era is decided by the imperial family and the government. During his administration, he is called the emperor of his particular era, for example, Emperor Meiji.
5. According to Pyle (1978: 49), "They [Dutch scholars] believed that Japan needed Western weapons and techniques in order to defend it; therefore it must avoid war with a Western power at least until it had a chance to strengthen itself – even if that meant giving in to foreign demands for the opening of ports."
6. A docu-drama film entitled *Nomugi-tōge* was produced in the early 1980s in Japan. The film reconstructed the life of a *jokō* (female factory worker) and her peers in a silk factory during the Meiji period. In contemporary Japanese history, the silk industry of the Meiji period is remembered as an exploiter of the *jokō* labor and their

architecture and transportation systems. Brick buildings began appearing, and steam engines and automobiles amazed the Japanese. The former Chinese calendar was changed to the western calendar system, and a new seven-day week with Sunday a holiday replaced the traditional ten-day cycle. Western dress impacted on the traditional Japanese style of dress commonly referred to as *kimono*.[7] A Japanese man dressed in a western suit with a pair of *geta* (traditional Japanese wooden sandals) was a familiar street scene of the early Meiji period (Sims 1973: 53; Yamanaka 1982: 39). Thus, Meiji symbolized an era of "tradition in transition" in various aspects of Japanese life-political, cultural, social, economic, historical, and technological. "It gave Japan a strong central government, committed to abolishing 'feudalism,' and eager for westernization and economic development" (Nakagawa and Rosovsky 1965: 314).

Throughout the Meiji period, westernization of Japan in many dimensions of life continued. Japan's adoption of western dress was a visible signature of that influence. Both Japanese men and women, to a varying individual extent, incorporated western fashion into their ways of life. The Meiji government eagerly promoted western fashion both in dress and hairstyle; the westernization of dress began with the military when western uniform styles were adopted. Later the association of the military and the western uniform was said to have been attributed to the wider acceptance and adoption of western dress by the general public (Fujii 1958: 212; Shibusawa 1958: 2). The presentation of Japan's "civilized" image to visitors from western countries and the demonstration of Japan's open attitude toward the new foreign trade relationship were important.

Thus, Japan's exposure to western ideas, material goods, and practice is a fairly recent development in its modern history, beginning less than 130 years ago. Today "the West," well domesticated[8] by the

female sexuality. In the near-slavery working condition, many *jokôs* died of tuberculosis and/or were raped by their male supervisors. The film's title symbolizes the name of a *tôge* (mountain path) where one pregnant *jokô*, who fled a silk factory, died in childbirth in the deep snow of northern Japan. When the film was introduced, it made modern Japanese re-think of sacrifices behind the economic success of today's Japan.

7. *Kimono* literally means wearing (*ki*) and item/thing (*mono*).

8. I use the word "domesticated" here to make a point. Western products did not simply replace the Japanese consumer market. The products and services were modified to meet the culture, environment, and physique of the Japanese. For example, McDonald's offers a teriyaki burger and tea along with their standard menu, and their name has been Japanized to Makudonarudo. Coca Cola sells "Coca Cola Light" in Japan: it is neither Coca Cola Classic nor Diet Coke, and the medium flavor

Japanese, fully permeates the daily consumer market: McDonald's, KFC, Coca Cola, Calvin Klein, DKNY, Nike, Revlon, Tokyo Disneyland, and T-shirts and blue jeans are all accepted in Japan. *Kimono*, the sole form of dress before the Meiji Restoration, is rarely worn today except for special occasions or holidays; western dress dominates Japan's everyday apparel scene. *Yôfuku* is the Japanese word for western dress, *yô* meaning western and *fuku* meaning clothing: *Wafuku*, similarly composed of two words indicating Japanese and clothing, is a Japanese word for *kimono*. These two words used to specify whether the topic of conversation or the object of observation in regard to apparel was western or Japanese. Western dress has become extremely common nowadays, and *fuku* without any reference to its country of origin simply means western clothing. Department stores that "once hired consultants to familiarize the Japanese with Western apparel now hire teachers to demonstrate how to put on *kimono*. And ...most young women are unschooled in the intricacies of dressing, walking, and sitting in *kimono*, and often their mothers do not know enough to help them" (Creighton 1992: 54).[9]

Japan's appetite for western ideas, goods, and practice has grown beyond the mission of the Meiji Restoration and the national goal of the post-World War II era, "catching up to the West." "As . . . material goods and customs associated with the once-exotic West have become a routine part of life" (Creighton 1992: 53), the coexistence of the West and the East has also become a natural part of Japanese identity. Like western dress, *yôshoku* a Japanese word for western food is no longer frequently used because *shokuji* indicates meals in general. Instead, the Japanese make a special effort to use *washoku* if the meal is indeed Japanese. Thus, through the help of western goods, foods, and services, ". . . Japanese define Japanese-ness by delineating what Japan is not" (Creighton 1992: 55). Today, the West does not denote an exotic concept or product in the Japanese consumer market, but an interest in the revival of Japanese tradition has evolved as the Japanese search for Japanese-ness.

---

gains the support of many Japanese who do not prefer a heavy soft drink flavor but are not as concerned about sugar-free dieting as many Americans. Blue jeans too have been redesigned to better fit the physical characteristics of most Japanese, who have longer torsos and shorter legs. And many retail stores offer while-you-wait alteration services to shorten the pant length. (See also Tobin 1992: 4.)

9. Shortly before the "coming of age" ceremony for which I was planning to wear a *kimono* (for the first time), my mother attended seminars for weeks to learn the basic skill of *kimono* dressing. She worked on dressing me for several hours, and still ended up with a wrong layering of collars. The sash, nevertheless, was state of the art.

While Japan's love and passion for the West continues, Japanese consumer goods, foods, and services that represent the images of "tradition" have been gaining a steady popularity among the Japanese consumers who grew up in a highly westernized, post-war market economy. Wooden toys and regional crafts are selling well. They bring to city folks a touch of nature, rural life, and disciplined artistry without having to leave the city. Restaurant guide books produce special issues on Japanese restaurants that serve authentic but casual food to suit those who have developed a McDonald's palate. Trips to hot springs, once considered a pastime for the elderly and thus not fashionable, are attracting more young visitors. Indeed, development projects in rural areas around hot springs are prospering, including the building of camping grounds and barbecue facilities for the use of youth. Similarly, train travel is making a come-back, this time on trains equipped with extra speed and furnished with a complete set of modern amenities. Lunch boxes that look lacquered but are easily washable are taking over from the once-admired Tupperware on store shelves. Today, all this market nostalgia associated with "old Japanese tradition," while the convenience of modern life is neatly packaged to go with them.

The Components of Japaneseness and the Degree of Japaneseness

Many consumer goods, foods, and services could be labeled Japanese simply because they may give an impression that they are not western. When it comes to people, however, there is a set of criteria that make up Japanese-ness and also determine the degree of a person's Japanese-ness. Despite the rapid wave of westernization that swept over Japan, especially in the material aspects of everyday life, three things have remained relatively unchanged: Japanese language, physical appearance, and location.[10]

First, the Japanese still speak Japanese, and that is their absolute mother tongue. Although English has been instituted as a mandatory second language in many secondary schools and universities, only a small fraction of students manage relative fluency. Business English too has shown a similar trend. Almost all western movies for television

---

10. Diana Forsythe reports a similar set of criteria that makes up and determines one's German-ness in "German Identity and the Problem of History" (1989). Her criteria include language usage, country of origin, and appearance.

are dubbed in Japanese, and books and manuals are translated into Japanese, but only in recent years have some TV stations begun offering a limited number of programs in English. Even in cases where a particular name, such as Maria, is taken from the West, *kanji* (Chinese characters) and/or *hiragana/katakana* (Japanese phonetic alphabets) are used to write it.

Second, the Japanese still look Japanese as a result of their genetic background. Because the Japanese have long favored endogamy, marrying within their own race, most Japanese exhibit similar physical characteristics, with only minor individual variations. In general, they have dark, straight hair, yellowish tinted skin, medium height (not many are under 5 feet, and not many are over 6 feet), and Japanese facial features. The Japanese say they can even tell other Asians from Japanese, often from the way they dress, wear their hair, or simply walk.[11] The physical characteristics can be modified to look more "western" through applying permanent waves and dye to the hair, using whiter shades of cosmetic foundation, or wearing high heels to extend height. When they discontinue those practices, however, people return to the original Japanese appearance with which they are born.

Third, the Japanese consider only those who still live in Japan to be Japanese citizens. Because the Japanese government is known to seldom grant Japanese citizenship to immigrants, the possession of Japanese citizenship is highly valued as a solid testimonial of one's Japanese-ness based on Japanese ancestry. *Nikkei* Japanese (Japanese-Americans), who neither live in Japan nor are Japanese citizens, are first viewed as Americans and then as descendants of Japanese who moved to America, despite the Japanese physical features they exhibit. The Japanese may make overseas trips, but most likely with a promise that they will return to Japan in a relatively short time. "Where is your home town?" and "Where does your family live?" are common questions Japanese ask each other when they meet for the first time. In a fairly racially homogeneous society, this is a way of measuring the degree of a person's Japanese-ness and insuring that the person with whom one is interacting is (or is not) a Japanese. In this respect, the most authentic Japanese is one who speaks Japanese as a mother tongue, was born to Japanese parents, and has Japanese citizenship.

---

11. I can often tell from a distance a non-Japanese-speaking Asian from a Japanese, simply by studying the amount of teeth that show in the speaker's mouth. Most Japanese words can be pronounced easily without showing a large portion of the teeth.

Re-visiting the Japanese Royal Family as an Ethnic Group

For the modern Japanese, buying a piece of "old Japan" is a convenient way of reviving their image of the past and tradition while materially satisfying their search for something exotic and not western: ". . . perceptions of the past are constantly reshaped by the present status quo and . . . a replication of current ideals is commonly projected onto past time" (Nagata 1993: 98). In their shopping enthusiasm, the Japanese are re-visiting the royal household, the symbol of ancient Japan, with a new consumer interest. During Japan's rapid westernization, the royal household has continued to practice its centuries-old customs, language, and traditions. The protected life of the royal household is remote from the rush-hour Tokyo scene; to the ordinary Japanese, the royal family is like an ethnic group from a distant place unaffected by the affairs of the modern world. Nevertheless, the members of the royal household meet all three criteria for Japanese-ness, and they are highly visible. Especially now the Shinto myth that the emperor is a spiritual deity has long been dissolved, the Japanese have nothing to be afraid of in buying a slice of that "exotic" lifestyle.

Here I provide a view of the royal household as an ethnic group and discuss why the modern Japanese find them exotic. According to Yinger (1985: 159, also Yinger 1976: 200), ethnic groups are "a segment of a larger society whose members are thought, by themselves and/or others, to have a common origin and to share important segments of a common culture and who, in addition, participate in shared activities in which the common origin and culture are significant ingredients." For the Japanese royal household, who had rigidly maintained their "pure" blood line through endogamy until quite recently, their common royal origin and culture are especially important.[12] Indeed, only three women have married into the royal household from outside the royal family boundary: the present Empress Michiko, and the Princesses Masako and Kiko. When the Empress, a commoner, married the present Emperor in the 1950s, there was a desperate outcry by the "blood" royal members. They had criticized her (some still do) for not fully understanding their unique

12. A similarity exists in the importance of common royal origin and culture between the Japanese royal household and the British royal family, as reported by Hayden (1987: 130–46).

custom, language, and tradition as do those who are royal born, and they feared her outside impurity would pollute the royal blood. Their protectionism is evident in the Japanese language, which separates the status of the royal household from the commoners. *Kôzoku*, a Japanese word for members of the royal household, is composed of two words literally meaning "imperial" and "race." *Kôshitsu*, another Japanese word for the royal household, translates as "imperial room." The commoners, on the other hand, are called *shomin* or *heimin*,[13] both indicating "a common people." Thus, these words imply the *Kôzoku*'s[14] perception of the royal household as a different race or as an ethnic group, whose everyday life within the protected imperial room is inaccessible to the *shomin*.[15] The reverse of this concept applies as well to the *shomin*'s perception of the *Kôzoku* as an "exotic" people. For the *shomin*, *Kôzoku* are a people they often hear about, but few have seen them personally.

As an ethnic group, the *Kôzoku* establishes its presence as a group differentiated from those outside of that organization (Yinger 1985: 158). Their ". . . dress, language, house-form, or general style of life" often convey identifiable royal characteristics (Barth 1969: 14; Nash 1989: 13). The dress of the *Kôzoku*, whether "Japanese"[16] or western style, is distinct from that of the *shomin*. The Japanese *kimono* worn by the *Kôzoku* during Shinto rites in the late twentieth century comes from a design worn by the imperial court of ancient times. When western dress is worn, regardless of what is currently fashionable

13. The same Chinese character used for *hei* of *heimin* is also used in other Japanese words that imply a person or an object without a level or a class. For example, the first Chinese character in *hirashain*, which describes a new employee who holds an entry-level position or an employee who never gets a promotion, is the same *hei* character in *heimin*. A single-story house is *hiraya*, literally meaning "level-less house." *Heijitsu*, a word for weekdays, also uses the same *hei*. Weekends, as opposed to *heijitsu*, are called *shukujitsu*, meaning holiday.
14. I am using an upper case K for *Kôzoku*. My intention is to establish the royal household as an ethnic group and treat its existence in the same manner as we approach such groups as the Hmong, the Inuit, and the Ainu.
15. I am not using an upper case S for *shomin*. Because this chapter approaches the *Kôzoku* as an ethnic group from a *shomin*'s perspective, the *shomin*'s ethnocentric bias of looking at an ethnic group as "the other" but not themselves is emphasized.
16. I have put the word Japanese in quotation marks because the *kimono* worn by the royals differs greatly from the *kimono* worn by the common Japanese. This is a type of *kimono* that in ancient times was worn only by the members of the imperial court. Thus, both in the past and the present, this *kimono* is strictly a royal costume, and thus qualifies to be studied as an ethnic dress or ethnic minority dress, both by the common Japanese and non-Japanese persons.

outside the royal land, the clothing designs must meet the dress code posed by the *kunaichô*, the Royal Household Agency. A woman's dress ensemble, for example, characteristically consists of a knee-length suit or a one-piece dress, a matching hat, and a pair of white gloves. The language of the *Kôzoku* is also identifiable; they speak the most honorific form of the Japanese language, which is rarely spoken (although comprehended) by the *shomin* today. The *Kôshitsu*,[17] their palace, is designed for a self-contained, isolated lifestyle. The vast land area in central Tokyo, where the *Kôshitsu* is situated, enables the *Kôzoku* of different generations to live together without struggling for their space, and its physical boundary is clearly marked and protected with a moat (Map 5.1).[18]

The *Kôshitsu* of the past had indeed maintained a relatively isolated lifestyle until the Meiji Restoration. When the Meiji politicians formalized the notion of common Japanese ancestry established in the Shinto myth as a nationalist ideology for political purposes, they brought the Emperor Meiji out of his "imperial room" and shaped his public image as a father figure in a way that would reinforce their political schemes. The symbolic manipulation of the emperor was furthered by the militarists during the Second World War. Emperor Showa was presented not only as a father figure, but as a spiritual deity with a supernatural power as well (Edwards 1989: 103–104; Bornoff 1991: 27–28).

Today, the emperor is no longer a political puppet or a pseudo-deity.[19] The mystery has been resolved, and his existence as a human being is a known fact. Thanks to modern technology, the life of the *Kôshitsu* can be viewed on a television series called *Kôshitsu Dayori*, which means "report from the *Kôshitsu*." This "visual ethnography" appears on NHK, an educational channel operated by the government.[20] The remaining Japanese television stations are publicly

17. In Japanese language, *Kôshitsu* means both the royal household as a cultural institution and the physical building in which the royal members reside.
18. The royal household is situated in the center of Tokyo, the largest and most populated city in Japan. The typical city life that takes place outside the moat — business, tourism, traffic, crime, pollution, entertainment — rarely touches the lives of the royal household. In Tokyo where trees are scarce, a "forest" of a substantial size exists inside the royal land, and pesticide-free organic vegetables are grown.
19. To the generation of Japanese who lived through the War, believing that Emperor Showa was (is) a deity, his death on January 7, 1989 meant a complex emotional drama. They were forced to realize and accept the fact that the emperor was not an immortal deity but a mortal human being.
20. Just like the National Geographic on an American educational channel!

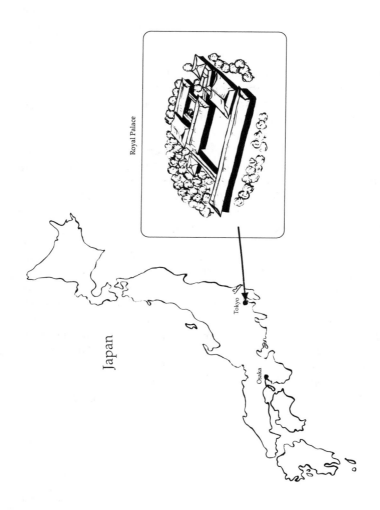

Map 5.1 Map of the Royal household in Tokyo.

owned, and they show the *Kôshitsu* only if the story is extremely newsworthy or scandalous.

The word "ethnic" often connotes a lesser degree (or lack) of political autonomy and power exercised by a group. Not only may the smaller population size prevent members of such a group from gaining full voice in the political arena, but they may be discriminated against as well. This concept, when applied to the present status of the *Kôshitsu* and the way the household is being treated by the *shomin* majority, illustrates the lack of respect or discrimination the *Kôshitsu* receives. The *Kôzoku* are small in size and possess little political power; indeed, they have little say in the Japanese legislature or the election of a prime minister, despite their royal status. Further, they live at the mercy of taxpayers, the *shomin*, for their everyday survival, and some *shomin* resent strongly the payment of both their tax for royal welfare and the mandatory NHK viewership fee. A televised funeral service of the last emperor, which took place on February 24, 1989, provides a good example. When all TV networks broadcast the funeral and canceled their popular programs such as dramas and game shows throughout the day, many *shomin* rushed to rental video shops and emptied their shelves for alternatives to viewing the funeral. They were not very interested in the sole affairs of an ethnic group. However, *Kôzoku* events, in which the *shomin* is also involved as an important participant, such as the 1993 royal wedding between the Crown Prince and a *shomin* woman, Masako Owada, whet their curiosity. They demanded every detail from the media on how the couple met, why she would want to marry him, and when and how the "inter-ethnic" marriage would take place.

The 1993 Japanese Royal Wedding and the Ritual Use of Dress

The royal wedding between the Crown Prince and Masako Owada took place on June 9, 1993. It was a rare kind of inter-ethnic marriage.[21]

21. My perspective on this marriage is similar to the interracial/intercultural marriages in the United States. Although these marriages are becoming more accepted and more common these days, marriages between a newly arrived ethnic minority group, such as the Hmong, and a white majority group is still rare. The ethnic group is so new to this country that its members often struggle to maintain their ethnicity and familiar cultural customs of their home land. The white majority are often reluctant (or afraid) to understand the culture, language, and customs of the ethnic group that are so foreign to their experience. When a marriage does occur between these two groups, however, extensive enculturation training is demanded. The burden

Indeed, only three such cases have been witnessed, all during the twentieth century: one occurred in the 1950s and two took place in this decade. In these cases a *shomin* woman married into the *Kôshitsu*, an "ethnic group," thus giving up the privileges and status she used to enjoy and exercise. The Japanese royal wedding exhibits this characteristic. When Ms. Owada, a person from the "majority" married the Prince, she sacrificed her right to freedom and privacy. As a Princess, she left her job as a career diplomat, and no longer speaks her "mother tongue,"[22] meets her friends as she desires, or shops for clothing by herself. She was even criticized for being outspoken on a television interview when she merely spoke in her previous manner of speech. She is now being constantly observed by royal guards who make sure she follows the cultural rules of the *Kôshitsu*.[23] Thus, "...ethnic identity is experienced as a moral commitment, making rejection of conflicting moral and legal commitments mandatory" (de Vos and Romanucci-Ross 1975: 369).

Shortly prior to the wedding, Ms. Owada was required to complete a fifty-hour princess education course offered by the *Kôshitsu*. Because of her unfamiliarity with the culture of the group, she was taught every subject necessary for smooth assimilation into the group; these subjects included Shinto rituals, ancient poetry, dress code and etiquette, the royal history, and the royal language (Powell 1993: 30). Ms. Owada surprised the Japanese *shomin* on a televised interview when she spoke fluently in the royal language. She successfully and quickly transformed her ethnic identity. The enculturation of a prospective group member ensures that the person understands an appropriate behavior that is expected for membership by the particular ethnic group (de Vos and Romanucci-Ross 1975: 368).

The 1993 royal wedding observed a strict Shinto religious rite. The bride wore a twelve-layer *kimono*, which weighted approximately thirty pounds (Figure 5.1). The *kimono* incorporated her color

often falls on the shoulders of those who must learn the particularities of an ethnic group, if the purpose of the group is to maintain their culture and ethnicity.

22. By "mother tongue," I mean two things. First, it is a standard Japanese language form the majority children learn in primary schools, not the stilted honorific language spoken to or spoken by the royal household members. Second, it is a casual form used in everyday conversation.

23. Approximately fifty assistants are assigned to the Prince and the Princess, including foreign relations consultants, house keepers, and jogging and tennis companions. At least one assistant must accompany the Prince and/or the Princess in their personal outings, such as concerts, research trips, and shopping (*Asahi Shinbun* 1993: 2).

© 1995 Masami Suga

Figure 5.1 Prince Naruhiro and Princess Masako in their wedding costumes, June 9, 1993.

preference of blue within the royal design allowance. This ancient imperial court *kimono*, although it is still called *kimono*, has not been commonly worn by the *shomin* (except as a theatrical costume or for the purpose of mockery); the *kimono* worn by the *shomin* consists of only several layers. Her hair-do was also uniquely *Kôshitsu*, and again not worn by the *shomin*.[24] With the sacred music of the Shinto religion and the royal wedding guests dressed in ancient court attire, the royal wedding recreated the ancient ritual of the *Kôshitsu* in this modern time. Especially for the bride, the wedding symbolized, both visually and culturally, her initiation into the ethnic group, ". . . a ritual in which the rebirth usually symbolizes rejection of actual ancestry and a pledge of allegiance to shared future goals of the new group" (De Vos and Romanucci-Ross 1975: 368).

Both in and outside of Japan, the ancient images of the *Kôzoku*, especially of the Prince and the Princess, were immediately broadcast and televised via satellite. Photographs of the couple appeared in the pages of Japanese and U.S. newspapers and magazines, including *Asahi Shinbun*, *Nippon Keizai Shinbun*, *Shûkan Josei*, the *New York Times*, the *Star Tribune*, and *Newsweek*. Journalists from all over the world rushed to Japan to observe and report the rare event. The court attire, as visual conveyers of royal symbols and customs, has made a lasting impression of the timeless and romantic royal life in the minds of many people. This impression was further strengthened by a tactful photographic technique that excluded many visible signs of modern, westernized Japan such as business suits and blue jeans.[25]

Following the Shinto wedding, the *Kôzoku* changed into formal western dress for another ceremony in which the Prince and the Princess reported their marriage and expressed their appreciation before the Emperor and the Empress (Figure 5.2). Again the western dress worn by the *Kôzoku* did not resemble the same western dress worn by the *shomin*. First, the dress, custom made by apparel designers specially hired by the *Kôshitsu*, had little to do with the fashionable style of contemporary western dress. Second, their formal western dress, with men in tuxedos and women in full-length gowns, was

24. However, dolls with the royal kimonos and hair-dos are displayed during the months of February and March in the homes of the *shomin* to celebrate Girls' Day on March 3. This practice may resemble the display of, for example, the Native American dream catchers in American homes.

25. Biased documentation (both literal and visual), in which a researcher/reporter intentionally omits the presence of modern western dress, for example, in a given cultural context helps further build the myth of an ethnic group (Collier and Collier 1986).

© 1995 Masami Suga

Figure 5.2 Prince Naruhiro and Princess Masako (right) in formal western dress reporting their marriage to Emperor Akihiro and Empress Michiko (left), June 9, 1993.

decorated with medals and ribbons that had been passed down for generations, a unique wedding tradition among the *Kôzoku* which does not mean much to the *shomin*.

Even when casual western dress is worn, for press conferences for example, the static image of royal life still continues (Figure 5.3). Royal women commonly wear knee-length suits or dresses, matching hats, and pairs of white gloves with little regard to their age, height, weight, social status within the household, or personal preference except in very minor ways. While the components of the ensemble may remain the same, the texture, surface design, and tailoring of the dress can show some timely fashion trends. It is still true today that while the modern *shomin* women take unisex apparel (jeans, pants, pant suits) for granted, the *Kôzoku* women do not appear in public functions wearing anything other than a skirt or dress. The only exception to this rule may be hiking clothes or sportswear worn within the immediate family. Thus, the image of the *Kôzoku* as an exotic people with their own customs living in a world far removed from the dynamic affairs of modern times becomes perpetuated, regardless of the forms of dress they wear.

The Royal Wedding is for Sale, Buy a Slice of Exotic Japan

We often find foreign cultures that appear "exotic" to our native eyes fascinating. A myth often perpetuates a stereotyped image of an ethnic group, maintaining the traditional culture and continuing the lifestyle of ancestors. The timeless image of this lifestyle indeed seems romantic. In reality, culture is a dynamic process, although the rate of change may differ from one group to another. Readily observable objects such as ritual dress and textiles that are used by generation after generation may trick the perception of an observer about that particular culture.[26] The "strange" but "beautiful" dress and textiles used in their rituals make us want to try and collect them. A similar phenomenon is taking place in Japan today.

The Japanese looked at the 1993 royal wedding the way a foreigner would and found it exotic (Creighton 1992: 53). They were drawn to the elaborate court *kimono*s worn by the Prince and the Princess. The

26. Indeed, the Shintoist wedding rite performed for the 1993 royal wedding is less than one century old, invented in 1900 for Emperor Taisho's wedding. However, the *kimonos* worn during the wedding trace their history to ancient Japan during the Heian era (*Asahi Shinbun* 1993: 3).

Figure 5.3 Princess Masako dressed in a less formal western dress, 1993.

twelve-layer *kimono* of the Princess particularly caught the attention of many women of marriageable age. Japanese fashion magazines, commonly read by young women in their 20s and 30s, specifically emphasized the beauty and timelessness of the ritual scene of the royal wedding. In the fast-paced modern Japanese life, where fashions can change overnight, many Japanese felt a strong sense of nostalgia when seeing the royal wedding, which visually re-staged an ancient Japanese tradition. Even the sacred Shinto ritual, often thought tedious and boring by the youth, gained a new "fashionable" status.

The Japanese wedding industry quickly foresaw a market potential in this trend. They took advantage of growing Japanese interest in the revival of Japanese tradition, which is also reflected in the wedding business. Like the consumer market, images from the West play a major role in wedding services provided for wedding ceremonies and receptions. For example, "gondola weddings" offer an exchange of wedding vows on a gondola boat from Italy in a little pond artificially built within a hotel or a wedding palace garden. This is based on romantic Italian lore that a couple who kisses under a bridge in Venice become united. In a "space wedding," a groom and a bride appear to the audience from a background heavily filled with theatrical smoke and illuminated with a laser lighting show. "Chapel weddings" may resemble what we commonly associate with a western wedding; a couple is wed by a minister in a chapel situated in a hotel or a wedding palace. However, this is a wedding style which has little connected to the religions of the West. In many Japanese weddings, western wedding gowns, which the Japanese most often associate with Christian weddings, has become a fashion necessity for all brides, whether they are Buddhists, Shintoists, Christians, or Atheists.

In a highly westernized wedding market, entrepreneurs in the wedding industry invented a Japanese tradition that can be conveniently catered to while satisfying consumers' instincts to buy something Japanese and exotic at the same time. The 1993 royal wedding met all four prerequisites for successful marketing. First, the royal household is unmistakably Japanese. Not only does it fulfill all three criteria for Japanese-ness, language, physical appearance, and location, but it also symbolizes the old Japanese tradition, which the modern Japanese are so eager to re-capture. Second, the royal household is famous. Not only does its centuries-old history give its royal presence special aura of privilege, but the affairs of the household are also highly publicized in modern Japan, just like the lives of celebrity entertainers. Third, the royal household is exotic.

The royal household maintains its language, culture, and tradition and survives as a unique cultural institution in this age of technology and world economy. Finally, the royal wedding involved Ms. Owada, a commoner with whom potential consumers can easily relate. Ms. Owada made the presence of the royal household less exclusive and distant and its image more accessible to the Japanese.

The wedding industry has begun offering a rental imitation twelve-layer *kimono* to couples for their wedding along with other standard costumes commonly rented out by the industry. Whether the wedding is Japanese or western in style, hotels and wedding palaces that specialize in providing wedding services are well stocked with a variety of costumes.[27] For those places, the larger their costume collection is, the better they can serve the clientele and generate profit.[28] A typical Japanese wedding consists of three or more costume changes during the course of a wedding and a reception. For example, a couple may wed in a Shinto ceremony, with the groom being dressed in a black *kimono* and a bride in a white *kimono*. Then they may change into more colorful *kimonos*, a white suit and a western wedding gown, and finally a tuxedo and an evening gown for the reception.

For modern convenience, certain simplifications were made to a twelve-layer *kimono*. Instead of layering all twelve *kimonos*, one *kimono* with twelve layers of different colors showing at the collar and sleeves was invented. The modification was successful, for today's weddings require a theater-like quick costume change and today's brides are not accustomed to wearing heavy, bulky apparel. Thus, "icons of tradition have been recast to fit the realities of contemporary Japanese life and tastes" (Creighton 1992: 56). Finally, a groom and a bride who don head-to-toe costumes made to look ancient and imperial are the center of a wedding reception, which is professionally

27. I use the word "costume" to emphasize the rarity of *kimono* being worn as everyday apparel in modern Japan. Just as "Halloween costumes" worn only once a year are called costumes, *kimono* worn only for special occasions also qualify for this category of apparel.

28. Extra garments worn during a wedding reception add to the social value of the wedding; the number of garments rented for the wedding also indicates the economic cost of the wedding that a bride's family (most often) is able to provide financially. In a similar way, a standard formula for determining the cost of the wedding ring that a groom presents to his bride is said to be two and one-half times of his monthly salary (Creighton 1992: 45). The Japanese custom that adult children live with their parents until marriage and that the parents are also expected to financially support their children until marriage, makes such a demand possible (*Asahi Shinbun* 1993: 4).

catered, spot-lighted, and narrated.

In a twelve-layer *kimono*, a Japanese woman can temporarily experience the timelessness of the *Kôzoku* life, just as in a romance novel. It is fantasy, a convenient visual celebration of stardom. She has no intention of living her actual life in the *Kôshitsu*, or go through a princess education course as Ms. Owada did prior to her marriage; all she needs to do is to buy a slice of exotic Japan, nicely pre-packaged and facilitated by the wedding industry. No training, practice, or rehearsal is required for the event, and the customer-friendly feature appeals to a generation who grew up with the television, for whom quick fun and an elaborate production have become a way of life (Edwards 1989: 135). The twelve-layer *kimono*, the national symbol of ancient Japan, is now available for sale. The modern Japanese can re-visit their past, re-discover their tradition, and re-define their Japanese ethnicity through the means they know the best – buying.

References

Asahi Graph (1993), Kōtaishi, Masako-sama Goseikon (*The Wedding of the Crown Prince and Ms. Masako*), Asahi Shinbun, June 20.
Asahi Shinbun (1993), "(The Royal Wedding Special Report)," June 9, pp. 1–8.
——, "Kōtaishi-sama, Masako-sama, katayose Paradel (The Wedding Parade)," June 10, 1993, pp. 1, 27.
Barth, F. (ed.) (1969), *Ethnic Groups and Boundaries: The Social Organization of Culture Difference*, Boston: Little, Brown and Company.
Bornoff, N. (1991), *Pink Samurai: Love, Marriage and Sex in Contemporary Japan*, London: Pocket Books.
Collier, J., and Collier, M. (1986), *Visual Anthropology: Photography as a Research Method*, Albuquerque: University of New Mexico Press.
Creighton, M.R. (1992), "The Depâto: Merchandising the West While Selling Japaneseness," in J. Tobin (ed.), *Re-Made in Japan: Everyday Life and Consumer Taste in a Changing Society*, Binghamton, NY: Ballou Press.
de Vos, G., and Romanucci-Ross, L. (eds) (1982), *Ethnic Identity: Cultural Continuities and Change*, Chicago: The Wenner-Gren Foundation for Anthropological Research.
Edwards, W. (1989), *Modern Japan Through Its Weddings*, Stanford, CA: Stanford University Press.
Fujii, J. (ed.) (1958), *Japanese Culture in the Meiji Era, Volume III, Outline of Japanese History*, trans. H.K. Colton and K.E. Colton, Tokyo: Obunsha.
Forsythe, D. (1989), "German Identity and the Problems of History," in E. Tonkin, M. McDonald, and M. Chapman (eds), *History and Ethnicity*, London: Routledge.

Hayden, I. (1987), *Symbol and Privilege: The Ritual Context of British Royalty*, Tucson: University of Arizona Press.

Nagata, J. (1993), "From Indigene to International: The Many Faces of Malay Identity," in M. Leven (ed.), *Ethnicity and Aborginality: Case Studies in Ethnonationalism*, Toronto: University of Toronto Press.

Nakagawa, K., and Rosovsky, H. (1976), "The Case of a Dying *Kimono*," in M.E. Roach and J.B. Eicher (eds), *Dress, Adornment, and the Social Order*, New York: John Wiley & Sons.

Nash, M. (1989), *The Cauldron of Ethnicity in the Modern World*, Chicago: University of Chicago Press.

Nippon Keizai Shinbun (1993), "Kōtaishi-sama, Masako-san, Yuinō no gi, (The Bridewealth Ceremony of Ms. Masako)," April 12, p. 1.

—— (1993), "Kōtaishi-sama, Masako-sama, Kekkon no gi, (The Wedding of the Crown Prince and Ms. Masako)," June 9, p. 1.

Powell, B. (1993), "The Reluctant Princess," *Newsweek*, May 24, pp. 28–39.

Pyle, K.B. (1978), *The Making of Modern Japan*, Lexington, MA: D.C. Heath and Co.

Shūkan Josei (1993), "Special Wedding Engagement Coverage," June 22, pp. 1–76.

Shibusawa, K. (ed.) (1958), *Japanese Life and Culture in the Meiji Era*, trans. C.S. Terry, Tokyo: Obunsha.

Sims, R. (1973), *Modern Japan*, Sydney: The Bodley Head.

Star Tribune (1993), "Future Emperor and Empress Wed in Japan," June 9, pp. 1A, 6A, Minneapolis, MN.

Tobin, J.J. (1992), "Introduction: Domesticating the West," in J.J. Tobin (ed.), *Re-Made in Japan: Everyday Life and Consumer Taste in a Changing Society*, Binghamton, NY: Ballou Press.

Yamanaka, N. (1982), *The Book of Kimono*, Tokyo: Kodansha International.

Yinger, J.M. (1985), "Ethnicity," in R.H. Turner and J.F. Short, Jr. (eds), *Annual Review of Sociology*, Vol. 11, Palo Alto, CA: Annual Reviews.

6

Becoming a Bunu Bride: Bunu Ethnic Identity and Traditional Marriage Dress

Elisha P. Renne

Adofi mi fe, aso ba mi gb'omo
Adofi is what I want, the cloth that helps me to carry children

— Bunu marriage song

The Bunu Yoruba, an ethnic sub-group of Yoruba-speaking peoples of southwestern Nigeria, reside in the area just west of the confluence of the Niger and Benue Rivers in central Nigeria. However, a strict association of Bunu ethnic identity with residence in this area would be misleading. Prior to the establishment of British colonial rule in the area in 1900, the Bunu consisted of many small kingdoms with their own local identities rather than an over-arching Bunu identity. Further, while being born and residing in Bunu District are important elements of contemporary Bunu ethnic identity, many Bunu people travel and work outside of the district, where they may stress more generically ethnic – such as Yoruba – or national – Nigerian – identities. Nonetheless, most retain ties with kin in Bunu towns and villages where they were born or raised, returning home during the Christmas holidays when various ritual performances – funerals, chieftaincy installations, and traditional marriages – are observed. These visits are part of process whereby an ethnic identity, based on an association with a particular place, group of people, and culture, is continually being constructed and reproduced.

In this chapter, I focus on the performance of one of these rituals,

117

Map 6.1 Map of confluence area indicating Bunu Yoruba and neighboring ethnic groups. Map by Danna Yamashita-Berry.

B. Bailey '95©

Figure 6.1 Bunu bride, wearing *adofi* cloth, catching water from a small gourd, on entering her husband's house (Mrs. Omosuwa Shehaye, Olle-Bunu, May 1988). Drawn by Rebecca Bailey© from a field photograph by Elisha P. Renne.

traditional marriage, and on the ways in which its continued, if changing, practice by women contributes to the constitution of a Bunu ethnic identity. In performing traditional marriages, Bunu women make use of several old, blue-black cloths, formerly woven in Bunu. Unlike neighboring ethnic groups such as the Owe Yoruba of Kabba who have stopped using cloths which were locally woven by women (Aina 1968) on the wide, vertical looms associated with women's weaving throughout Nigeria (Eicher 1977; Lamb and Holmes 1980) in traditional marriage performance, Bunu women have saved many of the cloths which they wove in the past and which are now irreplaceable. These blue-black handwoven marriage cloths are kept by older women and are borrowed for use by new brides.

Bunu women have also incorporated a new marriage cloth, known as an *adofi*, into their marriage traditions. These predominantly black cloths decorated with intermittent red and white warp stripes are presently woven by the few active weavers in Bunu, who substitute industrially spun thread for handspun cotton. Each woman performing a traditional marriage must commission the weaving of an *adofi* cloth which, unlike the other marriage cloths, she personally owns and has embroidered with her name (Lamb and Holmes 1980: 234). As only Bunu women who have performed traditional marriage can publicly wear them (Ibejigba 1985), these cloths have become a metonym for Bunu-ness (see Figure 6.2).

Some non-Bunu women might disparage the wearing of *adofi*, associating its simple patterning and three-color scheme with old-fashioned, rural backwardness. Yet the insistence of Bunu women on the continued use of traditional marriage cloths conveys a sense of moral superiority, in contrast to outsiders who have failed to maintain their traditions (Moore 1986: 301). Thus while Bunu District remains geographically isolated and under-developed compared with neighboring districts with their own associated ethnic groups, Bunu women throughout the district have made a virtue of their relative disadvantage. Their positive evaluation of a common, Bunu identity – represented in this case by the continued use of traditional handwoven marriage cloths – is reinforced by contrast with the moral laxity of outsiders who don't keep their old cloths. This tendency toward cohesion among Bunu insiders in opposition to non-Bunu outsiders, here distinguished by cultural practice, is reflected in the historical experiences of the Bunu and neighboring ethnic groups as well.

The Historical Construction of Bunu Ethnic Identity

The Bunu people's proximity to and historical relations with ethnic groups such as the Nupe, the Ebira, and the Igala who also reside in the confluence area of central Nigeria has led to considerable exchange of ideas, objects, and practices (Obayemi 1980; Picton 1991).[1] While the Bunu people are linguistically related to Yoruba sub-groups to the southwest – speaking a dialect of Yoruba sometimes referred to as O-kun Yoruba[2] – and thus sometimes called the Northwest Yoruba, they may share as much, culturally, with their non-Yoruba speaking neighboring groups.

There is a further delineation of this Northwest (or O-kun) Yoruba identity, for the Bunu are considered to be one of four Yoruba sub-groups, which also include the Owe, Ijumu, and Yagba. Each group speaks a slightly different dialect and, while living in close proximity (see Figure 6.1), their distinctive terrains and geographical locations in relation to major trading and governmental centers has influenced their history and development. For example, in 1908 the Owe Yoruba town of Kabba was chosen as the provincial headquarters of the colonial government, in part due to its location in relation to the major urban centers of Lokoja, Okene, and Ilorin. It consequently benefitted from colonial and post-colonial government development projects to a greater extent than relatively isolated towns and villages of Bunu District[3] which remain largely without electricity and paved roads. This economic disparity, resulting from the Bunu residents' distance from political centers of power as well as the district's hilly and forested terrain which makes development extremely expensive, helps to explain the particular form of ethnic identity which has emerged.

1. For examples of these cultural interchanges, see Picton (1980) on Bunu and Ebira handwoven cloth; Renne (1990: 110) on Nupe and Bunu women's spirit possession cults (*ejinuwon*); Renne (1995) on Kiri chiefs' acquiring chieftaincy regalia from Igala kings (the story of Ajon); and Miachi (1990) and Obayemi (1980) on the influence of Igala and Ebira masquerades on southern Bunu masquerade performance.
2. They were called O-kun Yoruba because of their frequent use of the word *o-kun* in greetings. The term *o-kun* probably derives from the Nupe word *oku*, "a common salutation, [meaning] welcome, hail" (Banfield 1969: 68).
3. In 1987, the former Bunu District was known as the Bunu Development Authority Area. The area is referred to as Abinu or Bunu by residents. I have used the term Bunu District in this chapter for simplicity's sake.

However, these identities within identities – Yoruba, Northwest Yoruba, Bunu Yoruba – are themselves somewhat artificial (Picton 1991) as such categorizations did not, as is also true for the nation-state of Nigeria, exist prior to British colonial rule.[4] Present-day boundaries of the Bunu District and the emergence of a single Bunu ethnic identity were initially a result of colonial officials' predilection for amalgamating groups and areas in order to streamline their administration. Despite this policy, however, there is evidence that local people in various parts of the district sought to shift boundaries and establish separate identities and alliances throughout the colonial period. This example comes from an assistant district officer's report of 1935:

> In the south of Bunu District there is a group of villages on the Lokoja-Kabba road, Chokochoko, Akpata and Obajana which claims that its original settlers came from Aworo District, and which wishes to come under the jurisdiction of the Olu Aworo. This claim is under consideration. (Squibbs 1935)

In the pre-colonial period, the area now known as Bunu District was made of up independent mini-states, small kingdoms each with their own political leadership and territorial domain surrounding population centers of various sizes (Krapf-Askari 1966a; Obayemi 1976). Kingdoms in the north were collectively known as Ikiri while the central kingdoms of Olle and Iluke and the southern kingdoms of Oke Meta and Oke Mehon were part of the group known as Abinu (Obayemi 1976: 256). The amalgamation of these independent mini-states within a single district during the colonial period was marked by continual disputes over the delineation of boundaries, the distribution of political offices such as the selection of the Olubunu (the king of Bunu), and the siting of government buildings such as courthouses among people living in the three major district areas.

Yet despite their disagreements, historical grudges,[5] and distinctive identities associated with discrete landscapes, a common Bunu identify has been forged. For while the Bunu (or *omo Bunu*, "children of Bunu") disagree among themselves, these differences pale in

---

4. See Peel (1983) for an account of the historical constitution of Ijesha Yoruba identity.

5. For example, people continue to nurse intra-Bunu resentments toward the village of Iluke in central Bunu. Villagers were believed to have collaborated with the Nupe, as evidenced by a cache of Nupe ammunition later discovered there by Sir William Wallace in 1897 (Squibbs 1935).

comparison to their historical disagreements with outside groups such as the Owe Yoruba and Nupe who in the nineteenth century conducted extensive slave-raiding in the Bunu area (Mason 1970). This sense of common oppression at the hands of outsiders coincides with the sense of moral superiority associated with the continued practice of Bunu traditional marriage, mentioned earlier; both are fundamental elements in the constitution and maintenance of Bunu ethnic identity. The remainder of this chapter focuses on the latter element, the performance of Bunu traditional marriage and its associated dress.

Bunu Traditional Marriage and the Cloth Called Adofi

During my first trip to Bunu District in November 1987, I stopped at the southern Bunu Yoruba village of Oke-Bukun along the Kabba-Lokoja road, where I visited Sarah Omonibi, a woman in her fifties, the one remaining weaver in the village. She showed me the cloth which she had recently finished weaving, the marriage cloth called *adofi*. She had woven this cloth, she said, in preparation for the performance of her traditional marriage, *gbe obitan*.

This first visit alerted me to the continued importance of traditional marriage ritual for Bunu Yoruba women, despite the many changes in its actual practice. As I interviewed older Bunu villagers about the use of *adofi* cloth and other named marriage cloths in traditional marriage performance, they told me that formerly all women had woven marriage cloths, using white and indigo-dyed handspun cotton yarns. At present in Oke-Bukun, only Mrs. Omonibi weaves, making *adofi* cloths from industrially-spun thread for the other village women performing traditional marriage.

In the past, I was told, traditional marriage was an integral part of the process of bringing a young woman along with her marriage cloths to her husband's house.[6] Now women wait until they and their families have accrued the necessary funds to perform this ritual, which requires expenditures comparable to that of Bunu men taking a first chieftaincy title. This delay means that some Bunu women may not perform traditional marriage until long after they have actually moved to their husbands' houses and had children. Indeed, some village women are grandmothers before they become Bunu brides, although it is still

6. This configuration of marriage steps was affected by British colonial officials' introduction of procedures for court divorce in 1918 (Renne 1992a).

preferable and more prestigious to perform the ceremony when relatively young.

I wondered why Bunu women continued this ritual, even when its performance was sometimes far remote in time from other actions associated with marriage. However, two aspects of this ritual provide clues as to its meaning and importance. First, it is performed by women in order to acquire a distinctive status, *obitan*, similar to that of contemporary male Bunu chiefs and related to the former system of titled women chiefs (Renne 1990). It distinguishes them from other women, for example, by qualifying them to take leadership roles in women's affairs (such as trading and dispute settlement) and to participate in village-wide decisions made by male chiefs. Second, it distinguishes Bunu women from non-Bunu women who do not perform this ritual and, despite their different situations, unifies those who do. Thus, it provides a social and material link between older and younger Bunu women and between Bunu village residents and Bunu out-migrants who must come home to perform this ritual. While Bunu women did not explicitly say that they performed traditional marriage in order to maintain a Bunu identity, they contribute to this process through their actions.[7] This unique identity is evidenced by the wearing of *adofi* and the thirteen other marriage cloths, carried in the tripartite basket, the *abo obitan*, on the eve of the bride's marriage.

The Marriage Basket and Thirteen Marriage Cloths

While the *adofi* cloth is worn by women throughout the district, there are several other named marriage cloths used in Bunu. The different types and names of these cloths vary, depending on where in Bunu they are used and who is describing them. Indeed, the variety and origins of these cloths reflects the cumulative quality of Bunu ethnic identity; for example, several narrow-strip cloths called *ojuedewo* are of Nupe origin.

One group of distinctively named warp-striped cloths of predominantly black, indigo-dyed, handspun cotton yarn were woven

---

7. Ironically, one man who was actively involved in studying Bunu traditional culture and promoting Bunu ethnic identity nonetheless disparaged the contribution of women to this process, remarking that soon women would abandon the backward practice of traditional marriage. His comment suggests that claims over what constitutes a particular ethnic identity not only have political implications in the national arena but have consequences for local gender relations as well.

in Bunu for use in traditional marriage (see Table 6.1). Generally, these cloths were woven personally or commissioned by individuals rather than having been woven for sale in the market, although one cloth collected by the Niger Expedition in 1843 at Egga, attributed to Bunu weavers, closely resembles a Bunu marriage cloth known as *ketekenin* (Johnson 1973; Renne 1992b: 93). When such cloths were sold, prices ranged from three to five times as much as prices paid for predominantly white cloths. This differential reflected the extensive expense and labor involved in indigo dyeing as well as the quantity of indigo needed to dye cloth black. Indigo enhanced a cloth's value, much like gold-plating.

Table 6.1 Thirteen Named Cloths Kept in Marriage Basket

Cloth name	Description
Top basket	
Atufu	Predominantly dark blue, with tiny white and reddish-brown stripes
Awere	Predominantly dark blue, with tiny white stripes
Ojuedewo	Predominantly dark blue, with white checking
(2 types)	Predominantly dark blue, with white, magenta (silk) stripes
Maabo	Predominantly dark blue with red bands
Orun pati	Predominantly white, with blue and red edging
*Orun pada**	Predominantly white, with tiny red stripes
Oja (2)	Red and white sashes
Bottom basket	
Ojuedewo	Predominantly dark blue with white
(4 types)	Predominantly dark blue with ikat patterning
	Predominantly dark blue with ikat patterning
	Predominantly dark blue with wide magenta silk stripe

I was allowed to document the contents of one tripartite basket (*abo*) in which the bride's thirteen marriage cloths were stored during a marriage performance in southern Bunu (see Table 6.1). Two cloths in the upper basket, *atufu* and *awere*, consisted of two panels woven on the wide horizontal loom, predominantly of indigo-dyed handspun cotton. The *atufu* cloth had tiny warp stripes of white and reddish-

Figure 6.2 Bunu brides distributing water around the village (*e mu obitan ponmi rakale*) (Mrs. Janet Ogunibi and Mrs. Kehinde Ogunibi, Apaa-Bunu) wearing *awere* cloths as wrappers with two *ojuedewo* cloths on shoulders, *oja* cloth at waist, and *orun pada* cloths on their heads (photograph by Elisha P. Renne in Apaa-Bunu, December 1987).

brown (from natural brown cotton known as *elepon*); its two panels were joined with elaborate embroidery, although its edges were left with a self-fringe. The *awere* cloth had tiny white warp stripes, its two panels joined with a simpler embroidered finish, and its edges were hemmed. The provenance of these two cloths is unknown although it is likely that they were woven by northern Bunu (Kiri) women weavers. Two narrow-strip handwoven cloths called *ojuedewo* which I was told had been obtained from Bida (in Nupeland) were also in the top basket. They both consisted of predominantly indigo-blue cotton; one had white warp and weft striping, and the other had white and magenta silk warp stripes.[8] Another cloth said to have come from Nupe was called *maabo*, which was made from two broad panels of indigo blue with red warp stripes; this cloth was in the top basket as well. All the cloths attributed to Nupe weavers were hemmed.

Two predominantly white marriage cloths were also kept in the upper basket. One, called *orun pati*, was woven with a type of bast fiber (Picton and Mack 1979: 31–2) called *kese* which was available in the region. It consisted of two panels woven with alternate narrow warp stripes of bast fiber and natural cotton, which were embroidered along the top edge and corners and had edges hemmed in dark-blue thread. While I was told that this cloth had been commissioned from weavers in Kiri (northern Bunu), I was unable to locate any women who had actually woven this cloth, the woman in Akutupa who specialized in its weaving having died. The other predominantly white cloth, *orun pada*, may have been woven as a substitute for the scarce *orun pati*, although its color scheme was slightly different. It consisted of two panels of natural cotton with narrow red warp stripes which were joined and left with a self-fringe.

The two remaining cloths in the upper basket were long sashes of machine-woven gingham cotton cloth in red and white (*oja*) which were used as waistbands (see figure 6.2). The four cloths in the lower basket were all of the narrow-strip *ojuedewo* type, in various combinations of blue and white cotton, and magenta silk.

In addition to these cloths used in southern and central Bunu, other types of marriage cloths were used in Kiri (northern Bunu) towns and villages. They include the Bunu cloths: *elese*, a two-panel dark indigo blue cloth of handwoven cotton with white warp stripes, and *ketekenin*,

---

8. The magenta thread, *alharini*, is described by Lamb and Holmes (1980: 40) as an imported waste silk from north Africa; it is called *galura* in Bunu.

which is similar in color but patterned with many fine, white warp stripes. Two other cloths used in northern Bunu were said to be purchased in Bida (Nupe): one cloth called *meri meka* which is blue with white warp and weft stripes and another called *maabo gandon*, also a narrow strip cloth in blue and white cotton. Any of these cloths might be carried in the marriage basket, though the number of cloths inside – thirteen – remained the same.

One other marriage cloth is used exclusively in northern Bunu, a white cloth of finely handspun natural cotton with an elaborate knotted fringe, called *yisala*. This unusual white cloth is stained at its center with camwood (another reddish dye), the resulting blotch said to resemble a child. It is used only briefly during the trip to the market, after which it is whisked away for safe-keeping (Renne, 1995); Like the *adofi* cloth, it is not stored in the marriage basket.

In the past, young Bunu women acquired these marriage cloths in several ways. They could be woven by the woman herself, commissioned from other weavers by providing yarn and/or cash, given by an older woman, or could be borrowed or rented. Of the fifteen marriage cloths, the *adofi* cloth was most commonly woven by the new bride. Twelve out of thirty southern Bunu women (aged forty-five to over eighty years old) who formerly wove said that they had woven their own *adofi* marriage cloth. Nonetheless, young women remained dependent on older women for the indigo-dyed cotton skeins necessary for its production. This was because older women controlled both the indigo-dyeing process and the proceeds of cloth sales, the latter derived largely from the labor of these same young women who served them in an apprentice-like capacity.

Before the mid–1950s when Bunu girls began attending primary school, most young girls worked as apprentices (Renne 1992b), learning to weave and to spin cotton in preparation for indigo-dyeing. They generally obeyed their mothers, for these women were the most likely sources of the black thread or cloths that were necessary for a young Bunu woman to marry.[9] These gifts of black thread or cloth were the reward for the years of labor which young girls had supplied.

At present, now that cloths of indigo-dyed handspun yarn are no longer being woven, these cloths are stored by older women who lend them out to women performing traditional marriages. *Adofi* cloths

9. See Aremu 1982; Brett-Smith 1990; and Renne, 1995 for discussions of the significance of the color black in handwoven marriage cloths.

and occasionally *orun pada* cloths are woven on commission from the few remaining weavers in the area. Making arrangements to borrow these cloths and the marriage baskets and calabashes (the *igba obitan*) is an important step in traditional marriage preparations, for it is the public display of the baskets which contain the thirteen marriage cloths that mark the ritual move of a bride to her husband's house.

Becoming a Bunu Bride

While sequentially similar, each performance of traditional marriage (*gbe obitan*) is unique. A woman performing traditional marriage may be old or young, with the timing of its performance depending on her own resources, the stability of her marriage,[10] and whether or not she has children. Indeed, of the seven women I saw "become a wife," four were in their forties, one was a grandmother, and all seven had children prior to performing traditional marriage. Although virtually all village women living throughout Bunu District aspire to perform this ritual, the actual number and elaboration of steps involved in "bringing a wife" vary, depending on where the ritual is performed and the situation of the bride. Nonetheless these performances all included certain objects, such as thirteen named marriage cloths and the three-part marriage basket (*abo*), and have a similar format.

The performance of traditional marriage in Bunu villages may be divided, for analytical purposes, into three parts which emphasize the metamorphosis-like quality of this process whereby women are re-made into *obitan*, wives. Its performance, which serves to celebrate the bride and to distinguish her from women who have not acquired this status, is both an ordeal and an accomplishment (Barber 1991: 105–16).

In southern Bunu, becoming a Bunu bride consists of a series of steps which take place over a three-month period. The traditional marriage described here was performed for two women in their mid-twenties who were marrying two brothers who lived in their father's house. Since this performance took place shortly after I moved to Bunu, my perception of the actions and the actors differed from my

10. Some Bunu men seek to discourage their wives and kinswomen from performing this ritual on the grounds that it is an un-Christian and backward practice, but many village women do so because church marriage does not convey the same social prestige and authority.

observations of a traditional marriage performance for an older woman that took place in a neighboring village six months later. Nonetheless, the earlier traditional marriage was the most elaborate I witnessed in terms of time and activities involved, making it an appropriate example for discussion (see Renne (1990) for a full description of this marriage).

Preparation and Separation

Several activities took place which served to distinguish the two brides from other village women prior to officially moving to their husbands' house as Bunu brides. Their hair was specially plaited in the distinctive style associated with Bunu brides (*e dirun obitan*, see Figure 6.3), and they were honored at dances and made special sacrifices.

In the afternoon of the marriage eve, the *igba obitan* (the set of three carved, dark blue calabashes used to support the marriage basket, containing the thirteen marriage cloths) was taken about the town (*e gbe igba obitan rakale*) by an older kinswoman, visually announcing that the marriage was soon to begin. Evidence that the necessary marriage cloths had been assembled is critical, for according to one older woman, the *igba obitan* and its contents are the most important things that a wife brings to her husband's house.

Around 9 p.m., preparations were made to conduct the brides (actually women acting as the brides), each concealed in a large satin burnous (*ibori*) to their husbands' house (*gbe obitan re ile oko*). After much negotiation, mock arguments, and singing, both surrogate brides arrived at the house by midnight. The real brides who had already arrived then went to the back of the house where water was poured onto the roof (*e somi howo obitan*); each bride caught the water in her hand and washed her face with it (see Figure 6.1) before crossing the threshold.

Meanwhile, men from the village had gathered in the front of the house for the marriage dance (*ere sakara*). Soon after, the two brides — wearing black *adofi* cloth wrappers, wax print blouses, and necklaces (*akunpa*), their heads covered and faces practically veiled with cloth — emerged from the house, accompanied by women from their age group. They slowly danced in a circle, and then returned to the house. The brides appeared twice more that evening, once wearing expensive machine-embroidered lace outfits and then in *aso oke* (handwoven strip-cloth) outfits. The dancing and singing went on until 6 a.m. when those remaining finally went home to sleep.

Figure 6.3 Bride (Janet Ogunibi) having her hair plaited by an age-group member (Apaa-Bunu, December 1987). Drawn by Rebecca Bailey© from a field photograph by Elisha P. Renne.

The Liminal Period

In the three-month interval between ritually being brought to their husbands' house, their mock return to their natal homes, and the final return to that of their husbands, the brides performed various activities depicting their roles as wives — including cooking, sweeping, carrying water, and three ritual trips to the market, the latter two events including the wearing of traditional marriage cloths in prescribed ways.

One morning, six days after coming to their husbands' house, the brides were taken to the stream to fetch water (*e mu obitan ponmi rakale*). The brides wore *adofi* wrappers and blouses (*buba*), and when they arrived at the stream they were washed and rubbed with camwood. Then, their *adofi* cloths were replaced with the dark blue marriage cloth (*awere*) wrappers, secured with a narrow red and white checked sash (*oja*) and with dark blue *ojuedewo* and blue *maabo* cloths placed on either shoulder. Large brass bracelets (*adangbara*) used in Bunu traditional marriage were placed on their wrists (Krapf-Askari 1966b), and the *akunpa* marriage necklaces were place on their necks. A woman of the same age then took another marriage cloth, the white *orun pada*, which she folded and coiled and then placed on the head of one bride, repeating the process for the other. Small black pots (*oru*) filled with water were placed on each bride's head. They were then accompanied around the village where they distributed water, after which they returned to their husbands' house (see Figure 6.2). Later the same day the brides, dressed in *adofi*, presented a special meal to their husbands and went about the town, thanking people receiving new names.

Two days later, the brides made their first "trip to the market" (*e mu obitan e woja*), wearing white *orun pati* marriage cloths as wrappers with blue *ojuedewo* cloths on their shoulders and carrying their *igba obitan* calabashes on top of a coiled, white *orun pada* cloth on their heads. On arriving at the market, two kinswomen who had performed the *gbe obitan* ritual led the brides around a large tree in the marketplace, calling out various items for sale. After circling the tree three times,[11] these two women removed the wives' cloths and marriage necklaces and rubbed the brides' bodies with camwood.

---

11. In Olle-Bunu (central Bunu) and Akutupa-Kiri (northern Bunu), they walk around a stone; in all three cases, a spirit *ebora* is believed to reside within the tree or stone.

Figure 6.4 Bunu brides returning from market wearing *awere*, with *ojuedewo* cloths, carrying the *igba obitan* (December 1987). Drawn by Rebecca Bailey© from a field photograph by Elisha P. Renne.

Different marriage cloths were taken from the *abo* (marriage basket) and the brides were redressed with dark blue *awere* and blue *ojuedewo* cloths. They were again led round the tree and then returned home (see Figure 6.4).

Two additional trips to the market were performed four days and eight days later. One bride wore the dark blue *atufu* marriage cloth with an *ojuedewo* cloth while the other wore a blue-black *awere* marriage cloth with an *ojuedewo* cloth.

Reincorporation and Conclusion

On the appearance of the third new moon since the wives were taken to their husbands' house, the brides and their kinswomen and *egbe* members prepared to complete the *gbe obitan* ritual. Dressed in everyday wax print wrappers, they made a mock return to their natal homes (*obitan hasu*), but were begged to return to their husbands by their husbands' kinswomen. This they finally did, marking the conclusion of their traditional marriage performance. The next morning the brides, wearing the black *adofi* wrapper, wax-print blouse, and *akunpa*, went about the town thanking people for participating the night before. On the following day, again wearing their *adofi* cloths, they traveled by taxi for the first time in three months to a neighboring village to greet their kin and to show that they were full-fledged Bunu wives through their public wearing of *adofi* cloth.

Discussion

The fact that Bunu village women perform traditional marriage using old, inalienable things – the three blue-black calabashes and marriage baskets and black cloths – distinguishes Bunu traditional marriage from traditional marriages performed elsewhere in Yorubaland (Layne 1989; Heath 1992). These ancestral marriage items, used since the "beginning of time," materially represent a sense of continuity and group unity, despite the fact that aspects of traditional marriage performance are changing and that various intra-Bunu disputes – over land ownership, village names, and resource distribution – persist (Weiner and Schneider 1989: 6). The use of old things such as marriage cloths conveys a "given-ness" to traditional marriage, which in turn contributes to a seemingly "primordial" perception of Bunu ethnic identity (Newbury 1988: 13), as something which is unchanged and conceived "from the beginning." This association of an essential Bunu-ness with the use of traditional things was articulated by one southern Bunu village woman:

> Things like *aso obitan* (marriage cloth), civilization cannot change it, because it is the type of cloth that has been used *"lataye-baye"* – from the beginning – of the traditional marriage ceremony. Therefore it has to remain like that. It is *igba* – tradition. (Kolawole 1991)

Yet at the same time that Bunu women and men assert this fundamental quality of traditional marriage dress and identity as things that civilization cannot change, some people acknowledge that changes are occurring in traditional marriage practice and in marriage cloth use. They recognize the pressures which lead young people to seek their fortunes outside the district that have affected young women's ability (in terms of time and interest) to perform this ritual. For example, I saw one young Bunu woman who was living outside the district return to her village to perform the visit-to-the-market sequence of traditional marriage. However instead of taking two weeks to go to the market, all three visits were condensed into one visit in one day.

This acknowledgment that traditional marriage practice in Bunu is changing is an important reminder that both tradition and ethnic identity, despite the timelessness which these words imply, are the result of historical processes which are constantly changing. Regardless of these changes, many Bunu women living outside the district as well as women living within it continue to perform traditional marriages, which stress their social, economic, and political ties to a particular group of people, language, and geographic place. In the case of younger women, its performance offers a sense of grounded-ness and source of prestige in an economic climate in which opportunities for higher education and white-collar employment are becoming increasingly difficult for rural women to attain.

For the older women who encourage and orchestrate the performance of traditional marriage, their actions reflect their own needs and strategies to counter the benefits of urban employment with familial comforts. These women do not consciously perform traditional marriage and use handwoven marriage cloths with the deliberate intention of constituting or preserving a Bunu ethnic identity. Unlike colonial and post-colonial officials, they do not have the political authority to organize meetings which decide, for example, district boundaries or the distribution of federal development funds; decisions which have provided, it has been suggested, the impetus for

reifying ethnic identity in Africa (Newbury 1988: 15).
Yet despite their lack of authority and official political incentives, Bunu women have played a role in constructing and unifying a district-wide identity, through their insistence on the performance of traditional marriage and brides' ownership of the *adofi* marriage cloth. Indeed, the *adofi* marriage cloth has been likened to something like a Bunu national flag. Thus while these women's activities are less of an instrumental political strategy – using ethnic solidarity to legitimate demands for federal funding – and more of an attempt to constitute social and moral ties between women of different generations residing within and outside of Bunu District, their actions, including the preservation of traditional marriage dress, are nonetheless significant in the construction of a Bunu ethnic identity.

References

Aina, S. (1968), *Marriage Customs of the Yagba People*, Kano: Local Government Printing Press.

Aremu, P.S.O. (1982), "Yoruba Traditional Weaving: Kijipa Motifs, Colour and Symbols," *Nigeria Magazine*, vol. 140, pp. 3–10.

Banfield, A. (1969), *Dictionary of the Nupe Language*, Farnborough: Gregg Institute Press.

Barber, K. (1991), *I Could Speak Until Tomorrow: Oriki, Women and the Past in a Yoruba Town*, Washington, D.C.: Smithsonian Institution Press.

Brett-Smith, S. (1990), "Empty Space: The Architecture of Dogon Cloth," *RES*, vol. 19/20, pp. 162–77.

Eicher, J. (1977), *Nigerian Handcrafted Textiles*, Ile-Ife: University of Ife Press.

Heath, D. (1992), "Fashion, Anti-Fashion, and Heterglossia in Urban Senegal," *American Ethnologist*, vol. 19. pp. 19–33.

Ibejigba, S. (1985), *Traditional Marriage Practices in Bunuland, Kwara State: Olle as a Case Study*, unpublished essay, Ibadan: University of Ibadan.

Johnson, M. (1973), "Cloth on the Banks of the Niger," *Journal of the Historical Society of Nigeria*, vol. 6, pp. 353–63.

Krapf-Askari, E. (1966a), "Time and Classifications: An Ethnographic and Historical Case-Study," *Odu*, vol. 2, pp. 3–18.

—— (1966b), "Brass Objects From the Owe Yoruba, Kabba Province, Northern Nigeria," *Odu*, vol. 3, pp. 82–7.

Lamb, V., and Holmes, J. (1980), *Nigerian Weaving*, Hertingfordbury: Roxford Books.

Layne, L. (1989), "The Dialogics of Tribal Self-Representation in Jordan," *American Ethnologist*, vol. 16, pp. 24–39.

Mason, M. (1970), "The Jihad in the South: An Outline of the Nineteenth Century Nupe Hegemony in North-Eastern Yorubaland and Afenmai," *Journal of the Historical Society of Nigeria*, vol. 5, pp. 193–209.

Miachi, T. (1990), "The Masquerade Phenomenon in Igala Culture: An Anthropological Analysis", unpublished Ph.D. thesis, University of Ibadan, Institute of African Studies.

Moore, S. (1986), *Social Facts and Fabrications*, Cambridge: Cambridge University Press.

Newbury, C. (1988), *The Cohesion of Oppression: Clientship and Ethnicity in Rwanda, 1860–1960*, New York: Columbia University Press.

Obayemi, A. (1976), "The Yoruba and Edo-speaking Peoples and Their Neighbours Before 1600," in vol. I, J.F.A. Ajayi and M. Crowder (eds), *A History of West Africa*, London: Longman.

——— (1980), "States and Peoples of the Niger-Benue Confluence Area," in O. Ikime (ed.), *Groundwork of Nigerian History*, Ibadan: Heinemann Books.

Peel, J.D.Y. (1983), *Ijeshas and Nigerians*, Cambridge: Cambridge University Press.

Picton, J. (1980), "Women's Weaving: The Manufacture and Use of Textiles among the Igbirra People of Nigeria," in D. Idiens and I. Ponting (eds), *Textiles of Africa*, Bath: Pasold Research Fund.

——— (1991), "On Artifact and Identity at the Niger-Benue Confluence," *African Arts*, vol. 24, pp. 34–49; 93–4.

Picton, J., and Mack, J. (1979), *African Textiles*, London: The British Museum.

Renne, E. (1990), "Wives, Chiefs, and Weavers: Gender Relations in Bunu Society," unpublished Ph.D. thesis, New York University.

——— (1992a), "Polyphony in the Courts: Child Custody Cases in Kabba District Court, 1925–1979," *Ethnology*, vol. 31, no. 3, pp. 219–32.

——— (1992b), "The Decline of Bunu Yoruba Women's Weaving," *Textile History*, vol. 23, no. 1, pp. 87–96.

——— (1995), *Cloth That Does Not Die: The Meaning of Cloth in Bunu Social Life*, Seattle: University of Washington Press.

Squibbs, L. (1935), "Organization of Bunu District, Kabba Division, Kabba Province," file SNPH 25254, Kaduna: Nigerian National Archives.

Weiner, A., and Schneider, J. (eds) (1989), *Cloth and Human Experience*, Washington, D.C.: Smithsonian Institution Press.

7

Why Do They Call it Kalabari? Cultural Authentication and the Demarcation of Ethnic Identity

*Joanne B. Eicher and
Tonye V. Erekosima*[1]

Introduction

The Kalabari people who have lived on islands in the Delta of the Nigerian Atlantic coast for at least 1,000 years wear dress ensembles that distinguish them from their neighbors. Some items and outfits affirm their ethnic identity in ways that are often so subtle as to mislead even the "expert" outsider; an instance is a director of a prominent North American art museum in the 1980s, who refused to access an historic textile prized and identified by the Kalabari as Kalabari because he said it was not African.

What accounts for the discrepancy between the Kalabari claim and the director's dictum? How does this relate to dress and ethnicity? The answer emerges from Kalabari history, geography and culture. As traders in a global marketplace, they established a reputation for independent spirit and were selective in their taste for trade goods. Their competitiveness and fierce pride, as members of one of the smaller ethnic groups in Nigeria, resulted in a continued effort to distinguish themselves visually from others, and produced their unique Kalabari forms of dress.

---

1. We participated equally in this chapter.

In this chapter we will analyze a selected group of material artifacts, imported textiles and ensembles of dress that the Kalabari use. None are technically indigenous but each has become identified as Kalabari through cultural authentication and resulting use. The construct of cultural authentication applies to specific articles and ensembles of dress identified as ethnic and considered indigenous when the users are not the makers or when the material used is not indigenous in origin. Many examples of Kalabari material culture illustrate this concept, but we will use one major example: Kalabari men's formal, everyday dress [2]

Kalabari Origins and Sociocultural History

Numbering less than one million among the total Nigerian population of 90 million, the Kalabari are identified linguistically as Ijo, the fourth largest linguistic group among an estimated 250 in Nigeria. Although originally of Ijo stock, they call themselves Kalabari and not Ijo. They migrated about one thousand years ago (Alagoa 1972; Erekosima et al. 1991) from a largely freshwater community in the central Niger Delta where farming was supplemented by seasonal fishing, to the island of New Calabar in the eastern saltwater side of the Niger Delta, where they took up fishing and trading as their principal occupations (Alagoa 1972). No longer able to grow their own food, the settlers developed an extensive salt-making industry by extracting salt from ocean water. Salt, along with abundant supplies of fish, was traded northward to the Igbo hinterland for root crops and livestock. Their trading network also extended westward toward Benin and the Yoruba country for commodities such as handwoven cotton textiles. This network was well in place by the time the Europeans appeared at the end of the 1400s (Periera 1937; Alagoa 1970). Early European documents indicate that New Calabar (also called Elem Ama and Old Shipping) on the Rio Real was a major trade center for Portuguese, Dutch and English (Barbot 1746; Periera 1937; Ryder 1965). By the 1880s they had dispersed to other islands to establish the towns of Abonnema, Bakana, Buguma and Tombia, along with several satellite

---

2. In earlier work, we analyzed the cut-thread textile called *pelete bite* made by Kalabari women from imported Indian madras. The latter is used for both men's and women's wrappers, masqueraders' face coverings, and as funeral bed decoration for an esteemed female elder (Erekosima 1979; Erekosima and Eicher 1981; Eicher and Erekosima with Thieme 1982; Renne 1985).

communities including Degema, Ido, Ifoko, Ke and others that became a part of the Kalabari city-state (Horton 1963).

Migration from a freshwater to saltwater environment brought not only economic but also political and social changes to the Kalabari. Leadership changed from the traditional Ijo pattern where the oldest man is head of the community, to one where the most able adult of the community become in charge (Alagoa 1972). As economic rights shifted from family-held land to communal fishing territories, inheritance was no longer strictly within the family. With each of these changes, enterprise and skill emerged as important indicators of success along with accumulation of wealth. Tienabeso (1984)

Map 7.1 (Map of Africa) Map showing location of Kalabari area within Nigeria. Courtesy of M. Catherine Daly from (1984), "Kalabari Female Appearance and the Tradition of Iria," unpublished Ph.D. dissertation, Minneapolis: University of Minnesota, p. 26.

claims such entrepreneurial acumen characterized King Amachree I who prospered through mud-skipper fishing. He founded the royal dynasty of the Kalabari that has been in continuous existence for over 300 years. In the 1990s, the Kalabari still live on islands in the southernmost part of Nigeria. These islands are spread out about four degrees above the equator, in an area of mangrove swamps and high humidity with an annual temperature range of 70–90°F. Men and women work in a variety of professions and occupations in nearby Port Harcourt, the capital of Rivers State, and elsewhere in Nigeria. Wage earners who work away from their home communities return, whenever possible, to participate in community celebrations and family rituals which encompass both Christian and indigenous belief systems.

Kalabari Ethnic Identity

We will focus on the transformation in Kalabari ethnic identity that became tied specifically to the period of intensive encounter with Europeans in their demand for slaves from the Niger Delta, particularly in the seventeenth to nineteenth centuries. This period marked an expansive recasting of Kalabari social organization and culture that made it possible for the Kalabari to cope with several challenges. One challenge was to ensure that they did not become victims of the relentless demand for African labor to work the plantations of the Americas; instead, they relied on their age old skills of trading and became intermediaries for hinterland sources of the export labor. This assertion of independence (Geary 1927; Hutchinson 1858; Jones 1963), economic strategies of refusing credit (Dike 1957), ceremonial demands of imposed protocol (Barbot 1746), and direct military defensiveness (Dike 1957) forced the Europeans to recognize their autonomy.

The Kalabari not only struggled for this critical autonomy but were pitted against similar rival communities. The Bonny, Nembe, and Okrika peoples, also of Ijo stock, similarly migrated from the central Delta and settled in the saltwater eastern Delta several centuries ago; these groups also obtained guns for protecting their trade routes and market sphere in what became a period of intense inter-ethnic destabilization in the Niger Delta (Dike 1957; Jones 1963).

The Kalabari cultural group was preserved by a radical restructuring of its internal social order (Eicher and Erekosima 1993). A male hierarchy of rigidly structured political ranks was established and enforced; the traditional family structure was turned into a semi-autonomous trading and defensive corporation called the War Canoe House; kinship was no longer sanguinally based, and leadership evolved around enterprising acumen and wealth; a men's dancing society (*ekine*) was organized around masquerade displays that incorporated all men of every age who valued and acquired cultural competency (Horton 1963); and a secret policing organization high-handedly eliminated those among the thousands of immigrants brought into the society who failed to learn the Kalabari language. A similarly well-fashioned hierarchy of women's place in society was established as the society's procreator and creatively renewing agency (Daly 1984; Daly, Eicher, and Erekosima 1986; Michelman 1992).

Reviewing Kalabari sociocultural history contributes to understanding how their dress, primarily composed of elements derived from their role as traders, can be seen as being specifically Kalabari. For several centuries[3] the Kalabari participated in a world economy, as illustrated by items of dress and textiles that still come from both West Africa and as far away as India, Italy, and England. Hats and textiles were imported from England and India; European-styled shirts and gowns had origins in England and possibly Portugal. The original version of the *attigra* gown came from within Nigeria and a later version was made from Indian velvet. The trading practices of the Kalabari allowed Kalabari men to exhibit their success through items of dress as depicted in photographs and supported by written accounts (Erekosima 1989; Erekosima and Eicher 1994; Eicher forthcoming). As traders, they acquired access to a plethora of non-indigenous items which they selected and recombined creatively.

By using these imported items of dress and textiles, social changes were communicated in visible ways. Kalabari men and women, elites, and families and other structures of ethnicity found ways to manipulate textiles to create meaning for members of their society in the new order. An interplay of historical forces, newly emerging social structures, and the skill of entrepreneurial traders and highly creative artists defined Kalabari ethnicity of the eighteenth and nineteenth centuries. Throughout the twentieth century, pride in being Kalabari has continued and remains vibrant and viable as the twenty-first century approaches, even as changes continue to occur in Nigeria and among the Kalabari.

---

3. We have outlined their history in more detail elsewhere. See Erekosima (1989), Eicher and Erekosima (1993), and Erekosima and Eicher (1994).

What is Ethnicity?

People such as the museum director who flatly stated that the cloth the Kalabari make from Indian madras is not African hold a view that what is ethnic must be completely indigenous. For some, the word ethnic represents an unchanging pattern or artifact of exotic lifeways, something coming from the past. Some also consider the "ethnic" concept as merely a fashionable invention used for giving an appearance of "traditionality" to products (Sollors 1989).

In contrast, we agree with Stern and Cicala that ethnic cultural resources are often as ingrained in the history of ethnic groups as they are made relevant to contemporary situations. Ethnicity combines both cultural stability and change in dynamic interplay, and supports a process by which folklife expressions are "continually added to the pool of a group's cultural resources, which, in turn, are used to examine [and adapt to] new problems and concerns" (Stern and Cicala 1991: xii). A balance of available resources with demands for relevance emerges as people try to make meaning out of their lives when they nod to their past, and also acknowledge the present, by wearing their extant forms of dress. As Burke points out, ethnic expressions, whether in verbal or material form, reflect and artistically treat a problematic situation (1947: 296).[4]

Dress as a demarcation of ethnicity is not merely a static product of an ethnic group, but allows ethnic group members to provide solutions to problematic situations that characterize, project, and sometimes even parody everyday life through efforts to reconcile their real and ideal worlds. Specific types of dress, food, legend, ritual,

---

4. A more constricted approach touts ethnicity or its creative expression as emerging ubiquitously in the context of concrete social relationship where it is constantly negotiated. One exponent of this contemporary viewpoint says it is "therefore an identity which resides not within the individual person or even the particular group, but between individuals and between groups engaged in social interaction" (Staub 1981: 115). In contrast, another perspective holds ethnicity to be the product of abstract historical or external forces reshaping customary ways. Beatrice Weinreich (1960) and Elizabeth Mathias (1974) demonstrated respectively that Jewish Passover practices and Italian funeral rituals persist in American society, but are highly modified to reflect American culture's influences. We focus on ethnicity, however, as a response to modernity or other forms of massive external impact on a community's customary lifeways. We assume a posture midway between these two extreme approaches of the micro and macro levels of analysis and acknowledge both individual and collective quest for meaning in the context of historical conditions.

song, and ceremony permeate every facet of ethnic life. Selected adaptations may touch on the cultural dissonance between some prior practices and the introduction of novel forms; preservation of the ethnic community, rites of passage for incoming or upgraded generations, maintenance of some enclaves of belief or ritual, or effective requisite institutional changes in ethnic culture. For each area, individuals' creativity reshapes established forms, sometimes pushing beyond limits thought admissible. From these efforts, generally acceptable new forms emerge; such is the case of the Kalabari.

Cultural Authentication Process

We have termed the process of adaptation as a strategy of change, or cultural authentication process (CAP). In our first research on Kalabari culture which examined the cut-thread cloth made from imported Indian madras (Erekosima and Eicher 1981; Erekosima 1989), we identified four broad categories of inter-related steps in cultural authentication. These are respectively the procedures of selection, characterization, incorporation, and transformation (SCIT).

The first step is when a particular external cultural practice or product is *selected* as appropriate and desirable by members of another culture out of an almost unlimited number of other cultural options or offerings. The next step is when the selected item is *characterized* in some symbolic form within the meaning reference-frame of the receiving society. The item may be renamed by members of the culture, in their own language, choosing the item or process or translating in any other expressive form into the mapping system of order by which the members of the culture conceptually define or iconically portray their experiences and artifacts.

The third step occurs when the innovation occupies some functional role within the receiving cultural system by being *incorporated* toward meeting some adaptation need in the society, at either individual or collective levels, and often at both. The fourth step is when the adopted artifact or practice (which may initially have been foreign or else from another generation or other segment of the same society) is *transformed* in itself. This entails an accommodation of its old form and purpose to the new setting in a holistic way. The outcome of this final phase invariably involves a creative or artistic change that envelops the product and setting.

We emphasize that symbols that are available to a culture from both its past and present, and which are applied to its expression of ethnicity, "are not fixed points of tradition, but rather frames of reference and meaning within which ethnics respond to social, political, religious or economic pressures" (Stern and Cicala 1991: xiii). We focus on the political and social domains of the nineteenth-century era of the slave trade as it boomed and waned, and contend that the Kalabari used cloth to project their ethnic distinctiveness.

Kalabari Dress As Demarcation of Identity

The textile and dress items assembled from Kalabari history and their range of trading contacts resulted in a distinctive appearance. Kalabari cut-thread cloth (called *pelete bite*) is a textile peculiar to them which, although subtle in its effect, differentiates its wearers from other Rivers people of the Niger Delta as being Kalabari.[5] Details of the Kalabari women's blouse and double wrapper set called *bite sara*[6] (Iyalla 1968; Daly 1983, 1984) separate them from their neighbors, in regard to imported textiles selected and combined and their chosen colors. Our example, however, will focus on the dress of Kalabari men which involves not only details but also garment shapes and styles.

5. The creation and use of *pelete bite* resounds with ramifications reaching to every aspect of Kalabari life. Through the symbolic patterns that they execute on this cloth (using the simple tools of a razor blade and needle and perhaps a pen-knife), textile artists transform the cloth to become an emblem peculiar to the Kalabari alone and one that represents all Kalabari. The intricate delicacy of the work aside, the patterns the Kalabari women impose on the delicate cloth by pulling and cutting one thread at a time, have been estimated to number at least thirty-five (Renne 1985). These depict themes of objects in nature, and indigenous man-made artifacts as well as foreign products of European culture. The Kalabari cosmos is graphically depicted in this supple medium, including rattle-seed and chess-board, wine-glass and the cross, a sisal mat and ladder, geometric shapes and sinewy reptile, and a pith-fan and metal chains. When brightly-colored ginghams from India are converted into *pelete bite* that the women design, they become most esteemed for use on the highest festive occasions by both men and women. A dark indigo variant of Indian madras, however, serves as pre-eminent mourning cloth tied by Kalabari women. These illustrate the crucial role of the Indian hand-crafted textile in Kalabari life and identity.
6. The most frequent example is a white eyelet blouse with madras wrapper.

The Political Domain of Kalabari Men

Political Ranks

Kalabari men's dress indicates a hierarchy that parallels age-grade and political status with rules of dress for their ensembles of top garment and wrapper. *Asawo* or "the young men that matter" wear the shirt called *etibo* with an Indian madras wrapper. The *opu asawo* or "gentlemen of substance" wear the upper garment called *woko* with either wrapper or matched trousers and appropriate accessories of hat, cane, and jewelry. The *alabo* (chiefs) wear the gown called *doni* over a shirt and wrapper plus a hat and cane. The King (*amanyanabo*) and paramount chiefs who are at the peak of the political hierarchy have gowns called *ebu*, of Indian madras with a matching wrapper underneath, an outfit reserved for them by custom. To be worn at ceremonies by any member of the elite are the gowns called *attigra* with an appropriate shirt and wrapper underneath, as well as hat and handheld accessories. All of these have been described in detail elsewhere (Erekosima 1989; Erekosima and Eicher 1980, 1994) and are depicted in Figure 7.1.

The pertinence of these forms to Kalabari ethnicity is twofold: first, internal cohesiveness of the in-group is consolidated, and second, distinctiveness from the outgroup (those seen as non-Kalabari) is secured. Internally, the multi-layered and criss-crossing "discourse" of authority and power groupings is integrated through visual patterns of dress by using various design strategies. Political ranks in the descending order of chiefs, gentlemen, and "youth that matter," for instance, are marked by a parallel ranking in their outfits. The *doni* gowns of the chiefs are made of either thick, multi-colored woolen or brightly-colored silk fabrics. They reach the ankles, have four studs, and are worn with formal hats like the English top hat and with shirts underneath that have cuffs folded back under the sleeves of the gown.

The gentlemen's dress (*woko*) is made consistently of less-colorful gabardines and serges, which are of generally plain hues and not as thick as the printed woolens used for chief's attire. They reach to the knee or mid-calf with elbow-length sleeves and have just three studs. They are worn over a simple undershirt or "singlet" with either straw hats or another style called a "smoking cap."

The young men's shirt (*etibo*) is generally made of light-weight cotton and is often plain white or another light color such as yellow.

Figure 7.1 Kalabari men's ensembles (left to right): *etebo, woko, doni, ebw, attigra.*

These shirts reach to the knee and have long sleeves that are folded twice on a diagonal (exposing more of the forearm than the shirt and gown of the *doni*). They have only one stud that may or may not be fastened at the neckband, and hats are not mandatory.

Use of a cane, umbrella, or walking stick is allowed for either the *etibo* or *woko* ensemble; for *doni* and *ebu*, one of the three is required. The overall effect of these outfits is an increasing registration of presence, bulk and dazzle as one goes up the hierarchy which runs parallel to the accumulation of power and influence in the political order. The chiefs administer the polity, the "gentlemen of substance" advise on policy and help to project the interests of societal segments as well as the entire state, and the "young men that matter" actively help with execution of decisions and programs.

Competing Kin Groups

This strict hierarchical order is counter-balanced by the War Canoe House units which each chief heads as leader of his kin-group. The War Canoe Houses engage in degrees of regulated competition, being semi-autonomous trading corporations with their own self-defense capability. In the past the chiefs secured their own boats and trading spheres when out on expeditions to obtain slaves from Igbo and other traders coming to the Atlantic coast from the Nigerian hinterland. The Kalabari chief's challengers were generally the traders from the neighboring Bonny, Okrika and Nembe city-states, as well as marauding pirates and unattached slave-raiders.[7] These House units also kept particular cloth symbols to represent them, all of which came from outside sources. The King Abbi Group of the Kalabari royal family retained a Yoruba woven cloth called *ikaki bite*, and later probably lent patronage to production of this cloth by the Igbo women of the town of Akwete, north of the Kalabari islands. Aronson (1980a) contends patronage of the Akwete weavers occurred when the westward route to Yoruba territory became less accessible in the nineteenth century during the period of the British blockade of the Atlantic coast against the slave trade.

The George Amachree House appropriated "real india" (the Kalabari term in English for madras plaid textiles woven in India) as its emblem. The Horsfall Family and (Dodo) West Group of Houses

---

7. An exhaustive account of this turmoil and intense rivalries that existed between these societies is provided by Dike (1956) and Jones (1963).

chose for themselves the handwoven West African cloths called
egennebite (an indigo striped textile from the Egenne tributary),
onunga (the handwoven, narrow-strip cloth from the Yoruba people
in western Nigeria), and *akraa* (also narrow-strip weaving from the
Ewe people of Ghana). The John-Bull House and Ombo Group of
Houses also chose a distinctive yellow Indian madras plaid (called
epe injiri) and an indigo and white Indian madras plaid called
amasiri. The John-Bull Family also used a specific emblem of an
applique design of a mangrove tree and roots. The Tariah Family of
the Birinomoni Group of Houses similarly chose an emblem of an
elephant design embroidered on Indian madras. These segmental
demarcators are offset by the white cloth headtie (*ogborigbo*) selected
by Amachree I, the founder of the reigning dynasty, which stands as
authoritative symbol of the entire Kalabari political order along with
the *ofo* (a handheld ritual object).

Lineage distinctiveness was therefore partly conveyed by display
of power and wealth in dress, textiles, and household furnishings
obtained in trade. Oral testimony by Kalabari informants documents
how family heirlooms of textiles, coral, and gold are exhibited at the
death of a chief. As the twentieth century developed, conspicuous
display at a funeral was expanded to include the burial of any
prominent elder, either male or female, and the practice has continued
into the 1990s (Eicher and Erekosima 1987, 1993; Daly 1987).[8]

Collective Polity

Cutting across the kin-groups of War Canoe Houses was the Kalabari
community's Dancing Society (*Ekine*) which represented all Kalabari
males of outstanding accomplishment. Chosen for their acquired
wealth or excellence as a dancer, drum-lore expert, warrior, or
wrestling-champion, these celebrities were integrated into a
leadership corps for the community ostensibly to display their skill
at dancing.

A gown called *attigra*, originally of handwoven cotton with
embroidered Islamic motifs, which was imported from northern

---

8. Field data collected by Eicher (1988) indicates that the practice of display of
family heirlooms of cloth and ornament most probably began first with chiefs.
According to accounts given to Eicher, large displays of cloth and other personal
possessions were heaped on the corpse of a chief with a majority of the possessions
buried with the corpse. Later, the practice of display was apparently extended to other
deceased elders and the burying of possessions terminated.

Nigeria, served as peculiar cultural symbol for this group, and was worn with an enormous hat called *ajibulu*. This inverted boat-shaped hat made by the Kalabari had the mystique of the ram's beard embedded in it (for power) as well as the finery of plumes and tinsel (for beauty) and adorned the head of its wearer almost like a crown. The Kalabari later introduced another version of the *attigra* made of Indian velvet embroidered with gold or silver metallic threads. Either form was worn with opulent accessories of coral beads and a necklace of tiger's teeth. The outfit was considered complete when a fan was held in one hand and an elephant tusk in the other.

Materials available to the Kalabari came from many sources. Cloth for wrappers worn by both men and women came from India (cotton madras, silk and velvet), England (printed woolen flannel), the former Gold Coast, Ghana, and Yorubaland (narrow strip handwoven cloth), and the adjacent Igbo town of Akwete (wide vertical textiles known for a design called "ikaki" or tortoise). Coral beads were said to be imported from Italy and elephant tusks most likely came from southern Africa, via Europe.

Male shirts especially appear influenced by Englishmen's styles of the middle nineteenth century (Case 1987). The influence of English traders is also shown in the variety of men's hats, such as top hats and fedoras. However, it is Indian madras, which the Kalabari call *injiri*, that the Kalabari adopted almost as a "flag" of group identity (Erekosima 1979). They use it in birth and death rituals and for the most revered dress of their chiefs (Erekosima and Eicher 1994). Using six yards in a wrapper set, women buy eight yards and routinely give the remaining two yards to their significant male family members, usually a brother or husband. The men wear it for a wrapper with the appropriate top garments. Thus, this cloth represents significant ritual and cultural aspects of Kalabari existence (Petgrave 1992; Eicher, Erekosima and Petgrave 1994).

The Cultural Domain

In other research, we drew from a variety of historical sources to establish the independent character of the Kalabari and their pronounced taste in dress (Eicher and Erekosima 1994; Eicher, forthcoming). Our evidence ranged from an interview in the 1980s with a prominent Niger Delta historian to observations as early as 1678 by Jean Barbot (1746), with several other commentaries in between. Professor E.J. Alagoa (1986) compared the Kalabari with his own people from the Rivers area, the Nembe: "The Nembe people tend to be much more informal and not to care so much about their appearance. They themselves have that feeling about being different from the Kalabari in this regard."

His statement reinforced the observations of Dapper, who traveled through the area in 1676 and noted that the Kalabari were "very particular" in their taste regarding dress, for they rejected as many as two or three hundred copper armlets from a barrel if they found them not well-made (quoted in Talbot 1926: vol. 1, p. 241). Barbot (1746) stated that the "Blacks of Calabry" make brass rings for the arms or legs which they polish "as fine as gold." Hutchinson (1858: 101), de Cardi (1899: 507) and Waddell (1970: 420) respectively commented about the "air of independence" the "majestic" stature and the "dandified" appearance of the Kalabari men they saw when visiting New Calabar.

As the Kalabari polity has become formally absorbed into the much larger contemporary nation-state of Nigeria and its independent people have faced intensive pressures to become "modern," a compelling question arises: has the ethnic distinction disappeared? Evidence suggests it has not. Rapid change has occurred in certain cultural sectors while past practices are retained in others, especially in the domain of basic values and rituals. Kalabari funerals are a case in point. In the domain of ritual and beliefs, at least, the older generation of men have resisted change and cling now to the demarcations of dress that expressly show them to be Kalabari. Similarly, the younger generation of men who have received extensive western education, live and work in thriving metropolitan centers and generally fit an image of being contemporary middle-class, also mark their continuing ethnic identity through the traditional dress when attending funeral events. This is ethnicity still kicking strong.

Dressing in Kalabari fashion continues into the 1990s, especially when Kalabari men and women travel to island homes, for social etiquette carries the expectation that "traditional" garb will be worn by adults of all social strata when attending cultural events, paying respect to families in mourning, strolling about the town, or attending church services on Sunday. Although there are wide variations in income and social standing, Kalabari adults prefer Kalabari dress for ethnic affairs. Those with less money may have only one outfit while those with more may have a large wardrobe, but a basic outfit with a wrapper of Indian madras is considered necessary.

Whether wealthy or poor, Kalabari adults take pride in wearing Kalabari dress for weekend activities and in reaffirming their ethnic identity (Daly, Eicher, and Erekosima 1986; Erekosima 1989; Eicher, forthcoming).

The Ritual Domain of Kalabari Funerals

The Kalabari have substituted a current convention of staging mandatory funerals at weekends in their towns for the former ceremony of *ada seki* (the communal dance of *Ekine* society men that marked the end of the eight-day weekly trade cycle). In the 1990s, most Kalabari family members consider a funeral celebration and burial "at home" to be mandatory for any Kalabari person who dies anywhere on the globe. The funerals serve as a key vehicle for continued sociopolitical education to preserve Kalabari identity through the use of traditional Kalabari dress and ceremonies.

When in mourning, the immediate family of the deceased (males and females, children and adults) meet special dress requirements for taking the body from the mortuary to lie in state for the initial wake, for the burial, the last wake, the family parade, and the final funeral dance (Eicher and Erekosima 1987; Erekosima 1989; Erekosima et al. 1991). Unmarried adolescents may wear western dress to attend dances where contemporary popular music is played, both African and western. However, teenage family mourners wear traditional outfits to dance, to visit, and to pay respects to the dead.

Wakes ordinarily occur on Friday night, with interment the next morning after church services if the deceased was Christian. A full-fledged funeral for an elder includes lying-in-state rituals, a post-burial parade of family members around the town, and a final close-out ceremony one week later (Eicher and Erekosima 1987). As a participant observer, Erekosima (1989) gathered data on men's dress that can be used to showcase the strength of continuing Kalabari ethnicity. He studied attendance at wakes, burials, and dances that routinely occur on weekends in Kalabari towns. Each weekend, many Kalabari men travel from Port Harcourt where they work to attend funeral events.

Erekosima compared numbers of male pedestrians on King Amachree Road in Buguma, a main thoroughfare in the cultural island capital of the Kalabari people, and analyzed their dress (whether European or Kalabari) in the middle of the week and on the weekend

(1989: 422). Using data collected over four weeks,[9] he observed 4,421 male pedestrians over a period of two hours for each of the days indicated. He found that from two to four times the number of males ages 5 to 75 appeared on the road on Friday nights and Saturdays as on Wednesdays, as is shown in Table 7.1.

Table 7.1 Number of Male Pedestrians Observed for All Indicated Weekdays

Week	Wednesday	Friday Morning	Saturday Evening	Saturday Afternoon	Sunday Evening	Sunday
1	44	186	178	197	179	109
2	151	312	220	233	111	100
3	70	231	350	175	123	117
4	105	454	268	221	149	138
Total	370	1,183	1,016	826	562	464

Data collected on the type of dress worn by male pedestrians were categorized as Kalabari traditional dress, European dress, or other Nigerian dress. Kalabari traditional dress included men's ensembles of trousers or wrapper worn with the shirt known as *etibo*, the top garment known as *woko*, or the gown known as *doni*. European dress included shirts and trousers or shorts (also known as "knickers" in Nigeria), the "French" or safari suit (short-sleeved jacket and trouser outfit of matching fabric) or "English suit." Other Nigerian dress encompassed the traditional attire of Yoruba and Hausa males, modern Nigerian fashions such as the *danchiki* worn with trousers, and miscellaneous outfits such as track suits, uniforms of police or scouts, or the rags of the mentally ill. All of these forms of dress were observed.

As shown in the Table 7.2, a sharp rise in the use of Kalabari dress in Buguma occurred on Friday evenings in contrast to Wednesdays. On Friday nights, wake-keepings either begin for the deceased who

9. He collected data for seven Wednesdays and weekends, but eliminated three. Two had heavy rain that cut down travel to Buguma, seriously curtailing activities, and the third weekend involved the government month-end sanitation Saturday curfew when Nigerian residents are confined to home compounds to engage in mandatory clean-up activities. See Erekosima (1989: 414–34) for summary of methodology. He and an independent observer had high congruence in their counts.

Table 7.2 Percentages of Adult Males (15–75) Wearing Kalabari, European and Other Nigerian Dress Over Two Months of Empirical Data Survey

Type of Dress	Wednesdays	Fridays	Saturdays	Sundays
Kalabari	28	51	56	32
European	56	42	38	56
Other Nigerian	16	7	6	12

will be buried the next morning or mark the final wake-keepings for the winding-down ceremonies of the previous week. The percentage of men wearing Kalabari dress increased slightly on Saturdays when either burials or family parades and final "round-ups" took place. By Sunday evening, the percentages for types of dress worn almost paralleled those of Wednesday. Concomitantly, the European outfits worn by 56 percent of the males aged 15–75 on Wednesday, declined to 42 percent on Friday and 38 percent on Saturday, and increased again by Sunday. The same pattern was observed for those wearing "other Nigerian" outfits. The decline on the weekend may be because fewer people of other ethnic groups came to Buguma on the weekends, or those Kalabari who owned other ethnic outfits did not wear them on the weekend. Funerals were attended by Kalabari people wearing Kalabari dress and visually marked their identity as a collectivity (Erekosima 1989: 429).

Erekosima (1989: 430) also analyzed his data by age and type of dress worn as shown in Table 7.3:

Table 7.3 Percentages of Types of Dress Worn by Age Categories for Adult Male Pedestrians on Indicated Days

Age	Friday Evenings			Saturday Mornings		
	Kalabari	European	Nigerian	Kalabari	European	Nigerian
5–15	25	71	4	14	86	–
16–30	42	52	6	36	56	8
31–50	63	29	8	75	21	4
51–75	79	15	6	87	10	3

His data confirmed that on Friday evening and Saturday morning, a much higher percent of males aged 51–75 (79 and 87 percent respectively) wore Kalabari dress than did males aged 5–15 (25 and 14 percent respectively) with the reverse case shown for those ages in regard to wearing European dress. Basically, older males were socialized to wear Kalabari dress and did so. A good number wore western dress journeying to and from their island home of Buguma. But for attending the wake and burial events, evidence of a radical switch to Kalabari attire confirmed that Kalabari men travel between two cultures: one is that of their traditional past, and the other is that of their current lives as Nigerians who are forging new identities in the context of modern industrial civilization.

Dynamics of Ethnicity

The Local Scene

The Kalabari used cloth emblems to distinguish themselves from other peoples around them. In general, they wore the same forms of dress as their immediate neighbors, such as the upper garment they called *woko*, but they alone championed plain and subdued greys, blues, beiges, and occasionally white. They avoided bright colors and bold patterns for this particular outfit. All their other neighbors, such as the Bonny, Nembe, Okrika, Ikwerre, and Igbo, wore this type of dress made with textiles of bright colors and bold patterns. Their meticulous dress etiquette also set the Kalabari apart from their neighbors. Both the Kalabari and the Bonny chiefs wore gowns called *doni*. However, the Bonny use three studs for their *doni* as well as their jumper or *woko*, which enables them to use the same set of studs. In contrast, the Kalabari have three button holes for their jumper or *woko*, but require four for their *doni* and need two different sets of studs. By interchanging their studs, the Bonny lose the flair of the top button hole-display that the fourth stud of the Kalabari *doni* permits.

The Kalabari insist on wearing an immaculate white shirt under the *doni* which has a single stud at the neck. This is not true for Kalabari neighbors such as the Ikwerre or Okrika who also wear the *doni*. Kalabari men were not known to have worn the *doni* with a long tie like Okrika men, but occasionally some men wore a bowtie as some early twentieth century photographs show.

The Kalabari were probably the center from which the *doni* was

Figure 7.2 Kalabari traditional men's dress includes the gown known as doni, worn in 1991 by Chief Emmanuel Erekosima. (Photograph by Carolyn Nqozi Eicher).

Figure 7.3 The meticulous etiquette is shown in the woko outfit worn by Chief O.K. Isokariari in 1991, standing in front of the statue of King Abbi Amachree IV. (Photograph by Carolyn Nqozi Eicher).

disseminated to neighboring communities. For example, around the 1920s several Kalabari tailors, well-known for their designs, introduced these *doni* outfits in Okrika by making them for prominent chiefs.

Comparing notable men of Bonny and Opobo with Kalabari notables, Erekosima analyzed Niger Delta men's dress in turn of the century photographs (1989: 362–5). He used two albums, providing a total of seventy individuals depicted in photographs from the period of 1870–1907. One album came from Jaja's Photo Studio in Opobo with forty-eight photographs, and the other came from the J.A. Green Photo House in Bonny with twenty-two. All sixty-one of the Kalabari men wore traditional dress whereas of the nine men from Bonny and Opobo, five wore European dress, two wore a mixed type and only two wore traditional Rivers apparel. His data revealed that the Bonny used the traditional Rivers gown called the *doni* far less than the Kalabari, which supports his thesis that this particular form of Niger Delta outfit most probably originated among the Kalabari.

Political differentiation by ranks among Kalabari men has become less significant today than when Kalabari society was autonomous and exercized full political powers. But the affinity for dressing to fit the ranked categories apparently remains and may have even grown stronger. Perhaps, in the rancorous social environment of multi-ethnic Nigeria, as the Kalabari find themselves a small minority, they feel threatened and have become defensive. Thus, dressing as Kalabari allows them to display their identity and status in the larger community.

No single ensemble of dress has arisen among Nigerians to symbolize a new and unified identity, but several new forms of fashion attire that represent a Nigeria-wide pattern are taking shape. They merge as a mix of designs drawn from long-standing ethnic patterns peculiar to ethnic societies such as the Yoruba and Hausa and even Senegalese or Sierra Leonians. Occasionally these examples of dress are used to commemorate specific events such as independence or to mark the solidarity of partisan political parties. However, they have not become expressly linked to an overarching collective or national identity; their use as a symbolic representation of national identity remains incomplete. Consequently, members of ethnic groups like the Kalabari and other Nigerian peoples wear their own ethnic garments as proven and familiar vehicles of attachment to the past. Perhaps by wearing ethnic outfits as a cushion of security, Nigerians feel better able to cope with the challenges of transition to industrial odernization. Such garments often emerged from the ancient ethnic ties of clan formation many millenia back, and later evolved in clothing forms during the eras of intra-African, Arab-Saharan, and European mercantilism as indigenous state-formation occurred. Erekosima's findings reveal that the impact of socialization regarding Kalabari identity has remained strong among the older population even though they participate in a different social order and political system in which they acquire new identities. Their dress at funerals constitutes a means of identification with their traditional polity.

A Global Scenario

Ethnicity among the Kalabari is related to a process of dynamic response deriving from a given cultural base which uses the demarcating symbol of dress to perpetuate an identity rather than to define a specific exclusionary agenda. The Kalabari model finds parallels in Japanese adoption of uniforms for all state officials during the Meiji restoration of 1868 which opened that society to modernization (Nakagawa and Rosovsky 1963: 59), in Gandhi's *khadi*-spinning movement in India as a form of resistance to British imperialism (Bean 1989), and in Mao's decree of a levelling form of dress for all Chinese during the inception of Communist rule on the mainland (Hawkins 1973: 113).

In the current political scene around the globe, in contrast, we have been shocked into discomfiture by ethnic leaders who choose to eliminate ethnic rivals through conflict. From Bosnia to Sri Lanka to Rwanda, the tragic genocides of the 1990s are examples of this. In the conflicts between Ireland and England, among the Somali, or between the Kurds and Iraqis, a similar pattern of struggle against a general repressive order asserts itself.

However, in the giddy triumphs of reconciliation and subsequent co-existence, we find yet another model. The Israeli-Palestinian rapproachment and the establishment of democracy in South Africa are other extremes in expression of ethnicity. Various cultural symbols around which historical forces, group interests, and individual fates and destinies have dramatically coalesced include religious tenets, social traditions, historical memories, blood bonds, or physical attributes. Agendas are woven around these, and leaders of ethnic groups use these agendas to embark on a strategy for declaring supremacy of their own ethnicity.

The Kalabari case represents a mid-range and more creative

response than a prescribed agenda. Using a visible marker, such as dress, to distinguish a group from others in a positive manner seems to point the way, with an instructive potential, to such other emerging forms as the "multicultural" accommodations currently gaining momentum in the Unites States. Various celebratory forms marked by folklike festivals have arisen in the United States which include ethnic dress. For example, the 1990 Festival of American Folklife focussed on the United States Virgin Islands, and Senegalese adaptations of African culture as organized by the Smithsonian Institution and the National Park Service (Seitel 1990). In St. Paul, Minnesota, the Festival of Nations changed from a biannual to annual event in the 1980s because of enthusiastic community response and support.

An urban fiesta dubbed the first "worldfest" was organized by the D.C. Committee to Promote Washington in 1993. Described by Asher (1993) as "the most eclectic block-after-block party this city could have hoped to host," it featured a "multi-cultural-multi-musical feast with an exceptionally diverse and mellow turnout." Its extraordinary panache, which revolved around an unlimited assortment of ethnic cuisine and a heady variety of traditional as well as contemporary entertainment displays, drew this understated conclusion from the reporter: "What helps diversity to click seems to be a chance to chill out and chow down—food, music, space and a town with, on a good day, so much to offer." (Asher 1993). Here stood a standard which was, indeed, adequately reminiscent of Kalabari funerals occupying the culture's apex today. Their savory symbolism is replete with fineries and pomp, but adds pain of loss as a kind of prototype.

Dress and textile items involve material goods that entered Kalabari life through trade with Europeans by the early 1500s and with other West Africans before that. These adopted, non-indigenous items exemplify cultural authentication, the process whereby borrowed objects become transformed so that they are indigenously meaningful and useful. They signify Kalabari cultural prowess of the past as an ethnic entity and are used to mark Kalabari identity in contemporary, multicultural Nigeria. The Kalabari exhibited creativity through the years in making new ensembles from imported materials to comprise the ranked system of men's dress, including the collage of items for the men's fanciful headgear known as *ajibulu*. Cultural authentication constitutes the basis for their arts of dress and the cut-thread textiles they call their own. Dress visibly distinguishes the Kalabari people from those around them and demarcates their ethnicity, albeit sometimes in subtle ways.

References

Alagoa, E.J. (1972), *A History of the Niger Delta*, Ibadan: Ibadan University Press.

—— (1986), interview, October 21.

—— (1970), "Long Distance Trade and States in the Niger Delta," *Journal of African History*, vol. 2, no. 3, pp. 405–19.

Aronson, L. (1980), "History of Cloth Trade in the Niger Delta: A Study of Diffusion," *Journal of Textile History*, vol. II, pp. 89–107.

Asher, R.L. (1994), "The Way to a City's Heart," *Washington Post*, May 6.

Barbot, J. (1746), "A Description of the Coasts of North and South Guinea and Ethiopia," in A. Churchill (ed.), *Collection of Voyages and Travels*, vol. 5, London: H. Lintot and J. Osborn.

Bean, S. (1989), "Gandhi and Khadi: The Fabric of Indian Independence," in A.B. Weiner and J. Schneider (eds), *Cloth and Human Experience*, Washington, D.C.: Smithsonian Institution Press.

Burke, K. (1947), *The Philosophy of Literary Form*, Baton Rouge: Louisiana State University Press.

Case, J. (1987), "Western Influence on Kalabari Dress," unpublished paper for Undergraduate Research Opportunities Program, Minneapolis, MN: University of Minnesota.

Daly, M.C. (1984), "Kalabari Female Appearance and the Tradition of Iria," unpublished Ph.D. dissertation, Minneapolis, MN: University of Minnesota.

Daly, M.C., Eicher, J.B., and Erekosima, T.V. (1986), "Male and Female Artistry in Kalabari Dress," *African Arts*, vol. 19, no. 3, pp. 48–51, 83.

—— (1987), "Iria Bo Appearance at Kalabari Funerals," *African Arts*, vol. 21, no. 1, pp. 58–61, 83.

de Cardi, Le Comte C.N. (1899), "A Short Description of the Natives of the Niger Coast Protectorate with Some Account of Their Customs, Religion, Trade, Etc.," in M. Kingsley, *West African Studies*, Appendix I, London: Macmillan and Co.

Dike, K.O. (1956), *Trade and Politics in the Niger Delta 1830–1885: An Introduction to the Economics and Political History of Nigeria*, London: Oxford University Press.

Eicher, J.B. (1988), field notes, Nigeria.

—— forthcoming, *One Hundred Years of Social Change among the Kalabari of Nigeria*.

—— and Erekosima, T.V. (1987), "Kalabari Funerals: Celebration and Display," *African Arts*, vol. 21, no. 1, pp. 38–45, 87.

—— (1989), "Kalabari Funeral Rooms as Handcraft and Ephemeral Art," in B. Engelbrecht and B. Gardi (eds), *Man Does Not Go Naked: Textilien und Handwerk aus Afrikanishen und Anderen Landern*, Basel.

—— (1993), "19th Century Patterns of Textile Use among the Kalabari of

Nigeria," paper presented at Cloth, the World Economy, and the Artisan conference, Dartmouth College.

—— and BobManuel-Meyer, O.D. (1994), "India in Africa: RMHK in Kalabari Life and Death," paper presented in Madras, February.

Erekosima, T.V. (1989), "Analysis of a Learning Resource for Political Integration Applicable to Nigerian Secondary School Social Studies: The Case of Kalabari Men's Traditional Dress," unpublished Ph.D. dissertation, Catholic University of America.

—— (1979), "The Tartans of Buguma Women: Cultural Authentication," paper presented at the African Studies Association Annual Meeting, Los Angeles, CA.

—— and Eicher, J.B. (1981), "Kalabari Cut-Thread and Pulled-Thread Cloth: An Example of Cultural Authentication," *African Arts*, vol. 14, no. 2, pp. 48–51, 81.

—— (1980), "Kalabari Men's Dress: A Sophisticated African Response to Culture Contact," paper presented at the African Studies Association Annual Conference, Philadelphia.

—— (1994), "Aesthetics of Men's Dress of the Kalahari of Nigeria," in M. DeLong and A.M. Fiore (eds), *Aesthetics, ITAA Special Publication no. 7*, Monument, CO: ITAA.

Erekosima, T.V., Kio Lawson, W.H., and McJaja, O. (eds) (1991), *A Hundred Years of Buguma History in Kalabari Culture*, Lagos: Sibon Books.

Evenson, S. (1991), "The Manufacture of Madras in South India and Its Export to West Africa: A Case Study," unpublished master's thesis, Minneapolis, MN: University of Minnesota.

Geary, W.N.M. (1927), *Nigeria Under British Rule*, London: Methuen Co. Ltd.

Hawkins, J.N. (1973), "The Schooling Society Chinese Style: Alternative Forms of Nonformal Education," *Educational Studies*, vol. 4, no. 3, pp. 113–23.

Horton, R. (1969), "From Fishing Village to City-State: A Social History of New Calabar," in *Man in Africa*, London: Tavistock.

—— (1963), "The Kalabari Ekine Society: A Borderland of Religion and Art," *Africa*, vol. 33, pp. 94–114.

Hutchinson, T.J. (1858), *Impressions of West Africa*, London: Longman, Brown, Green, Longmans and Roberts.

Iyalla, B.S. (1968), "Womanhood in the Kalabari," *Nigeria Magazine*, vol. 98, pp. 216–24.

Jones, G.I. (1963), *The Trading States of the Oil Rivers: A Study of Political Development in Eastern Nigeria*, Oxford: Oxford University Press.

Mathias, E. (1974), "The Italian-American Funeral: Perspectives through Change," *Western Folklore*, vol. 33, pp. 35–50.

Michelman, S.O. (1992), "Dress in Kalabari Women's Societies," unpublished Ph.D. dissertation, Minneapolis, MN: University of Minnesota.

—— and Erekosima, T.V. (1992), "Kalabari Dress in Nigeria: Visual Analysis and Gender Implications," in R. Barnes and J.B. Eicher (eds), *Dress and Gender: Making and Meaning in Cultural Context*, Oxford and Providence: Berg Publishers.

Nakagawa, K., and Rosovsky, H. (1963), "The Case of the Dying Kimono: The Influence of Changing Fashions on the Development of the Japanese Woolen Industry," *Business History Review*, vol. 37, pp. 59–80.

Pereira, D.P. (1937), *Esmeraldo de Situo Orbis*, London: Hakluyt Society.

Petgrave, M.D. (1992), "Indian Madras in Kalabari Culture," unpublished master's Plan B thesis, Minneapolis: University of Minnesota.

Renne, E.P. (1985), "Pelete Bite: Motif and Meaning," unpublished master's thesis, Minneapolis: University of Minnesota.

Ryder, A.F.C. (1965), "Dutch Trade on the Nigerian Coast During the 17th Century," *Journal of the Historical Society of Nigeria*, vol. 3, pp. 195–210.

Seitel, P. (1990), *Festival of American Folklife*, Washington, D.C.: Smithsonian Institution Press.

Sollors, W. (ed.) (1989), *The Invention of Ethnicity*, New York: Oxford University Press.

Staub, S. (Summer, 1989), "The Near East Restaurant: A Study of the Spatial Manifestation of the Folklore of Ethnicity," *New York Folklore*, p. 115.

Stern, S., and Cicala, J.A. (eds) (1991), *Creative Ethnicity: Symbols and Strategies of Contemporary Ethnic Life*, Utah: Utah State University Press.

Talbot, P.A. (1926), *Peoples of Southern Nigeria: A Sketch of Their History, Ethnology and Languages with an Abstract of the 1921 Census*, 4 vols., London: Oxford University Press.

—— (1932), *Tribes of the Niger Delta: Their Religions and Customs*, New York: Barnes and Noble.

Tienebeso, W.E. (1984a), *Buguma*, Port Harcourt: Rivers State Newspaper Corporation.

—— (1984b), *Some Events in the Life of Kariboye Abbi, Amachree IV, Amanyanabo of Kalabari 1863–1900*, Port Harcourt: Rivers State Newspaper Corporation.

Waddell, H. (1863), *Twenty-Nine Years in the West Indies and Central Africa*, London: Nelson.

Weinrich, B. (1960), "The Americanization of Passover," in R. Patai, F. Utley, and D. Noy (eds), *Studies in Biblical and Jewish Folklore*, Bloomington, IN: Indiana University Press, pp. 329–66.

8

Dress and Ethnic Differentiation in the Niger Delta

Barbara Sumberg

In this article, I examine the role of dress and textile use in establishing ethnic identity among sub-groups of the Ijo ethnic group who live in the delta of the Niger River in Nigeria (see Map 7.1 in previous chapter). Nash (1989) identifies the three most common boundary markers of ethnicity as blood, substance, and cult (pp. 10–11). Blood refers to kinship, the assumption of common descent that is exclusive to members of the group. Substance is the sharing of food, "the propriety of eating together . . . only one step removed from the intimacy of bedding together" and cult is a shared system of sacred symbols or religion.

In situations where this trinity, which constitutes the deep or basic structure of differentiation, is not outwardly apparent, the secondary symbols of dress, language, and physical feature become important for identification (p. 12). These attributes have a metonymical relationship with the elements of deep structure; they stand for it in the everyday world. They are meaningful as boundaries only when they are tied to the deeper core features. The secondary characteristic of dress and the importance of its use in showing group membership in the Niger delta is the focus of this chapter. I propose an increased significance for the use of dress and textiles in establishing ethnic identity in certain circumstances. In the modern world and in a situation where distinctions between groups or sub-groups are very fine yet still strongly maintained, secondary indices of ethnicity such as dress, language, and physical features move to the forefront as markers of ethnicity. Using a comparison between the Nembe and a neighboring Ijo sub-group, the Kalabari, I will describe and analyze the role of dress in ethnic differentiation.

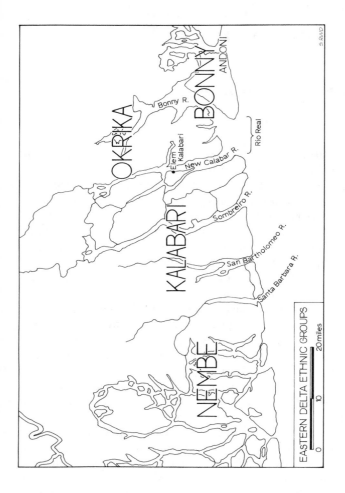

Map 8.1 Map showing the four city-states of the Eastern Niger delta. Courtesy of M. Catherine Daly, from "Kalabari Female Appearance and the Tradition of Iria," (1984), unpublished Ph.D. dissertation, Minneapolis: University of Minnesota, p. 30.

The Setting

Most of the Niger Delta is located in Rivers State and is inhabited by diverse groups of people. The Ijo ethnic group is spread over the lower reaches of the Niger Delta; the three large divisions of Western, Central, and Eastern Delta Ijo are further split into forty sub-groups or *ibe* (Alagoa 1966). The *ibe* are defined by common dialect, belief in a common ancestor, and worship of the same god.[1] Called part of the Ijo ethnic group, the people of Nembe, Kalabari, Bonny, and Okrika generally do not consider themselves to be Ijo though they share many characteristics with them such as riverain environment and political and religious organization, and speak many dialects of the same language (Williamson 1968).

The four city-states of Nembe, Kalabari, Bonny, and Okrika (see Map 8.1) are distinguished from the Central and Western Ijo by their development of a monarchical system of government, extensive early contact with Europeans, and their saltwater delta environment (Alagoa 1972). In addition, these four groups distinguish themselves not only from the larger Ijo group but also from each other (Alagoa 1972, 1976; Sumberg 1993) though they share some similar characteristics and history. Two of the ways in which they express this distinction are through dress and the use of cloth.

The history of migration patterns and settlement in the delta, combined with the relative isolation from the rest of the Ijo, sets the stage for the differentiation of the four city-states (Alagoa 1972). Competition for resources and trading relationships was a driving force in the economic life of the delta peoples during the period of burgeoning trade with the Europeans in the eighteenth and nineteenth centuries (Alagoa 1971). It was essential for the survival of the city-states that each maintain its independent identity and polity during this period of internal warfare and turmoil. Differentiation and separation are manifested in the varying traditions by which these groups are known.

Ethnic identity can be a flexible concept. A person's affiliation can change or be changed to suit different purposes. Erekosima (1991) states that Igbo women brought into Kalabari families to produce offspring for the family are no longer considered Igbo. Both they and

1. Alagoa notes that though these three factors are common, they are not the only possibilities and while language is important, it is not sufficient by itself to distinguish an *ibe* (1966: 280).

the Kalabari consider them and their children to be Kalabari when they have been properly educated and assimilated. This aspect of ethnic identity is present in Nembe today. Considered part of the minority group of Ijo by themselves and the government for official purposes, the Nembe will identify themselves with the larger group only when politically expedient. For most of the time, they are strictly Nembe people (Sumberg 1993).

The word Nembe describes a geographical area, a language dialect, and a group of people. Nembe is the name of the principal town of the present-day Brass Local Government. Nembe or Brass[2] is also used to refer to the entire area inhabited by the Nembe speaking sub-group of Ijo as well as the people themselves. An individual could say, 'I am Nembe' or 'I am a Nembe man' and anyone familiar with the delta would be able to place that person culturally and geographically. Historical accounts by European traders and explorers refer to the area as Brass and the people as Brassmen, based on their use of the word *ba-ra-sin* in trading, which means 'let go' or 'leave off,' indicating their unwillingness to accept a bad deal (Tepowa 1907: 42).

Kalabari territory adjoins Nembe on its western border and Okrika on the east. Unlike Nembe, the Kalabari territory had easy access and protected anchorage for trading ships. Contact and commerce with Europeans started earlier and had a bigger impact on development than in Nembe (Alagoa 1970: 321). The Kalabari were involved in the trans-Atlantic slave trade from its beginnings in the sixteenth century to its abolition in the nineteenth century. They also provided a major port for the export of palm oil subsequent to the slave trade.

Although Nembe also took part in the slave trade from an early date, this trade did not gain importance until the second quarter of the nineteenth century, when the British blockaded the more accessible ports of Bonny and Elem Kalabari in their attempt to end the slave trade (Alagoa 1964: 57). The remoteness of the port of Nembe, thirty miles inland up the Brass River, changed from a barrier to an asset during this blockade. By 1856 the palm oil trade had replaced the slave trade in economic importance, and the main port of the Brass region

2. The terms Nembe and Brass have been used interchangeably over the years. European traders knew the entire area and its population as Brass and the capital city as Brasstown until the late nineteenth century. At that point the name Brass came to refer to the coastal town of Twon and the inland city became known as Nembe, the inhabitants' name for the place and themselves (Alagoa 1964: 4–5). During English rule the area was known as the Brass Division, and today its title for Nigerian federal government purposes is Brass Local Government Area or BALGA. Today, it is not unusual to hear the coastal town called Twon/Brass.

was shifted to Twon on the coast. Due to poor natural harbor conditions and the dominance of the British-owned Royal Niger Company in the oil business, Nembe was never able to meet or surpass its neighbors in volume of trade (Alagoa 1964).

Today Buguma, the chief city of Kalabariland, is the second largest city in Rivers State. Buguma is more accessible to the mainland; the journey to Port Harcourt, the capital of the state and largest city, is a thirty-minute boat trip compared with two hours from Nembe. A road that connects Buguma to the mainland has also brought the city and its educational and economic opportunities closer.[3] Greater wealth of individuals and the community as a whole might account for the maintenance of some customs, such as *iria*,[4] (Iyalla 1968; Daly 1984) that are no longer practiced in Nembe.

The city-states of the eastern Niger delta are very closely related to each other as well as the larger Ijo groups of the central and western delta. The citizens intermarry, follow essentially the same traditional religious beliefs based on bush and water spirits, a war god, and a tutelary goddess, and determine ancestry and kinship ties by the same system.[5] According to Nash (1989), these three characteristics define ethnic boundaries and the secondary characteristics of language, dress, and physical features make them visible.

Language, dress, and cultural practice, closely related but distinctly different, are the major factors in Ijo ethnic differentiation.[6] All the Ijo speak dialects of the same language, some of which are mutually understandable (Williamson 1968); there are common features in

3. The greater wealth of the Kalabari was apparent to me after a brief stay in Buguma, where I observed more newly built many-storied buildings and prolific use of more expensive textiles during funeral celebrations than I recorded and observed in Nembe. Embroidered velvet, the most expensive cloth available in the market, is regularly displayed on Kalabari funeral beds and worn by female chief mourners (Sumberg and Eicher 1995). Out of the six funerals I attended in Nembe, I saw velvet displayed only once.

4. The Kalabari *iria* is analogous to the Nembe *ira*. Though different in actual practice, they both pertain to the celebration of successful childbirth.

5. The lineage system is based on the fact of children belonging to the mother's lineage except in the case of *eya* or "big dowry" marriage where, through a high bride price, the husband and his house gain control of the children. This means that when a man dies, all his property reverts to his brothers and uncles but not to his wife or children. Children inherit from their mother's male relatives (Jones 1963: 51–2; Sumberg 1993).

6. Physical feature is a far more nebulous concept, though it is perhaps used to separate the eastern groups from the rest of the Ijo. In Nembe one man pointed to another man on the street and said to me "That is a typical Ijo man, really black." This statement implied to me that Nembe people are perceived to be typically lighter than Ijo.

funerals (Alagoa 1967; Anderson 1987; Eicher and Erekosima 1987; Horton 1970) and ceremonies for women at the time of childbirth (Daly 1984; Aronson 1992; Sumberg 1993), and there is a style of dress which is different from the surrounding ethnic groups. A comparison of Nembe and Kalabari everyday and ceremonial dress and funerals follows.

Female and Male Dress

Female dress, except during the stages of *ira* and *iria* and in the lavish use of coral beads and other ornamentation, is essentially the same in both places. Adult women tend to wear a set of two wrappers with a blouse, jewelry, headtie, and handbag. At other times women wear a skirt and blouse or dress with accessories. In Nembe, printed cloth known as *wax* is worn on special occasions, while among the Kalabari wax is considered strictly everyday wear. The Kalabari attach much cultural significance to the wearing of *pelete bite* wrappers, which is the quintessential Kalabari cloth[7] while a cloth called *ondoba*, a blue, white, and yellow print of uncertain origin, is highly prized by the Nembe. This cloth is said to have arrived in Nembe with the Portuguese. (see Figure 8.1)

In Nembe I was told by a number of different people that 'There are no rules about dress, just customs.' Among the Kalabari there are definite rules, upheld by the old women who act as fashion arbiters and enforced by community censure (Daly, Eicher, and Erekosima 1986: 48). Kalabari male dress is more highly defined and prescribed; there are five categories of dress as opposed to the three of Nembe. The Kalabari *etibo* corresponds with the *opu shirt* ensemble of Nembe, *woko* with *angapu*, and *doni* with *dona*.[8] The two additional

7. *Pelete bite* is made by removing selected threads from imported Indian madras or *injiri* to create a wholly new design and look to the fabric. This art is practiced solely by Kalabari – women predominately, though not exclusively – and the resulting cloth is thought of as traditional Kalabari cloth (Erekosima and Eicher 1981). Nembe buy and wear *pelete bite*. One woman who opened her cloth box for me showed me two or three pieces she had commissioned to be cut in Port Harcourt. She had the dark threads removed from a black and white madras plaid, which is opposite from the way the Kalabari would wear it. They remove the light and white colored threads to achieve a darker design. *Pelete bite* was unknown among the other Delta groups (Eicher, personal communication 1993). The people of Nembe have no corresponding transformative textile art.
8. Along with a differentiation in styles, there is a different aesthetic at work. On viewing my slides upon my return from Nigeria, Joanne Eicher remarked that one particular Nembe garment/fabric combination would almost never be worn by a Kalabari man.

Figure 8.1 Nembe woman dressed in Nembe style, wearing wrappers of blue *ondoba*. Photograph by Barbara Samberg.

Kalabari garment types are *ebu* and *attigra*, both worn only by chiefs. *Ebu* is a long gown made of *injiri* and worn with a matching wrapper. It has a V-neck and a squared sailor collar in the back. Little or no jewelry is worn with it; the prestige of the garment comes from the cloth itself (Eicher and Erekosima 1993: 18). The richly embroidered and wide-cut garment called *attigra* was adapted from the Igalla of northern Nigeria and is worn during the performance of Ekine society masquerades (p. 25). This ankle-length gown is made of embroidered velvet or any suitably expensive and lavish fabric. It is worn with gold rings on all the fingers and often an elephant tusk is carried in the left hand while a fan is held in the right. A necklace of tiger's teeth and the hat called *ajibulu*, *azi* in Nembe, completes the outfit.[9]

Besides the different names, perhaps stemming from the language dialects, the different garments and more elaborate hierarchy signal an ethnic boundary. When I pointed to a photograph of Chief Naboyai of Nembe wearing an *ebu* he remarked that the garment is 'more a Kalabari style.' I did not see one worn during my stay in Nembe, though I saw many examples of rich *dona* at the chieftaincy installation (Figure 8.2). The Kalabari people were characterized by one informant as flashy dressers, more concerned and involved in appearance than Nembe (Sumberg 1993).

Ira and Iria

The *ira* of Nembe and the *iria* of Kalabari are ceremonies celebrating the procreative power of females. Though neither are practiced in the complete original form, part of the practice survives among the Kalabari in the 1980s and 1990s. The Kalabari *iria* is comprised of five stages, each with its distinctive dress and behaviors. The process starts at puberty and ends with the birth of an *iriabo's* (female in *iria*) first child. During this time a young girl is taught manners, comportment, and household management (Iyalla 1968: 216). She enters the fattening room prior to marriage (rarely practiced in the 1990s) and again after the birth of her child.

9. Eicher and Erekosima (1993) discuss body posture and carriage as well as the origins and meanings behind Kalabari dress. I was unable to uncover this kind of information during my field stay in Nembe, for a variety of reasons. There does not seem to be the richness of myth and lore surrounding dress and textile use, but this could also be a false assumption on my part. One woman said to me in reference to dress, "We used to have much more than the Kalabari but we sold them all of our riches and now we have none." Whether this statement was meant to be taken literally or metaphorically I'm not sure.

Figure 8.2 A Nembe chief wearing a *dona* with tophat, cane, and gold accessories at a chieftancy installation. Photograph by Barbara Sumberg.

In the 1990s, only the distinctive dress of the last two stages of *iria*, adult female dress and the assortment of particular wrappers, hats, and extensive jewelry worn after emerging from the fattening room after the birth of her baby, is seen in the context of *iria* ceremonies. The other forms survive as a type of display during celebrations such as a funeral or masquerade performance, but are not seen at other times. In Nembe, according to my informants, *ira* has disappeared altogether. When it was practiced, it was a far simpler ceremony which took place over the six months or so after a woman delivered a child. Family heirloom cloth and a special hairstyle were worn along with coral and chalk (Figure 8.3). The woman in *ira* walked about the town under an umbrella to receive the praise and presents that were her due. Members of the community were fed by the husband and mother of the new mother in thanksgiving.

Ira ceased being practiced about forty years ago in Nembe, based on the birth dates of my informants and their oldest children. Economic hardship is the reason given most often for its demise. The greater overall wealth of the Kalabari has perhaps contributed to the survival of these customs there.

Funerals

Nembe and Kalabari funerals share some common features and also have some disparate ones. All night wake-keeping on Friday and burial on Saturday are customary to both, as are laying out the corpse for public viewing in a cloth-decorated space, the firing of cannons, and the different types of burial for different types of deaths. Historically, some type of divination or animation of a specified object by the deceased's spirit for the purpose of answering questions about its death has been common to all the Ijo (Horton 1970: 57).

The main differences between the two groups' funerals for a person who has achieved old age and status are the public setting of and community contributions to a Nembe funeral and the degree of display in a Kalabari funeral. Public donation on the second day to the maintenance of the family and their obligations for the mourning period are unique to Nembe (Irigha 1986; Sumberg 1993), as is the display of the corpse in the public square from Friday night to Saturday afternoon. The family of the deceased are formally responsible for all the financial obligations in the other Ijo areas, including Kalabariland, although individuals give gifts to the family. The wake-keeping takes

Figure 8.3 Women dressed in the old *ira* style with coral and two wrappers. Photograph by Barbara Sumberg.

place in the family compound and is open to whoever wishes to attend.

Kalabari funerals are accompanied by a more lavish display of dress and textiles than funerals in Nembe. Among the Kalabari, selected female relatives of the deceased dress in *iria* style to express the position and status of the deceased and her or his family (Daly 1984).

The decoration of one to three Kalabari funeral rooms in the family compound for display of the body is common. The walls, ceiling, and bed of the first room are covered with red *injiri*, the second room displays handwoven West African cloths and other substantial textiles preferred by the Kalabari, while the third room is filled with embroidered velvet and silks from India. If the deceased was a Christian, white cloth is used in this room. If the family has sufficient wealth, up to seven rooms might be decorated (Eicher and Erekosima 1987). In Nembe, there is only one room in the family compound where the coffin rests for about six hours before being taken to the *duri-sun-wari*, the small pavilion in the public square used only for funerals. Of the three rooms I saw in Nembe, one was hung with *injiri* and two were decorated in white. When I asked if the white signified a Christian corpse, Chief Koki's relatives said yes, while Princess Oguara's family said no. White was used in her room because she had a special *juju* who demanded it. On another occasion I was told covering the bed in the *duri-sun-wari* with white did not signify Christianity in Nembe.

The dress of the Nembe and Kalabari chief mourners is significantly different. When the designated Kalabari chief mourner is male, he will wear a white *etibo*, *injiri* wrapper, a sash of *akwete* or *acraa*, and a turban of the same sash material on the day of the burial (Eicher and Erekosima 1987: 42). When the chief mourner is female, she is dressed as an *iriabo*. During the funeral itself and the following week of celebratory activities the chief mourner and other family members dress in prescribed ways in an elaborate hierarchy of association and meaning (pp. 42–4). In Nembe, the designated chief mourners are the only participants expected to dress in a particular manner.[10] They wear specific types of cloth tied in an archaic way and wear the coral beads of a chief (Figure 8.4). Their role is primarily symbolic of the spirit of the dead person and the transition to another life, rather than the

---

10. The widow of a deceased man is severely restricted in her choice of apparel but she does not actually participate in the funeral events.

Figure 8.4 Two young women dressed as *alabo* following a relative's funeral. They are wearing coral necklaces, wrappers tied in the old fashioned style, chalk on their faces and arms, and waist sashes. Photograph by Barbara Sumberg.

display of wealth and prestige as with the Kalabari (Sumberg 1993).[11]

In Nembe, *wax* wrappers are given by the family members, folded in triangles, and placed on the bed in the public square (Figure 8.5). No such practice is used by the Kalabari; in fact, to show *wax* at a funeral at all is considered extremely inappropriate because of prohibitions concerning its use as dictated by Owamekaso, the Kalabari tutelary deity (Eicher and Erekosima 1993).

Summary and Conclusions

Ethnic identification and pride is strong among the Ijo of Nigeria. The four city-states of the Eastern Delta hold both tightly and loosely to group identities that were forged in the difficult conditions that arose in the Niger Delta during the eighteenth and nineteenth centuries. These conditions of warfare and competition for trade encouraged the formation of self-identified ethnic groups that distinguished themselves from each other by their language, dress, and cultural expressions.

Differences in dress mark the boundaries between Kalabari and Nembe and visually identify membership in either *ibe*. Kalabari are known for their interest and skill in dress and adornment, and attribute this to the grace of their deity Owamekaso (Eicher and Erekosima 1993). Nembe are known for their more casual attitude toward life. A prominent Nembe man said in an interview, "The Nembe people tend to be much more informal and not to care so much about their appearance. They themselves have that feeling about being different from the Kalabari in this regard" (Erekosima 1989: 361). The diacritic of dress, sometimes considered to be of only superficial interest and importance, (Nash 1989) becomes one of the primary ethnic differences in this situation where related people hold themselves apart and in distinction from each other.

---

11. Daly quotes a Kalabari informant on this point: "It was a fantastic show of wealth. Everybody [the relatives] wanted to show what they had [cloth and coral]. Nobody compared notes [beforehand]. Everybody asked for a room to display . . .. I will put all that I have [into the occasion]. Before we could never afford even one room, when money was not throwing itself all over the place. Before it was more [a] communal show of wealth where now it's an individual [show]; brother and brother competing against each other. Just like *iriabo* at funerals. Everybody before would go and ask Aunty for cloth. Now you go and spy and then bring something bigger than that" (1987: 60).

Figure 8.5 Funeral bed in the *durl-sun-ware* in Bassambire, Nembe. Wax wrappers are folded into triangles and placed beside the corpse. The walls and ceiling are hung with other types of cloth. Photograph by Barbara Sumberg.

References

Alagoa, E.J. (1964), *The Small Brave City-State: A History of Nembe-Brass in the Niger Delta*, Ibadan: Ibadan University.
—— (1966), "Ijo Origins and Migrations: I," *Nigeria Magazine*, vol. 91, pp. 279–88.
—— (1967), "Ijo Funeral Rites," *Nigeria Magazine*, vol. 95, pp. 279–87.
—— (1970), "Long Distance Trade and States in the Niger Delta," *Journal of African History*, vol. 11, no. 3, pp. 319–29.
—— (1971), "The Development of Institutions in the States of the Eastern Niger Delta," *Journal of African History*, vol. 12, no. 2, pp. 269–78.
—— (1972), *A History of the Niger Delta*, Ibadan: Ibadan University.
—— (1976), "The Niger Delta States and Their Neighbors," in *History of West Africa to 1800*, vol. 1, J.F. Ade Ajayi and M. Crowder (eds), New York: Columbia University.
Anderson, M. (1987), "The Funeral of an Ijo Shrine Priest," *African Arts*, vol. 21, no. 1, pp. 52–7, 88.
Aronson, L. (1992), "Women's Masquerades: A Definition," paper presented at the Ninth Triennial Symposium on African Art, Iowa City.
Daly, M.C. (1984), "Kalabari Female Appearance and the Tradition of Iria," unpublished Ph.D. thesis, Minneapolis, MN: University of Minnesota.
—— (1987), "Iria Bo Appearance at Kalabari Funerals," *African Arts*, vol. 21, no. 1, pp. 58–61, 86.
Daly, M.C., Eicher, J.B., and Erekosima, T.V. (1986), "Male and Female Artistry in Kalabari Dress," *African Arts*, vol. 19, no. 3, pp. 48–51, 83.
Eicher, J.B. and Erekosima, T.V. (1987), "Kalabari Funerals: Celebration and Display," *African Arts*, vol. 21, no. 1, pp. 38–45, 87.
—— (1993), "Taste and 19th Century Patterns of Textile Use Among the Kalabari of Nigeria," paper presented at conference on Cloth, the World Economy, and the Artisan: Textile Manufacturing and Marketing in South Asia and Africa, 1780–1950, Dartmouth College.
Erekosima, T.V. (1989), "Analysis of a Learning Resource for Political Integration Applicable to Nigerian Secondary School Social Studies: The Case of Kalabari Men's Traditional Dress," unpublished Ph.D. thesis, Catholic University of America.
—— (1991), "Changing Patterns of Status among Kalabari Men," in T.V. Erekosima, W.H. Kio Lawson and O. MacJaja (eds), *Buguma 1984 Centenary Symposia on Kalabari*, Lagos: Sibon Books Ltd.
Erekosima, T.V., and Eicher, J.B. (1981), "Kalabari Cut-Thread and Pulled-Thread Cloth: An Example of Cultural Authentication," *African Arts*, vol. 14, no. 2, pp. 48–51, 81.
Horton, R. (1970), "Ikpataka Dogi: A Kalabari Funeral Rite," *African Notes*, vol. 5, no. 3, pp. 57–72.
Irigha, C. (1986), "Burial Customs of Nembe," unpublished Bachelor's thesis,

University of Port Harcourt.

Iyalla, B. (1968), "Womanhood in the Kalabari," *Nigeria Magazine*, vol. 98, pp. 216–24.

Jones, G. I. (1963), *The Trading States of the Oil Rivers: A Study of Political Development in Eastern Nigeria*, London: Oxford University.

Nash, M. (1989), *The Cauldron of Ethnicity in the Modern World*, Chicago: University of Chicago.

Sumberg, B. (1993), "Dress and Ethnic Differentiation in the Niger Delta," unpublished Master's thesis, Minneapolis, MN: University of Minnesota.

Sumberg, B., and Eicher, J.B. (1995), "India and West Africa: Transformation of Velvets," in J. Dhamija (ed.), *The Woven Silks of India*, Bombay: Marg Publications.

Tepowa, A. (1907), "A Short History of Brass and Its People," *Journal of the African Society*, vol. 7, no. 25, pp. 32–88.

Williamson, K. (1968), "Languages of the Niger Delta," *Nigeria Magazine*, vol. 97, pp. 124–30.

9

The Lady in the Logo: Tribal Dress and Western Culture in a Southern African Community

Deborah Durham

In 1990, a recurring topic at meetings of the Herero Youth Association, or *Otjira tjOmitanda*, in Mahalapye, Botswana was the design of a logo. Once selected, this logo would grace membership cards and one of the ubiquitous stamps that authorize communications in Botswana. Members of the Youth Association agreed that the logo should be unambiguous, communicating directly to viewers the nature of the group, its Herero membership and its purpose. And, although a final design had not been selected when I left Botswana in 1991, the central figure was certain to be a woman wearing the distinctive Herero long dress.[1]

It was generally agreed among the Youth Association that only this image could instantly communicate to all citizens of Botswana the Herero identity of the youth group, and that this would be the one unambiguous feature of the logo (other possible elements included a cow, a calabash for soured milk, and a caption in Herero reading *tiza ombazu*, "hold on to tradition"). But how unambiguous was this image

1. This paper was originally prepared for a panel on "The World at Home: Constructing Relations Between the Local and the Global through Everyday Goods and Practices" at the annual meeting of the American Anthropological Association, December 1992. Research in Mahalapye, Botswana, conducted between December 1988 and May 1991, was generously supported by a Fulbright-Hays Fellowship for Doctoral Dissertation Research, a National Science Foundation Dissertation Research Improvement Grant (No. BNS-8819432), and a Sigma Xi Grant-in-Aid of Research.

of a woman, and the "traditional" dress that she wore? What kind of tradition does that dress represent, to be held onto and to literally surround Herero? And what made that dress, apart from its instant recognizability, particularly appropriate for the Herero Youth Association, rather than the other distinctive Herero practices that were either not vetted or dismissed as unsuitable?

Before turning to describe this dress and its interpretations by Mahalapye Herero, a brief background on the community and the Herero Youth Association is in order. In 1904 Herero, living in what was then German South West Africa (today's Namibia) revolted against colonial rule. Many Herero fleeing the disastrous revolt in Namibia settled in Botswana. Although the bulk of these settled in the northwestern part of the country, small communities exist elsewhere, including the more densely settled eastern part of the country, where Mahalapye is located. There are perhaps 2,000 Herero in the "village" of Mahalapye (pop. over 30,000) which lies along the main rail line and road in Botswana some 200 kilometers north of Gaborone, Botswana's capital (Map 9.1). A sociological profile of Mahalapye Herero in education, employment, religion, wealth and involvement in national/state institutions would not differ significantly from that of their Tswana neighbors. Mahalapye Herero keep in contact with Herero in Namibia, Ngamiland, South Africa, and other settlements in southern Botswana through visits, changes of residence, phone calls, and letters. But Herero also have been intermarrying and intermingling with Tswana and other peoples in their neighborhood, and their residential ward is now very densely ethnically mixed.

The Herero Youth Association, started in 1985, is an association of young Herero men and women who are concerned with revitalizing a sense of being Herero. The group, or *Youthi* as they are often called, attempts to mobilize community activities, to re-energize Herero identity and to promote government-inspired goals of self-improvement. Most of the leadership is employed in government or private salaried positions. Although the "Executive Committee" is dominated by men, there are some women in the Youth Association's offices and the women are an important and influential part of the membership. While only one of the several women members wore the Herero long dress on a regular basis, the other women in the Youth Association either had a dress to wear on special occasions or would borrow one from a friend or relative. The Youth Association had been designing – and redesigning – a "uniform" for several years. As with the long-term project of the logo, although the details of the uniform

Map 9.1 Botswana

were debated and changed, the women's outfit was definitely going to be a Herero long dress.

The dress itself is unmistakable, and it is certainly true that it is recognizable throughout Botswana. Reminiscent of Victorian-era fashions, the voluminous skirts of the dress sweep the ground and, when properly supported by a number of underskirts, or petticoats, billow out solidly from the wearer's waist. The waist, tightly bound with a belt (which also serves to hold up the underskirts), is high, falling just under the bosom. The upper part of the dress is fairly snug, and has necklines of remarkable variety and elegance; all dresses button in a complex fashion across the left shoulder and under the left arm. The sleeves of most dresses billow out again, high and wide at the shoulders, falling to an exaggerated drop at the elbow, narrowing then flaring again at the wrist.

The dress cannot be worn without an equally distinctive headdress: this is an axiomatic feature of being Herero that must not be contravened. I was repeatedly informed that a woman would throw her long skirts up over her head rather than be seen in the long dress but without the headdress, and I saw a Tswana man brought to the chief's court for knocking off a Herero woman's headdress during a drunken argument. The headdress itself, the *otjikayiva*, is constructed out of two scarves; it is a high and intricate creation, with two *ozonde* or horizontal horns (the word is the same as for cattle horns), carefully shaped and constantly readjusted to be smooth and straight throughout the day (Figure 9.1).

Women always wear a short shawl over the dress, and properly dressed Herero must move with slow, almost ponderous, dignity and a deliberate decorum.[2] The position of the sitting woman in the Youth Association's proposed logo was held to allude to the distinctive bodily comportment of Herero women as well as to the dress, because only Herero women in Botswana, with their voluminous skirts, are able to sit cross-legged on the ground (where women generally sit) without displaying their thighs or genitals.

While most older Herero women in Mahalapye wear this dress, not all do, and only a minority of the women under 40 don the long dress on a daily basis. (Many of these younger women, however, dress Herero fashion for funerals.) The other women, those not wearing the long dress, clothe themselves in modern, western-style garments such as skirts, blouses, dresses, which generally cover the knees for modesty's sake but not the ankles. To Herero in Mahalapye, these more contemporary styles are not called "western" or "European," but are designated "Setswana" style, the style of the dominant ethnic group in Botswana; the question might be asked, *mo zara otjiherero poo otjitjuuana*? (Are you dressing Herero-style or Tswana-style?)

A contemporary and more or less international style, at least to outside observers' eyes, will be described "Setswana" for two

---

2. Hildi Hendrickson has done extensive investigation into the construction and history of the Herero dress in northwestern Botswana and Namibia (Hendrickson 1992). It is clear that appreciation of the dress as embodying Herero tradition varies across southern Africa, having different significance in the newly independent nation of Namibia, in the remote rural areas of northwestern Botswana (Ngamiland), and in the semi-urbanized town of Mahalapye in more heavily settled and developed eastern Botswana.

Figure 9.1 A Herero woman in Mahalapye, Botswana, wearing the Herero long dress (drawn by Rebecca Bailey© from a field photograph by Deborah Durham).

reasons: it is associated with the ethnic Tswana majority in the country, who dominate local and national politics, but it is also associated with Botswana, the modern nation-state of the Tswana. This is quite a different issue, for the Herero of Mahalapye consider themselves full members of that state, and will with the state in mind call themselves "Batswana," which means literally "Tswana people" (Durham 1993). It is the association of the "short" dress with the latter, with the nation-state, that is most important for understanding the contrast of Herero and Tswana dress.

Already I have called the Tswana dress style "international" in character: but is this so from a local, Herero perspective? Certainly a sense of modernity clings to the shorter dress, but modernity does not, as we so often assume, imply internationalism. Even more certainly, the Herero long dress represents a tradition in that it represents to Herero a continuity between the past and the present. But we must not take for granted the meaning and implications of that tradition, especially as it is imagined through the medium of clothing. Indeed, in an inversion of expectations, it is the long dress, the traditional style, that represents to Herero in Mahalapye international interactions and dynamism, and the shorter, modern dress that seems particularly local or, more exactly, regional. As I will demonstrate, the contrast between the long and short dresses, and between the tradition and the particular modernity that they enclothe, incorporates (almost literally, on the body) the way that Mahalapye Herero understand their current situation, and the situation of their country, in southern Africa past and present (see Comaroff and Comaroff (1987) for a similar example among the Tswana).

Let us start with the traditions. The notion of a tradition, or a traditional form, is a loaded one in contemporary western discourse, gaining its full meaning through opposition to a particularly construed modernity, to modernism and more recently to post-modern conditions. In some senses, "traditional" is an adjective used to characterize others, whether within or distant from western civilization. "Modern" then characterizes us, so that non-western cultures and marginal areas of the west are said to modernize as they discard local practices and adapt and appropriate western forms. But there is more than a structural opposition at stake here, more than the dichotomizing of us and them.

In an otherwise important and suggestive piece, one that has stimulated a whole generation of research and debate, Hobsbawm and Ranger provide what is almost a caricature of our notions of "traditions," at least the more self-conscious ones: "invented traditions" are discovered in "the contrast between the constant change and innovation of the modern world and the attempt to structure at least some parts of social life within it as unchanging and invariant" (Hobsbawm and Ranger 1983: 2).[3] The important thing here is that tradition is what is *represented* as unchanging, invariant, unresponsive to innovation and adaptation, in a context of change and variability.

A second aspect of tradition that is often taken for granted for the "other," not discussed by Hobsbawm and Ranger, is its specifically local nature, its narrow reference to a tightly circumscribed experience (which might be regional or ethnic). By contrast, modernism and modernity are definitely non-local: one can think particularly of the "International Style" in architecture, or experimentation with language in modernist poetry that is intended to escape local social fixtures. And modernity itself refers to the trans-national sweep of social, political and economic trends originating in Europe but thought to be global, or universal, in application. It is these aspects of self-conscious traditions, the represented invariance and unresponsiveness to change and the narrow, local reference, that do *not* characterize Herero traditional dress in Mahalapye, at least not to the Herero themselves.

There is no doubt that the loss of traditions, of practices that are associated with the past and that are important for sustaining a distinct identity within the modern state, is of major concern to Herero in Botswana. Most important among these is the perceived decline in Herero language skills (in favor of the Tswana language, the national language of the country) and the more infrequent use of the Herero dress by women. Both of these concerns were noted by members of the Herero Youth Association, and were perhaps more loudly rehearsed by older members of the Mahalapye Herero community. Now, insofar as these traditions are associated with a minority community and serve to mark it out, creating a form of homogeneity within and distinctiveness without, we might expect that the traditions would seem exclusively Herero. But in fact the dress (and to a much lesser extent the language) is portrayed by Herero — both old and young —

3. Some note must be made of Hobsbawm and Ranger's notions of "custom" and routine, which they place in opposition to invented traditions. Any anthropologist will have trouble with the concept of traditions that are functionally organic parts of a social order, "the motor and fly-wheel," or technologically necessary, contrasted with traditions that are not. Suffice it to note here that the Herero long dress emerged as distinctive only after the Herero revolt against German imperialism in South West Africa, at a time when consciousness of a Herero nation unified in culture and experience had just been formed.

with a complex history, and in the composition of that portrayal incorporates both the past and the present.[4] And as with the dress, the Herero experience itself is viewed by the people as historically dynamic and evolving.

On several different occasions, I heard and participated in discussions about the origins and development of the dress among Mahalapye Herero. Most striking was the emphasis upon outside sources, influences and non-Herero commentary. At a New Year's party, I overheard one woman explain to an elderly man that the long dress had been adopted by Herero to give respect to Queen Victoria, and that the dress was an imitation of hers. (It is worth noting that although Herero were colonized by Germany in the nineteenth century, they also interacted with many British from Cape Colony and Britain. After the war of 1904, refugees in Botswana lived under British administration.) The dress itself was thus represented as an adoption or adaptation from a particular western imperial power, indicating an admiration of the form, style, and (implicitly) the politics of Britain.

It is interesting to add in this respect that in Mahalapye close friends often construct identical dresses, or at least use the same fabric. This practice expresses their shared sympathies and tastes, but it also is symbolically and practically the outcome of a mutual venture, the joint purchase of a bolt of fabric and the mutual planning and sewing of the dress. The mutual venture, the inter-relatedness of interests, investments and activities, is made concrete for Mahalapye Herero in the actual form of the long dress. The dress invokes the complicated historical processes of interchange and interaction that account for modern Herero traditions.

But it is not just the relationship between Britain and Herero that is represented in the dress. At a funeral, I joined a group of women in a discussion of the history and conceptualization of the long dress. The British influence was not suggested here, but we discussed the German missionaries as introducers of western dress. The women also talked about possible Dutch influence on the headdress: I speculated to myself that perhaps one woman had seen the folkloric, flying-nun type hat in a picture somewhere, or was referring to an

4. Tswana residents of Mahalapye, on the other hand, often attempted to "debunk" the authenticity of the Herero long dress. They would often confide in me that, whatever Herero were telling me, the dress had actually been borrowed from missionaries. Tswana, that is to say, generally assumed that Herero believed that the long dress was "authentically" and exclusively Herero.

Afrikaner style of headdress (although most Mahalapye Herero did distinguish between European Dutch and South African Afrikaners). All these possibilities, the British, German and Dutch sources of style, are routinely considered and accepted. The dress construes a long inter-relationship of Herero with different Europeans for well over a century, an inter-relationship of which these Herero are clearly proud.[5]

It is worth mentioning that the historical complexity of the dress is complemented by humorous stories of how others, Tswana, Afrikaners, and Americans, see the dress. This has diverse ramifications for the creation of identity, but for the purpose of this paper these stories re-emphasize the fact that the Herero long dress is perceived to have significance and impact outside the more narrow domain of an exclusive Herero community.

And so what of modernity? How does the shorter dress style of contemporary Botswana serve to complement and contrast with the long history of the long dress? At the outset, it must be stated that everyone recognized the western origin of this style and its relatively international status; but this fact was very rarely articulated. The short dress, the modern style, was the unmarked and in many senses unremarked upon style. But it was at the same time treated and considered as a distinctively regional style, to be sharply distinguished from the fashions – and here I must emphasize the notion of quick change and evolution inherent in the word "fashion" (Veblen 1919, Barthes 1983) – of the European West. The region encompassing the Tswana style was Botswana, but more especially Botswana as a part of the southern African economy, dominated by South Africa. In Mahalapye and Gaborone, clothing was purchased from South African chain stores or ordered from catalogues with South African addresses (although sometimes these had American names: a popular catalogue was called *Ebony*). Apart from a few known local manufactures (such as those making school uniforms), clothes purchased from Botswana merchants were assumed to originate in South Africa. (In fact, in 1985 about 78 per cent of imports were made in or came through South Africa.) Home-made and locally-sewn clothing imitated closely the patterns of commercial goods (apart from the Herero long dress).

5. The interchange of style is not represented as entirely one-way. Herero, both women and men, enjoyed telling me of other non-Herero who would wear the long dress at Herero events. Among these non-Herero were German, British, and Tswana women.

When I talked to women and some men about women's modern dress styles, their distinctness from western fashion was often emphasized. These are the clothes that *we* wear, that *we* like, people often said to me. European fashions, worn by Europeans or by very well-traveled, cosmopolitan local people, were often explicitly disapproved of: the skirts were too short or too long, the styles did not flatter the figure, pants and shorts on women were ridiculous and clothes were often worn in a slovenly manner, un-ironed and sometimes dirty and without slips underneath. Indeed, most Herero in Mahalapye in 1990 were notably uninterested in the styles of European fashion or in what people were wearing in America or Europe or other parts of Africa. "Ghanaian" was a term of dismissal for many West Africa styles and "Afro-American" was an adjective of amusement for people with overly long hair.

Both the Herero long dress with its headdress and the modern dress style of Botswana incorporate many messages about the regional politics and economy, which are often stamped directly onto the fabric. A favorite cloth that was made into shirts, skirts, headdresses and long dresses praised the cars of Botswana (*Dikoloi tsa Botswana*). One woman's Herero dress was made of political cloth with Kenneth Kaunda's portrait all over it (Kaunda was then president of neighboring Zambia). Another locally-made cloth had prints of the basketry of Botswana, a promoted local industry; others simply featured maps of the country or continent. Among Mahalapye Herero, a print of their chief had a brief and very limited popularity: it was clearly superseded by the "cars of Botswana" print. While these patterns imposed on the modern dress style only confirm the local and regional interpretation of that dress, they emphasize again the openness of the so-called "traditional" Herero style, and its constant engagement in the world around it (and beyond: three of the most striking dresses I saw featured Polynesian motifs).[6]

A view of Herero tradition and identity as emerging in an ongoing interchange with a larger world, as experienced by the wearers of the dress itself, is part of how Herero understand their present situation in Botswana. Struggling with the contradictory tenets of a tribal

6. It is tempting to call Herero attitudes towards their dress "post-modernist," in the susceptibility of interpretation to fragment the dress into allusive and historically disparate components. But, of course, post-modernism demands a more ironic stance, and only makes sense as a condition when compared to modernism and some form of traditionalism. As Herero have gone through neither of these 'stages' they really cannot be placed in that category.

identity, taken for granted and irrefutable in most of the country, and with an acceptance of the liberal citizenship attributed to members of the nation-state (Durham 1993), the dress is one of the media of resolution. In (literally) and through the dress, Herero from Mahalapye configure their traditions as dynamic and interactive, evolving and changing – as invented as the traditions are and committed as they themselves are to an ethnic-national identity. By incorporating recognition of their "others" – sometimes in admiration, sometimes passing comment on them – into their own developing history, Herero conceive of themselves as distinctive and yet mutual participants in Botswana.[7]

I asked at the outset of this chapter why the Herero long dress would be an extremely appropriate image for the Herero Youth Association. There are other images that, iconically, could also serve: the *okuruo*, the sacred fire of Herero patrilines, would suggest not only connectedness with the past through the ancestors but a certain changelessness, a reproduction of the ancestral values and lives in the present. But the Youth are not committed to the reproduction of a static past, or of the present, for that matter. The Herero Youth Association has as its goal "consciousness-raising" (as it was explained to me in English), which I would argue involves constant reformulation of Herero past and present identities; it is also a group committed to improvement, to changing the conditions of life and advancing the lives and careers of its members. Most of the group's leaders were deeply engaged in the Botswana economy, through jobs or investments and some were directly involved in politics. Projects that they talked about included a day-care center that would free mothers to work and earn money, and prepare children for success in public schools and jobs. An interweaving of putatively age-old identities with the exigencies and potentialities of contemporary life is central to the actual goals of the Herero Youth Association, and this engagement in the national society, and indeed in the regional society, is experienced and interpreted in the "traditional" dress. The lady in the logo, tradition embodied (and enclothed), looks upon a very complex history that incorporates not only Herero but the world.

---

7. The situation is slightly more complex than represented in this paper. The other side of the tensions between tribal and citizen identities is also realized through the dress, as it is criticized as cumbersome, impeding Herero movement both literally and figuratively, in Botswana society (Durham 1993).

References

Barthes, R. (1983), *The Fashion System*, trans. M. Ward and R. Howard, New York: Hill and Wang.

Comaroff, J., and Comaroff, J.L. (1987), "The Madman and the Migrant: Work and Labor in the Historical Consciousness of a South African People," *American Ethnologist*, vol. 14, pp. 191–209.

Durham, D. (1993), "Images of Culture: Being Herero in a Liberal Democracy (Botswana)," unpublished Ph.D. dissertation, University of Chicago.

Hendrickson, A.H. (1992), "Historical Idioms of Identity Representation Among the Ovaherero in Southern Africa," unpublished Ph.D. dissertation, New York University.

Hobsbawm, E., and Ranger, T. (eds) (1983), *The Invention of Tradition*, Cambridge: Cambridge University Press.

Veblen, T. (1919), *The Theory of the Leisure Class: An Economic Study of Institutions*, New York: B.W. Huebsch.

10

"The Fairest of Them All": Gender, Ethnicity and a Beauty Pageant in the Kingdom of Swaziland

Carolyn Behrman

Introduction

In her discussion of representations of whiteness in the black imagination, bell hooks writes of the "looking relations" (1992: 340) between white supremacists and black slaves. Using Foucault's concept of the gaze, she finds socio-political meaning in the structured ways that people see each other. In this chapter I wish to raise for consideration the possibility that looking relations focusing on ethnicity and gender between two groups of people can be used as political tools within one of those groups.

I intend first to profile some of the defining features of ethnicity and gender in Swaziland which I encountered in 1991. Basic demographic information is presented along with a necessarily abbreviated discussion of perceived differences between ethnic groups and genders as expressed to me by Swazi men and women in interviews.

I then introduce the idea of dual gender systems. The notion of dual systems is a common one in Swaziland (dual legal, governmental and marriage systems, to name a few). Based partially on colonial legacies, these set of systems have grown and developed elaborate interconnections since Swaziland's period as a British protectorate. Elsewhere (Behrman, unpublished), I propose that dual *gender* systems exist in Swaziland which resemble these other sets of systems and that men and women construct and negotiate their identities in the gray area or dialectical space between these two systems.

For my purposes here, dual gender systems are used as a structural model or guideline. Images of women in Swazi public culture, the print media, and interview exchanges will be examined focusing on issues of fashion and beauty, and in particular on the Miss Swaziland Beauty Pageant. Using the idea of dual gender systems as a guiding principle, I will explore the significance of ethnicity in a seemingly nearly homogenous society for the ongoing construction and negotiation of women's gender identities.

Swaziland at the time I lived there in 1990–1991 was a country of approximately 800,000 people, over 98 percent of whom were ethnically and racially black Swazis. The vast majority of these people lived in ranch-like homesteads scattered across the rural landscape of this tiny southern African country. They were by and large agriculturalist-pastoralists living what Swazis would call "traditional", and anthropologists would further classify as patrilineal, virilocal lifestyles. In a country with a total land mass approximately the size of the state of New Jersey, rural residents had fairly easy and consistent access to print media in the form of Swaziland's two daily newspapers, one women's magazine, radio and, for the well-off, television (Map 10.1).

Swaziland appears on the surface to be culturally unified, a country without significant ethnic differences. When asked to discuss ethnic groupings in interviews, most respondents pondered the question before replying and although most settled on racial/ethnic categories, some insisted on discussing variations in church groups (Zionist, Protestant, Catholic, Baptist, evangelical vs. Nazarene). Fewer than two percent of the population were "colored," European, Indian or non-Swazi African residents. Colored residents make up less than half of this roughly two percent (Government of Swaziland 1988). A term borrowed from South Africa, colored includes anyone with some mix of African, Portuguese, British, Afrikaaner or Indian ancestry; most were Swazi citizens and fluent in siSwati. There were some colored farmers in rural areas but the colored population lived for the most part in urban areas and pursued wage employment. One black Swazi man interviewed said he didn't "understand their culture" but felt that colored people shared his. Another explained to me that colored Swazis are "mixed people so even their culture is mixed."

Initially motivated by the observation that colored and white European women appear far more frequently than two percent of the

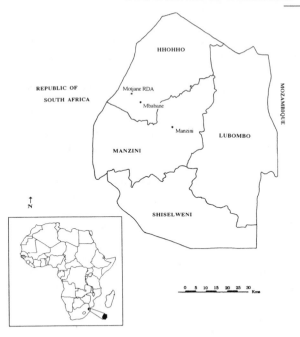

Map 10.1 Swaziland

time in Swazi print media,[1] I designed a survey-interview on ethnicity and gender. To get at underlying assumptions about ethnicity and differences in gendered identity according to ethnicity, I asked both men and women to consider the various racial/ethnic groups present in Swaziland and suggest occupations in which men and women in each of these groups might be found. Summarizing the results of eighty-eight in depth interviews, the consensus was that black Swazi men could undertake work in a wide variety of areas including farming, the civil service, business and industry, law and law enforcement. Black Swazi women were assigned most often to teaching, household and farm work, handwork and office work. Both men and women in the ethnic/racial black Swazi group had a wide range of options regardless of the ethnic group of the interviewee. By contrast,

1. White women appearing in Swazi newspapers and magazines tend to be non-local anonymous models or world- famous women such as Princess Diana and Demi Moore. While this, along with the fact that photos of foreign royalty like Princess Diana clad in bathing suits were preferred, is interesting, it is more appropriately the subject of a different paper.

colored men were generally associated with auto mechanic work and colored women with modeling, tailoring, clothing design and retail clothing sales – in other words, with fashion work.

In this nearly homogenous setting, colored women occupied a special niche in the public consciousness. They were associated with female self-presentation, beauty and glamour. In actuality, I found colored women in a variety of mainly urban occupations, including the fashion industry but also business office work, banking, legal work and non-clothing retail sales work. However, the public association of this group of women with the glamour and fashion sector was made clear in the person of Miss Swaziland 1991, a colored woman named Jackie Bennett (see Figure 10.1).

Dual Systems of Gender

The concept of dual systems in Swaziland has a considerable historical background. Even summarizing this background here would take too much space so I will offer one illustrative example in the hopes that a verbal picture might be worth several thousand words of explanation. This example concerns systems of marriage which evolved out of Swazi experience during the colonial and missionary period. Marriage in Swaziland in 1991 could be contracted according to two parallel but basically independent systems (Nhlapo 1987). A system here refers to a complex of institutions, cultural structures and assumptions. The first system was civil marriage which was a codified legal contract much like marriage in the USA. The couple decided in advance whether or not to be married in or out of community of property. No other marriages were permitted for either partner during the tenure of the present marriage, and inheritance rules as well as the responsibility for any children of a civil marriage were governed by the codified law and formal court structures.

The other system was referred to as customary marriage. A customary marriage was contracted through a series of ceremonies which formed an unwritten contract between families. The husband was permitted other wives and the rights of the wife over her children, inheritance and control of property were severely restricted. Disputes were handled by the families, who could appeal to the area chief for a ruling if necessary. There was no barrier to a couple contracting both forms of marriage, but the gray area between the two systems could be used, particularly by men, to manipulate women who were bound by both contracts. For example, a wife's property could be usurped by a husband even if they were married out of community of property if she had also contracted a customary marriage.

Focusing on the relationship between men and women in my interviews, I encouraged the people I spoke with to take into account the fact that information about gender is encoded in other systems and institutions. When asked to talk about women's roles in relation to men's, interviewees characterized the appropriate position for women as supportive to men or as strikingly independent of men. In the former case, respondents included references to women's legal minority status in many issues, their responsibilities for raising children who officially belonged to the families of the children's fathers, and the generally supportive rather than primary nature of many tasks. These included food production, washing and ironing, homemaking, and assisting their mothers-in-law. In the latter case, they talked of women's complete responsibility for the care, education, clothing and feeding of their offspring; the separation of men's and women's cash incomes within the household was also cited. Women in Swaziland often did not know, and felt they had no official claim to, the income of their husbands; money was contributed to the household when the earner felt it was appropriate, and in this matter men and women were felt to have different levels of obligation.

At the risk of oversimplification, two ideational systems of gender relations emerged as dominant in the Swazi gaze. In one, women were supportive/dependent members of family fabric, most appropriately woven into the traditional family settings supporting elders, men and children as cooperative participants. In the other, women were seen as independent actors obliged to draw on many resources in order to function properly as workers and mothers in the face of some resistance from men. While these distinctions can be framed across traditional versus modern and rural versus urban lines, it is important to recognize that there is not a perfect fit between these sets of concepts. There were forces in Swaziland's "modern" sector (certain missionary churches, the "suburban housewife" image transmitted across the airwaves) which encouraged the image of women as dependents. Similarly, aspects of traditional life in 1991 supported the image of the strong and independent woman. Rural areas were largely populated by women, and women did the majority of the subsistence farming which supported rural households. In the polygamous or extended family homestead, a woman was expected to take primary responsibility for the daily care, feeding and support of her children.

The husband might have multiple households among which he divides his obligation or he might be absent altogether while working for wages "in town." It is vital to recognize that the two gender systems were both part of most black Swazi women's experiences. This duality allows for a space – a gray area – within which identity could be negotiated. In this gray area between these two gender systems lay the issues of personal appearance and the politics of beauty, the politics of public and self representation.

Identity and Image

Representations of women in public culture in terms of beauty and fashion heavily influenced the personal process of negotiating these dual gender systems. Here are a few essential examples of images raised in the print media:

• The independent woman is represented by a nineteen-year-old black woman from the Picture Profile page of The Times of Swaziland Sunday (September 8, 1991). The caption says she "calls herself a scholar. She likes movies, reading novels and playing squash." She is dressed in a mini-skirt, short jacket and sunglasses.
• Mini-skirts were generally considered daring but more controversial still was the wearing of trousers by women. In The Times of Swaziland Sunday (February 3, 1991), the picture captioned "What's the big fuss about pants?" depicts two slender young black women approximately 15 years old in neat and stylish trousers and blouses.
• The press did not exclusively focus on the independent woman. A traditionally clad couple celebrate their marriage in a photo in The Times of Swaziland (November 6, 1991). The focus of the picture is the woman's hairstyle, dress and finery.
• A large group of teenagers in /emahiya/ (traditional dress) inspect each others hair and dress while milling in a courtyard before Reed Dance. They are overseen by an officious male elder in a The Times of Swaziland photo (August 29, 1991).

How were issues of gender identity negotiated around or through these images, and how was ethnicity implicated or used in these negotiations? "Consider the case of Miss Swaziland 1991 (see Figure 10.1). Jackie Bennett does not have a typical Black Swazi surname; Jackie is colored." Photo spreads like this one in both Swazi papers over several days showed Miss Bennett wearing the latest in slightly

Figure 10.1 "Here she is . . .." Miss Swaziland, Jackie Bennett. (*The Times of Swaziland Sunday*, October 20, 1991.)

shocking fashion. As assumed representatives of fashion but not of traditional Swazi status, colored women were felt to be freer to experiment in terms of self-presentation, at least in the opinions of the Swazis I interviewed. The black Swazi women who adopted or experimented with these fashions and looks adopted some of that freedom but as a member of an ethnic group different from the possessor of these fashions, they were also able to remove them and move closer to the image of the supportive/dependent woman. There was pressure not to completely adopt the image encouraged in these photos. A black Swazi friend of mine chastised another woman publicly for wearing legging-like trousers under her skirts too soon after the death of her own mother.

Beauty and fashion trends attributed to colored women were adopted, regulated and re-defined by women and men in mainstream Swazi culture in order to transmit a variety of different messages. In Figure 10.2, the editor of the Woman to Woman page of the Swazi Observer appears to be expressing a major contradiction in the public image of women by placing these images of fashion in ethnically exotic visage beside an article and pictures addressing the serious-minded, powerful black Swazi woman. But these images are compatible, and they are intended for the same audience of black Swazis who negotiate the gender systems and favor the independent woman image.

Figure 10.3 provides an example of the ways that modern fashion images associated generally with the colored woman can be re-defined in the black woman's repertoire and used to transmit the predominate Swazi message of harmony between progress and the past. The advertisers here have deliberately juxtaposed two images of women according to stereotypes of traditional and modern. The images of women recreate the same dichotomous interaction of concepts implied in the name Royal Swazi Airlines – tradition and modernity apparently peacefully juxtaposed and linked.

This message is revealed again in the two photos published in *Dzadze* magazine shown in Figure 10.4. The Emakhosikati, their royal majesties the wives of the King of Swaziland, offer a toast at the King's birthday party and, in the lower photograph, participate as leading figures in one of the most important traditional ceremonies of the Swazi calendar, the Reed Dance. The Emakhosikati embody these negotiable images with dignity and grace. In both guises they represent the national goal of harmony between conflicting forces of change and the existing structures of power.

Figure 10.2 Contradiction? ("Woman to Woman," *The Swazi Observer*, March 2, 1991.)

Figure 10.3 Advertisement for Royal Swazi Airways highlighting two images of young women in Swaziland. (*The Times of Swaziland*, April 10, 1991.)

Emakhosikati

Figure 10.4 Their Royal Majesties, three of King Mswati's wives offer a toast to the King in "modern," "western" fashion and lead the procession at the annual Reed Dance, a "traditional" ceremony celebrating Swaziland's young women. (Dzadze (Sister), *The Swazi Mirror*, May 1991).

Conclusions

Laurel Rose (1992) suggests that ideologies of harmony are guiding principles in social, economic and political relations in Swaziland. My final point is that in the negotiation of gender identities within the structure of dual gender systems I have set forth, ethnicity serves a pivotal role in maintaining harmony. Colored ethnicity becomes a device by means of which other issues such as gender are negotiated between mainstream black Swazi men and women. Women in this ethnic mini-minority of colored Swazis are transformed through the politics of harmony into something to which one can ascribe undesirable concerns (such as immorality or excessively rapid change in response to trans-national pressures), and through which one can experiment with potentially desirable concerns (like increasing employment opportunities for women and revealing or daring dress and make-up trends) without committing oneself. In other words, in this country where ethnic differences are in reality very small, an extremely small ethnic group of women have become a metaphor or symbol by means of which a larger group maintains harmony while negotiating change.

References

Behrman, C. unpublished.

Dzadze, The Swazi Mirror, May 1991.

Government of Swaziland (1988), *Annual Statistical Bulletin*, Mbabane: Central Statistical Office.

hooks, b. (1992), "Representing Whiteness in the Black Imagination," in *Cultural Studies*, (eds) Grossberg, Nelson and Treichler. London: Routledge.

Nhlapo, T. (1987), "No Cause for Optimism: Bigamy and Dual Marriage in Swaziland," in *Women and Law in Southern Africa*, (eds) Armstrong and Ncube, Harare: Zimbabwe Publishing House.

Rose, L. (1992), *The Politics of Harmony: Land Dispute Strategies in Swaziland*, African Studies Series 69, New York: Cambridge University Press.

The Times of Swaziland (1991), August 29.

The Times of Swaziland (1991), November 6.

The Times of Swaziland Sunday (1991), October 20.

The Times of Swaziland Sunday (1991), September 8.

The Swazi Observer (1991), March 2.

11

The West African Origin of the African–American Headwrap

Helen Bradley Griebel

Over the centuries, Americans of African descent have been called by a number of names, including derisive epithets. More generally, and until quite recently, they were called "Negroes" or "colored people."[1] Now, in the last years of the twentieth century, they call themselves "blacks," "people of color," or "African-Americans." Concerning the latter term, a question is raised about this communal appellation: what remains "African" about African-Americans? To help answer this question, I examine a single object of African-American material culture: the headwrap.

The headwrap is a piece of cloth wound around the head, usually completely covering the hair and held in place either by tucking the ends of the fabric into the wrap or by tying the ends into a knot close to the skull. This distinct head covering has been called variously "head rag," "head-tie," "headkerchief," "turban," or "headwrap;" I use latter term here. The headwrap is an article of dress almost exclusive to women of African descent.

Since the 1970s, African-Americans have been claiming that they wear the headwrap because they are descendents of West Africans. They contend that the headwrap is an authentic West African object, and is thus theirs by right of ancestry. African-Americans are correct in claiming any West African object as part of their heritage; but are

---

1. Here I refer specifically to people of African ancestry from the United States of America and not to people of African descent from other regions of the American continents. Throughout this text, references to African-American will mean a citizen of the United States.

they correct in claiming that the headwrap is particularly West African? In another essay, I focus on the culturally specific way in which women of African descent wear the headwrap, and I establish the practical and symbolic functions of the headwrap in the United States (Griebel 1995). In this chapter, I will document the headwrap's origins. My purpose is two-fold: to offer proof of a West African origin for the headwrap, and, by establishing the rise in popularity of the headwrap among West African women during the seventeenth century, to demonstrate a connection between the West African tradition of wearing this particular head covering and its continued use by African-Americans. In essence, we are examining an item of dress worn by large numbers of West African and African-American women in order to determine the cultural links between the two groups. These links include the material form of the item, but extend as well to less overtly recognizable cultural characteristics.

I will begin the discussion with a review of scholarly arguments concerning the retention or loss of West African material culture in the Americas, and then summarize statements by others who assert that the headwrap is an African item, but who offer no proof. Next, I will review several hypotheses that suggest the headwrap was introduced into West Africa by outsiders. Finally, because no one to date has provided a systematic study that gives evidence for the headwrap's origins, I will focus on that task, concluding with reflections on the headwrap's meaning since its public re-emergence in the 1970s during the black civil rights movement.

Surviving Beyond the Middle Passage

The study of African-American culture has been marked with controversy concerning what elements of West African culture survived for the peoples who were removed from their homeland and brought to a new continent where they found themselves in a position of bondage to people of alien cultures. All cultural groups constantly undergo change; certainly, much of the West Africans' material world changed in the Americas, just as the material culture of their emigrant European counterparts changed. Each group's material culture altered as it borrowed and adopted from the other, and as each group made adaptations to the new social and economic circumstances and to the new physical environment. The debate about African material survivals in the Americas, therefore, does not rest so much on

Figure 11.1 African–American woman in headwrap, (drawn by Rebecca Bailey© from a field photograph by Helen Bradley Griebel, 1994).

"change" itself, but rather on the *degree* to which the material culture changed.

Numerous scholars argue that, because of the conditions of enslavement, the West Africans who were brought to the United States lost all vestiges of their material culture, and that it was completely replaced by European forms. For example, Porter wrote: "the slaves lost many of their tribal habits and customs, along with their technics, through a process which anthropology terms *acculturation*" (Porter 1943: 4). Porter based his argument on the theory proposed by Herskovits that, among other losses incurred by Africans in the Americas, "African forms of technology . . . had but a relatively slight chance of survival" (Herskovits 1941: 136). These scholars argued that the social features of enslavement such as lack of personal time curtailed traditional crafting forms, and that the new environment meant crafting had to be carried out with tools and materials different from those formerly used in West Africa. According to this reasoning, West African objects gave way to the objects of the more powerful European community. This was particularly true in the United States where whites were in the majority, unlike the situation throughout the West Indies, and certain areas of Central and South America where Africans were the majority. For blacks in the United States, all of these conditions resulted in new forms of objects not traditional to West Africa.

Nevertheless, Herskovits (1941), followed by others, deduced that although Africans in the United States were deprived from replicating most objects in African forms, they did retain deeply ingrained, often subconscious, patterns of thinking. Herskovits called these cultural outlooks "unconscious mental retentions" or "Africanisms." These terms mean culturally learned ways of doing, seeing, feeling, and perceiving in the world about us, which affect even the way we make and use material objects. The term "world view" encapsulates this definition.

World view can survive even under constant pressure to change, and even while people live in the midst of a more formidable social group. Adverse situations, however, usually do result in radical changes in the outward appearance of material objects. Using this concept, several scholars suggest that the crafts made and used by African-Americans relate to older African forms only in so far as they signify more deeply embedded aspects of African world view. That is, although the forms changed, the underlying functions and meanings of the objects did not; or, as Mintz and Price (firm believers in the tenacity of cultural world view) put it, "overall, direct formal continuities from Africa are more the exception than the rule in any African-American culture" (1992: 60).

Yet another group of scholars maintains that not only do African-Americans retain an underlying West African world view which perpetuates the fashioning and utilization of certain objects, but that they retain as well specific West African formal qualities in such objects. Thompson (1984), for instance, finds a continuation of West African designs in African-American textiles and in the formal layout of certain southern black cemeteries; he cites other scholars who locate objects among blacks in major U.S. urban communities (such as New Orleans, Chicago, Harlem, and Atlanta) which replicate in material form vestiges of West African cosmological belief (p. 131). Vlach (1990) directs attention to West African formal and technical continuities in a variety of African-American crafts and decorative arts, including architectural features, quilting patterns, and basketry methods.

Of the various categories of material objects examined by scholars, little attention has been paid to African-American dress and its relation to West African garments except in a cursory manner. Herskovits mentions clothing only as one of the fundamental objects supplied to "the slaves by their masters," dismissing the possibility that any item of West African dress might have survived because:

> ... it is natural that these should have been what was most convenient to procure, least expensive to provide, and, other things being equal, most like the types to which the slave owners were accustomed. Thus African draped clothes were replaced by tailored clothing .... (1941: 136–7)

Even so, one object of West African dress did survive, never falling victim to the vagaries of fashion over the centuries. Similar to some of the objects identified by Thompson and Vlach, the headwrap may be traced back to West Africa both in its style and in the underlying African world view which encodes that style. The headwrap is West African both in form and in the meanings and functions it embodies.

Scholarly Assumptions about an Item of Dress

When examining the headwrap, many scholars avoid theoretical discussions on survival, revival, retention, acculturation, and loss; instead, they simply assume that the headwrap began in West Africa and was brought to the Americas by enslaved Africans. In so doing, these scholars make casual allusions to African origins for the headwrap, but without giving any corroborating evidence. For example, in 1973 Brathwaite observes: "I have seen girls in the markets of Port-au-Prince who are Yoruba or Dahomean market girls, except for the lack of tribal marks. The headties persist, some of the hairstyles persist . . ." (1973, quoted in Mintz and Price 1992: 101). Or, Genovese (1974) writes:

> A curious historical irony surrounds the use of headkerchiefs or bandannas. Carried into the twentieth century in the rural South, it became a mark of servility . . . of everything to be exorcised, so far as militant blacks were concerned . . .. Yet originally, nothing so clearly signified African origins and personal pride. The whites transformed it into a badge of servility (p. 558). The custom of wearing those headkerchiefs originated in Africa and appeared most strongly in those areas of the New World in which African values retained their greatest strength. (p. 559)

Likewise, Miller and Smith state:

> Slave women wore kerchiefs as standard head coverings throughout the year. Headkerchiefs appear wherever black women were held in bondage throughout North and South America, the brightly colored material covering women's hair revealing culture ties to West African tradition. (1987: 119)

McCarthy notes, "Black women favored a turban or bandana. In New Orleans this took the form of a *tignon*, an elaborately folded madras square worn around the head, reminiscent of African women's head coverings" (1989: 466). And Mercer mentions "head-wraps" as "elements of 'traditional' African dress" (1987: 39). However, in none of these instances have hypotheses on the exact place and time of origin of the headwrap on the ancestral continent, and the reasons for its use there, entered the scholarship.

Unsupported Hypotheses

Before pursuing the West African evidence for the origin of the headwrap, we need first to summarize and dismiss several hypotheses which suggest that outsiders were responsible for introducing the headwrap to West Africa.

As did their ancestors, modern West African women today wear a variety of head gear; but just when, where, and why headwraps became commonplace remains unknown. Arabic sources, which might contain evidence of the headwrap before the coming of the Europeans, remain largely untranslated. These presumably valuable Arabic archives await research and translation by specialists. Meanwhile, we have a paucity of early literary or visual sources concerning West Africa before the time of European contact. This reality does not allow much supposition as to the headwrap's origins; several theories have been proposed which suggest that the headwrap was introduced into West Africa by Arabs or, more usually, by Europeans, but these have little historical backing.

An Arabic influence is possible, but if this is so it must derive from the male turban. In the late eighteenth century, Mungo Park, who kept an account of his travels inland from the Gambia River, explained the difference between the dress of Moorish men and that of non-Islamic African men: "The men's dress among the Moors [i.e., black Moslems] of Ludamar differs but little from that of the Negroes . . . except that they all adopted that characteristic of the Mahomedan sect the *turban* . . ." (Miller 1954: 117).

Perhaps the African woman's headwrap does derive from the male Islamic turban; however, since Islam is not the only West African religion, all African women who wear headwraps today do not do so as part of Islamic belief. Furthermore, as described by Park, female Moors adopted the veil, not the turban, as part of their religious faith:

> The head-dress is commonly a bandage of cotton cloth, with some parts of it broader than others, which serve to conceal the face when they walk in the sun; frequently, however, when they go abroad, they veil themselves from head to foot. (Miller 1954: 117)

Concerning Moslem dress, Sieber believes that "Quite possibly this type of dress appeared along the west coast [of Africa] as a costume of prestige rather recently" (1972: 29). Sieber bases his reasoning on accounts by eighteenth- and nineteenth-century European travelers, who reported seeing black males who wore Moslem attire as being primarily inlanders, not dwellers on the coast.

I also question authorities who, by stating that the headwrap originated in Africa, thereby imply that it was commonly worn at very early dates by enslaved West Africans in the Americas. Rather, all evidence which I have uncovered to date points to the headwrap not becoming widely popular in either West Africa or in the Americas until the eighteenth century, that is, not until sometime after European contact.

Several hypotheses may be made for Europeans introducing the headwrap in West Africa. First, the women taken in bondage during the slave trade may have been forced or induced to cover their heads as a gesture to mark them as subservient. We know that headwraps served such a purpose in the southern United States, where legal codes actually enforced these measures.[2] Second, it is possible that enslaved African women were forced to wear headwraps as a way to prevent infestations of lice in the inadequate African slave-holding pens, and later in ships' holds during the trans-Atlantic voyage. We know that sometimes the Africans' heads were shaven, presumably for the same reason. Later, in the quarters of enslaved people in the Americas where bathing facilities were virtually non-existent, headwraps no doubt continued to aid in combating the ever-present lice.

John Thornton offers two additional arguments for the European introduction. He advances the unlikely interpretation that European missionaries initiated the headwrap in West Africa to meet the Christian requirement that the female head be covered during mass (1992: 233). However, having women cover their heads is a Moslem practice as well. Thornton also proposes that the headwrap appears as "a result of the racially mixed new population of the coast and islands, because the hair form was looser and straighter and thus did not hold plaits as well" (p. 223), but West African women's hairstyles and ornamentation were never limited to just plaiting. In addition, Thornton's supposition does not explain why so many women who are not of mixed ancestry also have worn the headwrap.

The preceding theories on the origins of the headwrap each point to Arabs or Europeans imposing this type of cloth hair covering on West African women. Such assertions, however, are often presented in ahistorical and timeless contexts. They remain presumptive at best and ethnocentric at worst. The issue, then, is to chart more carefully the rise in usage of the headwrap.

Contrary to general opinion, I believe that the headwrap did not come to Africa as a foreign introduction. Rather, it is an indigenous African article of dress, which makes its first appearance on the West African coast (perhaps at the very staging centers where human beings were traded for cloth), and spreads from there to other African communities throughout the continent and overseas. An examination

---

2. See Griebel (1995 in Roach-Higgins et al.), "The African American Woman's Headwrap: Unwinding the Symbols" for a discussion of these codes, especially as they refer to women's head coverings.

Figure 11.2 Nanny holding child, 1848 (drawn by Rebecca Bailey©
from photograph in the J. Napoleon Collection, *Newsweek*©, 20
February, 1995).

of historical, eyewitness accounts and an analysis of cultural characteristics suggest that the headwrap began as a syncretic element of West African women's dress, a combination of West African aesthetics and world view with European material goods. In this case, the world view points to a pronounced aesthetic of the human head.

An Aesthetic of the Head: Material Form and World View

A demonstrably important aspect of any social group's material culture is its dress. One of the outstanding features of the West African headwrap, brought to the Americas and worn by millions of enslaved black women and their descendents, is that it has survived with only slight variations in its basic form for at least 350 years in both the ancestral lands and in the adopted American lands. In light of all that is known about racial slavery and its affects on those in bondage and their descendents, it must be asked how this object could have endured. Perhaps the answer lies in the significant fact that the headwrap survives not only in its material form, but also as a distinct marker of African world view.

As mentioned, although specific forms of material objects change, more deeply ingrained, culturally learned attitudes about manipulating oneself in this world are less susceptible to modification. Several characteristically West African attitudes bound, and continue to bind, West African people to African-American people. The most obvious and most often mentioned collective cultural characteristic is musical style. But West Africans and African-Americans also exhibit less overt manifestations of shared world view; for instance, scholars have long noted that each cultural group holds a pronounced belief in the power of ancestors over the lives of the living.[3] In addition, many scholars agree that, in each group, improvisation and call-and-response are decided criteria for judging successful performative presentations and individual style (Davis 1987: 16ff; Allen 1991: 85ff)

West Africans and African-Americans also share another seemingly indestructible cultural attitude: a concern for the importance of the human head. The retention of the headwrap is a concrete example of how those who were brought from West Africa to the Americas held

---

3. Sterling Stuckey writes: "Respect for age is the basis of much Black African culture and the principle inspiration for its art . . .. (1987: 333) The core of African culture . . . is based on respect for the ancestors and elders . . ." (p. 334).

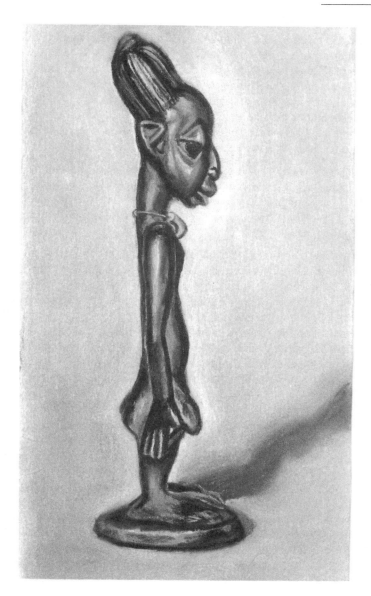

Figure 11.3 Yoruba Ibeji figure showing 1:4 head to body proportion (drawn by Rebecca Bailey© from an artifact in the North Carolina Museum of Art).

onto this cultural ideal. More unusual, perhaps, is the fact that down through the centuries African-Americans have continued to replicate its specific form.

Figural sculpture demonstrates that black African cultures have long had a heightened regard for embellishing the head. Although tropical African works of art are as diverse as the many social groups which populate the region, they are united by the dominance of the human head in figurative representations. Willett notes that in much West African figural sculpture:

> the head was greatly exaggerated in size in relation to the rest of the body, equalling about a quarter of the estimated over-all height of the figure. In the Greek and European tradition, the head would occupy only one-seventh or less of the overall height. (1958: 357; also see Willett 1993: 161–4)

This distinctive feature of tropical art is temporal as well as spatial. From the massive terra-cotta Nok (Nigeria) heads, dating from circa. 500 B.C. to 200 A.D., to more modern works, black African craftsmanship shows the human head to be the bodily part most obviously given paramount importance.

Regard for the head is manifested as well by early travelers' descriptions of the West Africans' penchant for ornamenting it. In the earliest period of contact, however, woven cloth was still a scarce item for all but the most wealthy and powerful. Therefore, instead of using cloth, most West Africans decorated their heads by a variety of alternative means such as elaborate hairstyles embellished with flowers, beads, shells, metal and feathers, by shaving the hair close to the scalp in ornamental patterns, or by applying clay to the hair and sculpting it into various shapes. The influx of available and inexpensive cloth, imported by the Europeans, permitted a natural adoption of cloth to meet these aesthetic needs and personal choices. In addition, by the last half of the eighteenth century, ready-made foreign headwraps were being imported into West Africa, apparently because of a demand for them. For example, "kerchiefs" are listed as a trade item to Benin in European merchant ship inventories: a "Cholet kerchief" and a "Nîmes silk kerchief" are listed in the cargo of a French vessel in the early 1770s; a Portuguese ship's document of the same period lists "4 kerchiefs" (Ryder 1969: 208, 210). It appears, therefore, that by the eighteenth century West Africans considered the headwrap a popular item of attire. But just how widely West Africans used it before that time remains unverified.

The Origin

To date, after reading several hundred accounts, I have located only one reference which offers certain proof that some West African women were wearing headwraps by the mid-seventeenth century. This evidence appears in Richard Ligon's account, published in 1657. Ligon set out from England to seek his fortune in the West Indies in the 1640s. On his way, he stopped at Cape Verde on the coast of present-day Senegal before proceeding to Barbados (Abrahams and Szwed 1983: 420). While at Cape Verde in 1647, Ligon describes in detail the clothing of one particular woman whom, he says, "wore on her head a roll of green taffatie, strip't with white and Philiamont, made up in manner of a Turban, and over that a sleight vayle, which she took off at pleasure" (Ligon 1657: 12).

The earliest European pictorial representations of West Africans show men wearing a variety of head coverings, including turbans. In contrast to male customs, and to Ligon's written report of a female headwrap, visual artists usually portrayed women without hats and with their hair close-cropped and unadorned. Written accounts, however, describe women from various West African regions as wearing a variety of hair-dos and hair decorations. Ligon gives one such account after he first categorizes the people of "high Africa; as of Morocco, Guinny, Binny, Cutchow, Angola, Aethiopia, and Mauritania, or those that dwell near the River of Gambia." He next gives a description of women's hairstyles from these places by comparing them to the hairstyles of women he saw at Cape Verde. Of the Cape Verde women, Ligon writes:

> Their haire not shorne as the Negroes in the places I have named, close to their heads; nor in quarters, and masses, as they use to weave it, which is ridiculous to all that see them, but themselves; But in a due proportion of length so as having their shortenings by the natural curles, they appeares as wiers [wires?], and artificiall dressings to their faces. On the sides of their Cheeks, they plat little of it, of purpose to tie small Ribbon; or some small beads, of white Amber, or blew bugle, sometimes the rare flowers that grow there . . .. (1657: 16)

Mungo Park, quoted earlier, made two trips inland from the Gambia River in 1795–1779 and 1805–1806. Park's comments about the West African people whom he encountered demonstrate that he was a traveler imbued with a highly developed curiosity. His account is unusually objective for the time, meaning that his perceptions about newly encountered people were not tinted with a Eurocentric bias. Park summed up the attire of a variety of people he met on his journeys in West Africa. He found clothing itself to be rather uniform throughout the region: "This account of their clothing is indeed nearly applicable to the natives of all the different nations in this part of Africa;" but significantly, Park added, "a peculiar national mode is observable only in the head-dresses of the women" (Miller 1954: 15).

Park's notes on women's head ornamentation are specific. His observations illustrate the obvious care with which women adorned their heads, and they point up the noteworthy fact that no single type of hair ornamentation was standard. Park's comments make it apparent that among West Africans, as among many other social groups, one of the ways by which people marked themselves was by styling their hair or wearing head decorations in a manner unique to their particular community.

> Thus, in countries of the Gambia [on the West African coast, between the Senegal and Gambia Rivers] the females wear a sort of bandage, which they call *falla*. It is a narrow strip of cotton cloth, wrapped many times round, immediately over the forehead. In Bondou the head is encircled with strings of white beads, and a small plate of gold is worn in the middle of the forehead. In Kasson, the ladies decorate their heads in a very tasteful manner, with white sea-shells. In Kaarta and Ludamar, the women raise their hair to a great height by the addition of a pad (as ladies did formerly in Great Britain), which they decorate with a species of coral, brought from the Red Sea by pilgrims returning from Mecca, and sold at a great price. (Miller 1954: 15)

I found no references to West African headwraps for the half-century following Ligon's account from Cape Verde; but by the eighteenth century, evidence for women wearing headwraps comes from a variety of sources and from several geographical locations. Mungo Parks's mention of the *falla* worn by Gambian women in the 1790s – "A narrow strip of cotton cloth, wrapped many times round, immediately over the forehead" – must be another example of the West African headwrap. Nearly a hundred years earlier, West African women already had brought the custom across the Atlantic to the Caribbean. This is documented in a painting by Danish artist Dirk Valkenburg in 1707, which shows a group of newly arrived enslaved Africans on the Dómbi Plantation in Suriname. Each of the females wears a headwrap high on the forehead and above the ears.[4]

While Valkenburg's painting seems to support the general assumption that the headwrap made its way to the United States via the West Indies, an advertisement in the *Charleston South-Carolina Gazette and Country Journal* (25 April, 1769) demonstrates that West African women also brought the custom of wearing headwraps directly from Africa to the colonies which later became the United States:

> RUN-AWAY from my Plantation at Goose-Greek a NEW-NEGRO WENCH, she had on when she went away a new oznaburg coat and wrapper, and a black striped silk handkerchief round her head . . . she is a middle sized wench, about 24 years of age, of the Guiney country, has her country marks on her face, and speaks no English . . . .. (Windley 1983: 644)

Comparative verification for this item of dress among blacks in the United States during the late eighteenth century comes in pictorial form. For example, Samuel Jennings, in his allegorical painting of 1792, *Liberty Displaying the Arts and Sciences*, portrays several African-American women, all but one of whom wear a headwrap. Another work, painted by an unidentified artist, illustrates enslaved people dancing on an unknown plantation, probably in South Carolina, about 1800.[5] In the painting, now titled *The Old Plantation*, one man wears a hat and the other African-Americans, of both sexes, are either bareheaded or wear headwraps. A wealth of documentation is available throughout the nineteenth and twentieth centuries as numerous writers and visual artists depict African-American women wearing headwraps.

I hypothesize, therefore, that the West African woman's headwrap comes into being sometime after the start of the European trade expansion in Africa. In exchange for European goods, often in the form of cloth, the West Africans traded human beings whose destiny was enslavement in the Americas. In the ensuing years, the exact forms of most West African material goods changed in the American social environments due to the circumstances of enslavement and because certain objects, particularly items of dress, usually are modified or abandoned as social groups come in contact with one another. But

4. The painting illustrates the cover of Richard Price's *First-Time* (1983), Baltimore: Johns Hopkins University Press, and is owned by the Royal Museum of Fine Arts, Copenhagen. My thanks to Dr. Robert Farris Thompson who pointed out to me the date of the painting.

5. The painting is in the collection of the Abby Aldrich Rockefeller Folk Art Center, Williamsburg, Virginia.

even as many other objects of West African material culture were changed or completely lost, the headwrap survived.

By the late eighteenth century, the headwrap was a nationally recognized characteristic feature of African-American women, marking their social and economic status as well as their ethnicity. The headwrap had become the consummate emblem of their positions in American society, perceived as such by those within the black communities and by those without, although often each group imbued its view with quite different qualifications.

Symbols of Africa

In the history of American dress, the African-American woman's headwrap possesses the lengthiest record of wear for any article of clothing donned by non-indigenous people. As an item of dress, the headwrap never went out of use although different groups of African-Americans might wear it for different reasons. The headwrap has been a ubiquitous form of head covering among black communities throughout South and Central America, in the Caribbean, and in the United States since at least the eighteenth century. It originated on the west coast of Africa, probably at the very beginning of a trade which compelled millions of Africans also to become Americans. In the United States, black women throughout the period of enslavement wore the headwrap – sometimes because they were forced to, sometimes because of personal choice. After the American Civil War and well into the twentieth century, many black women, particularly in the rural South, continued to wear it even in public. For urban and middle-class and northern black women, the headwrap usually became an item worn only in the home where it served as a "do rag" that protected a hair-do until it was time to show it off, or served as a convenient way to cover the head on a "bad hair day."[6]

6. Bebe Moore Campbell speaks of her grandmother wearing a "do rag" to protect her hair-do (1989: 155). Henry Louis Gates, Jr. says that men used do-rags to keep lye-processed hair straightened when they slept or played sports. He notes that the do-rag might be fashioned of a simple cloth or of an actual handkerchief (1994: 47).
    Anyone can have a "bad hair day," but Gates discusses the particular African-American concept of "bad" and "good" hair as he remembers it during his childhood in the 1950s: "'Good' hair was straight. 'Bad' hair was kinky" (p. 43). "Everybody I knew as a child wanted to have good hair. You could be ugly as homemade sin dipped in misery and still be thought attractive if you had good hair" (p. 44). Zora Neale Hurston appended a glossary to her 1942 essay, "Story in Harlem Slang," wherein she records no less than eleven different African-American folk terms for designating hair as either "good" or "bad" (pp. 94–6).

In presenting evidence for the West African origins of the headwrap, and connecting this to its phenomenal longevity in the United States, I have followed an old expression still commonly uttered by black Americans: "What goes around, comes around." Embedded in this folk saying is a particular notion of life and time as circular rather than linear as white westerners experience it. Americans of African descent perceive the inter-relatedness and interconnections of human behaviors and material objects as bounded by neither spatial nor temporal considerations. Directed by this Afrocentric approach, my attempt at establishing a place, a time, and a reason for the beginnings of the headwrap has been circular; it began with the period of enslavement,[7] moved backward in time to seventeenth- and eighteenth-century West Africa, and now moves forward to the last decades of the twentieth century in the United States.

During the modern black civil rights movement in the 1960s and 1970s, communities of African-Americans began assertively to define themselves in relation to their West African past. In that period, they rejected the terms "colored" and "Negro" and adopted the appellations "Afro-American" or "black." Some black Americans discarded their European personal names and gave themselves African names. Others converted from Christianity to Islam, a major West African religion before the coming of the Europeans. Meanwhile, black students demanded courses whose subjects were relevant to their historical and cultural experiences, paving the way for academic programs and departments in Afro-American (or, Black) Studies.[8] Not all blacks accepted all of these gestures, but everyone was aware that these moves were symbolically helping to shape a sense of self-empowerment for millions of disenfranchised Americans. And everyone realized that among that era's most potent symbols were those that ushered in an ongoing, collective, positive recognition of African-Americans' West African heritage. That is, it was a time for espousing symbols by which identities could be measured in terms of an ethnic beginning which was posited in Africa.[9]

7. Elsewhere, I demonstrate the various reasons why enslaved women wore the headwrap as well as the symbolic and practical functions it served during that period (1995 in Roach-Higgins et al.).

8. Huston Baker reviews the ferment during the formative years of these programs in *Black Studies, Rap, and the Academy* (1994: 1–32).

9. Henry Louis Gates, Jr. remembers: " . . .it was an exciting and sincere effort to forge a new communal identity among people descended from splendid ancient cultures, abducted and forced into servility, and now deprived of collective economic

Besides name changes, religious conversions, and demands for curricular restructuring, African-Americans utilized material objects as a means towards self and communal identification. Foremost among the outward, material emblems of renewed interest in ethnic ancestry were items of personal adornment. As is usually the case, young people often led the way in adopting these burgeoning fashion statements; by the mid–1960s, young men were donning kaftans in brightly colored, African-patterned textiles and wearing kofi hats, and both young men and young women were growing and arranging their hair into Afros.[10] By mid-twentieth century, older black women had abandoned the headwrap for public wear; in the 1970s, however, many young women consciously took up the headwrap as another potent sign of black empowerment. Daughters chose to wear in public what their mothers had so recently abandoned.

Through the 1970s and on into the 1990s, African-American men and women added and discarded an array of African-inspired clothes, jewelry, and hair-dos. Most items of dress adopted in the early years of rediscovering the West African past did not survive into the following decades. Looking back to that revolutionary period of the 1960s and 1970s, we can see that the kaftans did not last long as a daily fashion among the black American men involved in reclaiming their ties to West Africa, and within a decade African-American men and women had discarded the Afro and began braiding their hair or growing Rasta locks. Since then, younger generations have used other objects of personal adornment to carve out still other identities: athletic shoes, "X" T-shirts and baseball caps, and baggy trousers, to name a few.

In these many symbolic movements between perceived and real Africas and Americas, the headwrap alone persists. It is a tradition

---

and political power. We thought we had learned at last our unutterable, secret name, and that name was BLACK!" (1994: 186).

10. Several writers recently have reminisced about their politically active adolescences, and described how older relatives reacted with scathing humor to their youthful ideas about personal appearance. For example, Bebe Moore Campbell recalls wanting to graduate from college in her new Afro, whereupon her grandmother said the Afro made Campbell look like the "Queen of the electrified Zulus" (1989: 260). From the male point of view, Henry Louis Gates, Jr. offers his personal experiences about being the first black in his small West Virginia hometown to grow an Afro. He remembers that his father called the style "KKK hair:" "Knotty, Kinky, and Kan't-comby" (p. 186). Pertinent also is the entire chapter that Gates devotes to a discussion of African-American male and female hair "processing" during the 1950s (pp. 40–49), which was, of course, one of things the young blacks in the 1960s and 1970s were rebelling against.

which continues today in the last decade of the twentieth century, when black American women of all ages wear the headwrap for all manner of occasions. As such, the headwrap serves African-Americans as the fundamental symbol of self in relation to ethnic identity.

Conclusion

In the Americas, the woman's headwrap acquired meanings that it never possessed on the ancestral continent. Many of these meanings were conceived during the period of enslavement and its aftermath. When younger women in the 1970s re-adopted the headwrap, it acquired still other layers of meaning; for African-American women at the end of the twentieth century, the headwrap encodes two new significations, each symbolically denoting a form of ethnic identity particular to their social group. In winding a cloth about their own heads, modern Americans of African descent manifest in material form an identity, first with their enslaved forebears and, second with those who remained in West Africa. They valorize their American ancestors who wore these special forms of head coverings during their bondage; however, they also don and fashion the headwrap with the overt and specific claim that it is a traditional item of West African attire. The headwrap serves to memorialize those American ancestors who wore the cloth head covering as a mark of servitude to whites and as an emblem of social and economic privation; but modern black women imbue it with an additional symbol of ethnic identity, as a reclamation of their West African heritage. For black folks, the headwrap encodes in material form those dual souls that W.E.B. DuBois (1903) first identified: a soul forged in the crucible of racial slavery in America, and a far older African one.

References

Abrahams, R.D., and Szwed, J.F. (eds) (1983), *After Africa*, New Haven: Yale University Press.

Allen, R. (1991), *Singing in the Spirit: African-American Sacred Quartets in New York City*, Philadelphia: University of Pennsylvania Press.

Baker, H.A., Jr. (1994), *Black Studies, Rap, and the Academy*, Chicago: University of Chicago Press.

Brathwaite, E.K. (1973), "Cultural Diversity and Integration in the Caribbean," paper presented in 1973.

Campbell, B.M. (1989), *Sweet Summer*, New York: Ballantine.

Davis, G. (1987), *I Got the Word in Me and I can Sing It, You Know: A Study* in the *Performed African-American Sermon*, Philadelphia: University of Pennsylvania Press.

DuBois, W.E.B. (1903), *The Souls of Black Folks*, New York: Fawcett.

Gates, H.L., Jr. (1994), *Colored People*, New York: Alfred A. Knopf.

Genovese, E. (1974), *Roll, Jordan, Roll*, New York: Pantheon.

Griebel, H.B. (1995), "The African American Woman's Headwrap: Unwinding the Symbols," in M.E. Roach-Higgins, J.B. Eicher, and K.K.P. Johnson (eds), *Dress and Identity*, New York: Fairchild.

Herskovits, M.J. (1941), *The Myth of the Negro Past*, Boston: Beacon Press.

Hurston, Z.N. (1942), "Story in Harlem Slang," *American Mercury*, July, pp. 84–96.

Ligon, R. (1657), *A True and Exact History of the Island of Barbados . . .*, London.

McCarthy, B. (1989), "Clothing," in C.R. Wilson and W. Ferris (eds), *Encyclopedia of Southern Culture*, Chapel Hill: University of North Carolina Press.

Mercer, K. (1987), "Black Hair/Style Politics," *New Formations*, vol. 3, pp. 33–54.

Miller, R.M., and Smith, J.D. (eds), *Dictionary of Afro-American Slavery*, Westport, CN: Greenwood Press.

Miller, R. (ed.) (1954), *Travels of Park, Mungo*, London: J.M. Dent.

Mintz, S.W., and Price, R. (1992), *The Birth of African-American Culture: An Anthropological Perspective*, Boston: Beacon Press.

Porter, J.A. (1943), *Modern Negro Art*, Washington, D.C.: Howard University Press.

Roach-Higgins, M.E., Eicher, J.B., and Johnson, K.K.P. (eds) (1995), *Dress and Identity*, New York: Fairchild.

Ryder, A.F.C. (1969), *Benin and the Europeans 1485–1897*, New York: Humanities Press.

Sieber, R. (1972), *African Textiles and Decorative Arts*, New York: Museum of Modern Art.

Stuckey, S. (1987), *Slave Culture: Nationalist Theory and the Foundations of Black America*, New York: Oxford University Press.

Thompson, R.F. (1984), *Flash of the Spirit: African and Afro-American Art and Philosophy*, New York: Vintage Books.

Thornton, J.W. (1992), *Africa and Africans in the Making of the Atlantic World 1400–1680*, New York: Cambridge University Press.

Vlach, J.M. (1990), *The Afro-American Tradition in the Decorative Arts*, Athens GA: University of Georgia Press.

Willett, F. (1958), "Ife in Nigerian Art," reprinted in C.M. Otten (ed.), *Anthropology and Art: Readings in Cross-Cultural Aesthetics*, Austin: University of Texas Press.

—— (1993), *African Art*, New York: Thames and Hudson.

Windley, L.A. (1983), *Runaway Slave Advertisements: A Documentary History from the 1730s to 1790*, vol. 3, Westport, CN: Greenwood Press.

12

Traditional Palestinian Wedding Dress as a Symbol of Nationalism[1]

Yvonne J. Seng and Betty Wass

Village wedding dress from the beginning of the twentieth century has emerged as a symbol of Palestinian national consciousness and a source of national pride. Elevated from an agricultural context, it is worn proudly by city women and expatriates who, until recently, preferred western dress for all events. Revival in the use of village dress and the enactment of village wedding customs has taken on political meaning for many persons since the period of turmoil after the Arab-Israeli wars of 1967. Following the physical dispersal of the Palestinians from their homeland, dress and customs began to provide a link to the homeland. As such, garments, both those from the beginning of this century and their more modern adaptations, are cherished and accepted as traditional dress by contemporary Palestinian women. This traditional dress and the associated revival of the village wedding have come to serve as an expression of the zeal to maintain a national identity.

Two pre-mandate Palestinian wedding outfits from the regions of Bethlehem and Hebron originally led us to investigate the historical and contemporary cultural context of the ensembles. As background material, previous research on similar outfits was combined with interviews with ten Palestinian women who came from the regions

1. The initial research appears in Bishop, Y.S. (1982), "Two Middle Eastern Wedding Costumes as Vehicles of Traditional Culture," unpublished M.S. thesis, University of Wisconsin-Madison.

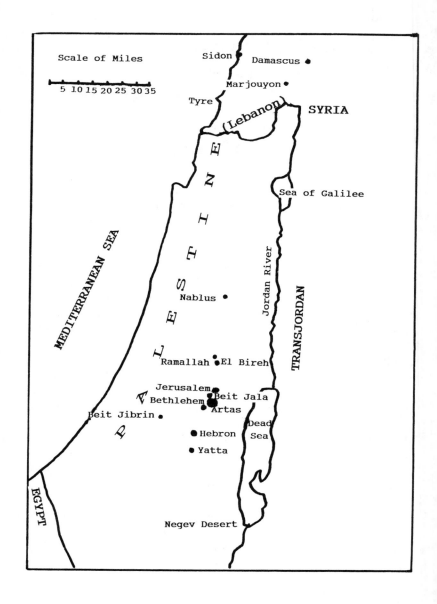

Map 12.1 Palestine. British Mandate (1920–1948).

where the dress originated but who now reside in the United States. They spoke about their perceptions of "traditional dress." In the conversations with these women, we found that the term "traditional" was laden with internal tension, for not only were hand-made, heavily embroidered garments from the beginning of the century considered as traditional, but so too were recently machine-made garments of modified shape and poorer workmanship. When this apparent discrepancy was addressed, the interviewees replied that both were considered traditional but that the older garments were considered to be *more* traditional, more evocative of a distant past. The latter part of the reply was often punctuated by a pause – what we might term a pause of association or evaluation – in which the properties which constituted tradition in these women's minds were formulated and weighed. This chapter addresses that evaluation in an effort to show the commonalities of tradition embodied in these garments, how the concept of tradition has changed, like the garments, over time, and how that change is linked to a search for national identity.

We shall look at what Shils (1981: 14) terms the "essential elements" or the components and characteristics of Palestinian wedding ensembles, historic and contemporary, which allow them to be described as "traditional" by Palestinian women. Since components of the garments are related to the wedding celebration, we will also look briefly at how parts of the garments have lost their form as the celebrations and ritual have changed or were forgotten. This is of particular importance when we consider that the original context of the garments is not known to many contemporary women, who are now turning to both the traditional gown and wedding as a reaffirmation of identity and community, and who are themselves adding new traditions to the historic pool. Finally, as the smallest element of the garments, we will underline the relation of the embroidery and the act of embroidery to the agricultural community from which it originated.

Tradition: Inherited or Invented?

The topic of tradition itself is currently undergoing reevaluation. In ethnographic research it has come to mean an item or action inherited intact from the past, "relatively invariant from generation to generation" (Dominguez 1986: 549). Collectors and exhibitors of traditional dress and other cultural artefacts have in general presented and reinforced this definition, which establishes a dichotomy between "traditional" and "modern" societies.[2] But, as indicated by the attitude of the informants towards the garments, the definition of what is traditional involves a selective process, for as long as an object contains certain determined elements it may still be considered as "traditional." Both process and definition are dynamic.

The adoption of a village dress as a symbol of the Palestinian homeland by women, many of whom were cosmopolitan and had never lived in an agricultural setting, epitomizes what Hobsbawm refers to as "invented tradition." In this framework, although focus is ultimately centered on the object, invented tradition also encompasses the ritual context in which the object evokes that sense of tradition. It "is taken to mean a set of practices, normally governed by overtly or tacitly accepted rules of a ritual or symbolic nature, which seek to inculcate certain values and norms of behavior by repetition, which automatically implies continuity with the past." (Hobsbawm and Ranger 1983: 1). This historical past need not be invented from a void, but may derive from a pool of objects, practices, and attitudes which are re-interpreted according to the perceptions of the group involved. Consequently, it may be adopted and re-interpreted by a sub-group or, conversely, it may originate within a defined community but take on more universal dimensions as the community undertakes a retrospective of itself.

Invention involves a point of recognition of the need to define oneself (as a community or individual) and the past (Hobsbawm and Ranger 1983: 6–7). This was particularly true with small dispossessed groups among whom feelings of rootlessness were replaced by those of nationalism.[3] Eisenstadt has emphasized that the "crystallization of symbols of collective identity, and the reconstruction of traditions" becomes more fully articulated during transitional periods, commonly marked by severe conflicts and struggles (p. 351). These transitional periods, in effect, often represent a rite of passage and may be broadly described in Turner's terms of "liminality" in which the initiate or ritualist is marginalized during a period of instruction undertaken both by practice and precept. Furthermore, Turner has posed that liminality occurs during transitional periods of history of the group as well as of the individual "when the past has lost its grip and the future has

---

2. See Baizerman (1990), pp. 233–40; Clifford (1988) pp. 215–52; Firth (1988).
3. See Trevor-Roper (1983). In this incisive chapter, he discusses the concept of a distinct Highland culture, including the adoption of the kilt and tartan patterns, as a retrospective invention.

not yet taken definite shape" (Turner 1980: 1). The ongoing experience of the Palestinians in relation to reclamation of land as a symbol of national identity may therefore be more adequately described as "liminoid," where "we take our crises and transitions into our own hands, ritualize them, make them meaningful, and pass through and beyond them in a spirit of celebration" (Turner 1982: 26). It is in this context that the village wedding both symbolizes the land and serves as a rite of passage on a microcosmic level.

Often, the perceived or invented tradition acquires validity through the act of being acted out; that is, through the participation of a focused group, it gains the stature of tradition which is further reinforced through later enactments. Research undertaken on the Quebecois conception of national identity would point to such consolidating re-enactments of tradition during the annual folklore festival, an event initiated at the turn of the century to consciously promote Quebecois cultural identity (Handler and Linnekin 1984: 276–82). Many of the traditions were "invented" at this time, and many objects which were described as traditional have been later shown to be spurious. A common characteristic of objects chosen to represent traditional national culture was that they were "natural." Their cultural value increased when a direct relationship could be established between the object and pre-industrial village life. The changing meaning or value that a group places on its past (or objects from its past) was further recognized by the city of Quebec in its restoration of the historic Place Royale: any changes had to be undertaken so as to accommodate any meaningful reinterpretation or re-evaluation by future generations of their understanding of their history of that area (pp. 280–1).

In a review by Dominguez (1986: 553) of an earlier work by Csikszentmihalyi and Rochberg-Halton (1981) of what possessions were considered by individuals to be "special", she states that rather than monetary value, "memories, associations, and experiences linking individuals to others and assisting them in their construction, development, and representation of the self" were the most dominant characteristics of the possessions. Again, these referential indices often arose from a sense of rootlessness and a search for community. In the case of the Palestinians, costume which evokes memories of land and land-based community ties have become the focus of tradition.

The Reclamation of Land and Identity

The association of the village wedding dress with the land is an immediate and potent symbol not confined to Palestine. In dispossessed communities in which land plays an important role, the often ideological content of tradition becomes most apparent when the group undertakes a self-conscious interpretation of its relationship to that land (Shils 1981: 195). Shils notes that views of the past may be "retrospectively reformed" and, by so doing, nationalist movements may unwittingly change the traditions they attempt to revive (p. 246). With the island communities of Hawaii, for example, a reclaiming of identity also took the political form of reclamation, if not physically then emotionally, of land which they had lost during the past century (Handler and Linnekin 1984: 282). Land and certain past rural traditions (language, crafts, and performance arts) became the focal symbols of Hawaiian relationships, and whereas the ritual meaning was selectively revived for some objects and places, for others meaning was acquired. Underlying this was an idealization of the past, of the agricultural community and lifestyle of which remnants remained but of which few people had any practical knowledge and to which fewer still realistically wanted to return.

For the Palestinian diaspora, however, land has become the central symbol in the national struggle between Jew and Arab in Palestine (Antran 1989: 73). For Arabs, this has meant a living history of imposed land settlement, fragmentation, and dispossession of land holdings, as well as social dislocation and disaffection. In Arabic, the term *watan*, meaning one's country or one's birthplace, also has the ideological overtones of "a land, a place, tangible and visible" (Lewis 1988: 41). For the agricultural workers, the *fellahin* who had lost their land and who now work in towns without having access to an urban lifestyle, commuting between village and town has led to a rootlessness in which land has become a powerful focus. Socially, today's *fellahin* are neither urban nor rural.

On a secondary level, the association with village wedding dress is that of community, of the idealized role of women, and of celebration. Not only the land itself, but also the sense of community associated with the land, the "self-reference, reference to others, the semi-conscious indexing of community, and the constant reminder of production, reproduction, and the generation of future possibilities" (Dominguez 1986: 554) place the village wedding gown as a "special" object. This association imbues the village wedding dress with tradition not only for a small group which directly identifies with the agricultural community, but also for a dispersed and diverse body which identifies with a larger community tied to the land.

Weddings themselves serve as a symbolic microcosm of the sociocultural order. They are a celebration of the future as well as the past, a celebration in which identity is reaffirmed, values re-instilled, and relationships cemented. They bring focus to bear on the family, the social and economic unit of Middle Eastern society, and subsequently upon women and their role within the family. Although the role of the wedding may be underlined as a socializing factor for the community as a whole, this is especially true for women. This phenomenon is not confined to the Middle East: referring to the rites of women in Romania, Kligman emphasized that the wedding "enacts social process in terms that are socially constituted and understood: a woman is alienated from her natal family and incorporated into the family of her husband" (Kligman 1984: 184). The critical focus of the ritual is therefore upon women, for the wedding signifies not only the reaffirmation of the identity of the community but also the redefinition of the woman who leaves the house of her family. This loss of household and birthplace is one with which many refugees and migrants can identify. Kligman further stressed the importance of oral tradition, especially in poetry at weddings, to inculcate women in their societal roles.

In Palestinian folk tales, the important relationship between oral tradition and weddings or marriage is also highly visible. In their anthology of tales recently collected from refugees living in the West Bank, Muhawi and Kanaana (1989) draw associations between women, oral tradition, and other avenues of creative and artistic energy. Women, they write, "observe the society and weave plots for the folk tales from the materials of daily experience" (p. 18). This, they claim, is partly due to their being omitted from formal kinship structure whereby they are left to define their own roles in society. "They do so through the tales, and in other forms of folklore that in Palestine are traditionally their domain: embroidery, basket weaving, pot making, and verbal arts like wedding songs and laments for the dead" (p. 19). These activities are usually those of women. Although men are not excluded, the telling of folk tales, for example, is usually performed by older women in a household setting, in a time and space set apart. The events and transformations are understood only by the use of imagination, not rational thought, which is the domain of menfolk (pp. 6–7).

As with the traditional folk tale, so too with traditional embroidery, narrative details, or "folk motifs" can fit into more than one plot context. Innovation of motifs was regulated by group consensus, and although a story could not stray far from the recognized plot outline, it was acceptable for different plot details to be "woven" into the same tale (p. 8). Variations of folk tales could be identified according to region. Many tales focus on family life, courtship, and weddings. The wedding, embroidery of the costumes, and folk tales are therefore part of a continuum of women's activities, a language *per se*. That these activities are considered to belong to the sphere of women is attested to by the language used in folk tales: the general form and the flourishes or embellishments are those derived from women's speech, even when the tales are told by men.

As a form of what Geertz (1983: 119) terms the "social history of the imagination," parallels may also be drawn between the embroidered Palestinian gowns and the "story cloths" of the Laotian Hmong artists living in Thai refugee camps. They are described by Peterson (1988: 6) as "key texts" that "enact concepts of historicity, cultural identification, intercultural communication, and collective action." The story cloths depict scenes, stories and activities from daily life, "a kind of encyclopedia of experience" (p. 13) which includes the recent loss of the homeland. Similar to the Palestinian embroideries, works of embroidered narrative have grown out of traditional textile cloths produced by women and used to identify an individual's clan, sub-group, and region. They differ from the Palestinian embroideries in that the narrative outline is drawn by male artists and then passed on to the female members of the family to be embroidered. Like their Palestinian counterparts, however, the market for these newly-traditional textiles also extends far afield from the refugee camps: they are made primarily for export to the Americas, a market which includes refugees and migrants.

Description of the Allen Collection Village Gowns

The two female wedding outfits studied here originated in two distinct regions in the southern Judean mountains, and are styles identified with the villages surrounding Bethlehem and Hebron.[4] They were

4. The outfits are also similar to those in documented collections of Middle Eastern clothing or textiles in the Annenberg Gallery, Los Angeles, The Textile Museum, Washington, D.C., The Museum of Folk Art, Santa Fe, and the ethnographic collections of the National Museum of Natural History, Washington, D.C.

Figure 12.1 Front view of Bethlehem dress.

Figure 12.2 Back view of Bethlehem dress.

purchased by the Helen Louise Allen Textile Collection at the University of Wisconsin from the estate of Alma Kjelland Kerr, who worked with the Red Cross as a coordinator of refugee and resettlement programs in Syria and Lebanon from 1919 to 1926, and again from 1948 until 1956. The garments were given to Mrs. Kerr at some unspecified date by refugees as gifts of gratitude. Each of the outfits is comprised of a headdress and a blue-black floor length, loose fitting gown worn with long, voluminous, triangular-shaped sleeves. Both of the garments are highly decorated, using a combination of various types of embroidery, printed fabrics and woven designs.

The Bethlehem garment (Figures 12.1 and 12.2) consists of thirty-nine pieces of cotton velveteen, cotton twill and plain weaves, and linen, silk, rayon and mixed metallic plain weaves. It was embroidered with silk and metallic couching and cross-stitching. The Bethlehem *thob malakeh*, or "queenly dress" with its distinctive embroidery was not confined to Bethlehem but was preferred throughout the surrounding villages as the dress of the wedding day.[5] The Hebron garment (Figures 12.3 and 12.4), simpler in design, consists of eighteen sections of cotton, linen, and rayon plain weave, and rayon satin weave fabrics. It is heavily embroidered using cross stitch (counted-thread work). Hebron itself was not known for its embroidery; the garment was probably produced in Beit Jibrin, a village ten miles northwest of Hebron, where the women excelled in this skill.[6] The headdress from the Bethlehem outfit consists of a stiff, truncated conical hat (Figures 12.5 and 12.6) covered with embroidery, whereas the Hebron headdress consists of a tripartite embroidered shawl with one of the narrow edges gathered into a halo-like band (Figure 12.7). Both of the headdresses have silver-plated coins or "sequins" attached to the front section; the Bethlehem hat also has several rows of coins which form a panel on the front. Each garment

5. The works of two anthropologists, Hilma Granqvist and Philip J. Baldensperger, were major ethnographic sources for information concerning weddings and wedding ensembles in pre-Mandate Palestine. Descriptions of Palestinian wedding garments and wedding customs are also found in various monographs and texts that have been written over the past sixty years (for example, Crowfoot and Sutton 1935; Crowfoot 1936; MacDonald 1951; Jones 1962; Stillman 1979; Kawar 1982; and Volger, Welk, and Hackstein 1987). The ongoing and extensive works of Weir (1969, 1970, 1973, 1989, Weir and Kawar 1975, and Weir and Shahid 1988) have added a body of much-needed research on both pre-Mandate village dress and the social environment in which this dress originated.

6. This village has been researched by Stillman (1979).

Figure 12.3 Front view of Hebron dress.

Figure 12.4 Back view of Hebron dress.

Figure 12.5 Headdress from Bethlehem outfit. Front view.

Figure 12.6 Back view of Bethlehem headdress.

Figure 12.7 Hebron headdress showing embroidered shawl section.

complex is completed by the basic accessories of a belt or girdle (a length of fabric folded on the bias), jewelry, shoes or slippers, and an opaque, face-concealing veil.

Significance of Traditional Dress to Present-Day Palestinian Women

In the twentieth century, western influence in Palestine brought about major changes in dress. In 1920, Palestine passed from Ottoman rule, which had lasted for approximately four hundred years, and became a British mandate. Western influence was already evident in the clothing of town-dwellers; by the end of the nineteenth century, women of Bethlehem and Jerusalem increasingly abandoned the traditional *thob malakeh* and were married in white western gowns. Both of these towns had large and prosperous Christian populations who maintained extensive contact with European relatives and business connections and were thus a conduit for European fashion. During the 1930s, the village wedding dress was also superseded by western gowns in rural areas. By the 1940s, the traditional village wedding outfit was worn only by a few women who were either interested in preserving their heritage or who lived in isolated villages, and the wedding itself became an accretion of both western and "traditional." Large numbers of European Jews had migrated to Palestine, part of which had been proclaimed as the Jewish national homeland in the Balfour Declaration of 1917, and further added to the European influence upon clothing of indigenous residents. Traditional dress was worn daily in the late 1940s only in the more isolated villages or by older women who had worn it since their youth.[7] In 1948, when much of Palestine was proclaimed to be the state of Israel, many Palestinian townspeople and villagers fled during the ensuing fighting and large bodies of immigrants settled in such cities as Detroit, Washington, New York, and Chicago.

To provide insight into both the meaning of the dress within its original context and to the meaning attributed by present society, ten women who came from the regions where the garments originated were interviewed in their homes, either in Madison, Wisconsin, or in the northern suburbs of Chicago.[8] All but three of the women had lived in or visited the Middle East within three years of the interviews, and all had been there within the previous fifteen years. Their ages ranged from twenty-three to seventy-five years and spanned three generations: women who had made and worn gowns similar to the

7. One informant stated that while she lived in Palestine in the 1940s she had attended several weddings in a wealthy *fellahin* family from Beit Jala, close to Bethlehem. The brides of that family continue to wear brightly colored traditional wedding outfits although they could afford the western gowns of their urban peers. After the weddings, fashionable western clothing was worn daily.

8. The ten women, who were considered highly informed about their culture, were selected from a more inclusive list of members of a Middle Eastern cultural organization. Women rather than men were selected because of their access to occasions at which the outfits were most likely worn and from which men were usually excluded by custom.

gowns in the Allen collection, those who remembered their elders wearing such garments but who eschewed them themselves, and those who had little, if any, practical memory of such outfits except in their revived form. Only one of the women, the oldest, had belonged to a family actively involved in agricultural production. For all these women the wedding dress, like the *kefiyyeh* or scarf headdress sported largely by their male counterparts as a political accessory, has come to be identified with a reaffirmation of the Palestinian community and nationalism. The two ensembles were identified by the interviewees as "wedding" or "festival" dress.

During the past twenty years, Palestinian village dress has taken on new meaning. Whereas once the garments were a sign of backwardness associated with village life, the wedding and festival garments now signify cultural pride. For some informants, the village wedding dress has taken on strong and definite political connotations, especially after the nationalistic sentiment which surfaced during the Arab-Israeli wars of 1967. Each of the expatriates who were interviewed owned one, if not several, hand-embroidered Palestinian *thob* or *shawal*. Although these garments are considered to be "traditional," with the exception of the oldest woman, none of the women had produced the garments themselves; rather, they had either been purchased ready-made in the markets of large towns or had been commissioned through a tailor on return visits to their home villages and to relatives living in the West Bank. According to the women, these types of dresses may be worn to political meetings and during demonstrations against Israel. For some the political connection was less overt, but the outfits were still associated with the land and the agricultural worker, the *fellah*. In the words of one interviewee, "the *fellaha* worked the land and we are fighting for that land."[9]

The "traditional" dresses presently worn by Palestinian women maintain a strong resemblance to the Palestinian dresses worn at the beginning of the century, but have undergone several noteworthy modifications (Figure 12.8). The garments show change in form, silhouette, materials and surface decoration. Immediately noticeable is the slimmer, more form-fitting and streamlined silhouette. The garments are constructed without the triangular side panels and voluminous sleeves, and long back zipper closures are used instead

9. It is noteworthy that the feminine form of the word, "peasant," was used to denote the relationship between the land and the worker, and once more points to the perceived relationship between women and agriculture.

Figure 12.8 Contemporary Palestinian dress (circa 1980).

of a front bodice opening to accommodate the garment to the body shape. The triangular sleeves are usually replaced with narrow, set-in sleeves. According to several women, these adjustments have given the garments a more western look which places emphasis on overtly flattering the body. The belt, which identified the family's affiliation and was used in field work, is often omitted or replaced by a narrower, grommeted version, and its function, like the sleeves, of holding keys, money, and personal odds and ends has been replaced by the modern shoulder bag. Transparent nylon headscarves, sometimes decorated with light metallic "coins" or sequins, replace the coin-laden embroidered headdresses, and linen-like synthetic blends are substituted for the cotton and linen fabrics which predominated at the beginning of the century.

Older informants noted that the garment was marked by its adaptability, a characteristic that was appropriate for the many varying activities that were part of village life. Most of the younger women, having never had occasion to wear the garment on a daily basis or at ceremonies which were part of the continuum of daily life in a village environment, were unaware of the practicality of the garment. Thus, in its more modern version, the reinterpretation of the outfit has lost some of the form which had practical and ritual meaning to its original wearers.[10] A case in point is the voluminous pointed sleeve, perhaps one of the most adaptable parts of the garment. What appears as an incommodious volume of fabric was actually a determined length which enabled the sleeves to be rolled up and tied behind the head by its points (or tassels). This unique arrangement thus freed the arms for heavy work and allowed for maximum movement without the structural weaknesses of a set-in sleeve with seams around the armscye.[11] When the woman wished to cover her arms after fieldwork at the end of the day or to go out in public, she easily lowered her sleeves to achieve the required observation of modesty.

In addition, the sleeves of the *thob* were used to observe specific Islamic social customs. According to Baldensperger (1900: 85), the sleeves were also used to cover the hands of a woman when greeting men who had returned from a long journey such as pilgrimage or conscription. The garments, therefore, were an accommodation to the practical work life of the village women and to prevailing social interdictions; they were also the sign of a modest and capable woman. The full range of activities in which the sleeves were used became more apparent during the wedding celebrations in which dresses were invested with new meaning and their parts took on added dimensions.

10. The *thob* has been worn in the Middle East since the medieval period (Stillman 1979: 26, 1972: 104). Whether the garment originated in the towns and was adapted by village women is uncertain, but it is indicated in literature and by informants that the garment was considered "rural" at the turn of this century.

11. A graphic example of this use of the sleeves may be seen in a photograph, possibly from Ramallah, at the beginning of the century, published in Weir (1989: 103). In it, two women are grinding wheat with a hand-mill and a young girl is embroidering. Their sleeves are all tied behind their shoulders to leave their hands free for these activities. See also page 92 for a similar example with young girls carrying baskets on their heads.

There, the sleeves were highly visible elements in the women's dances and, later, in the collection of gifts of money from wedding guests.

The omissions and substitutions are not simply the result of the ongoing process of fashion. Indeed, they are related not only to a loss of specific use and meaning of parts of the garments, but also to a change in events for which the garments are used and in the space in which these events take place. Two parts of the older garment, the sleeves and the lower back panel, were especially important in the artistic dance formations in which women participated on festival days. According to informants, although dancing still takes place at social events, these same village dances are no longer performed. The steps have been forgotten by many (or were never known) and although village or traditional dancing is being revived as an art form, involvement remains largely spectator rather than participatory. Moreover, the social value of the dances has changed. Young men and women (and their families) no longer rely on these gatherings to meet and speculate upon future marriage partners, and so the flirtatious use of the garments in the outdoor festivities has changed. A more overt emphasis is placed on the body in a social setting in which all men and women are not well-acquainted with each other, but are part of a larger, more diverse community with greater freedom of interaction.

The location of the celebration has also changed from the outdoor courtyard to a more confined indoor arrangement, and from the homes of relatives to a rented reception hall or restaurant. This too has wrought changes in the voluminous garments, which have been subsequently modified to a slimmer version without the bulk which would impede movement in indoor social gatherings. The bride, as the center of the marriage ritual, retains the option of wearing either the voluminous skirt of the western-style dress or the bulky sleeves of village *thob*, both of which encumber and impede her movements while simultaneously increasing the magnitude of her presence. Again, the sleeves of the village dress in particular were singled out as a hindrance; knocking over glasses, dragging in food, and generally rendering the wearer clumsy, the sleeves were seen as useless appendages. Not only was their meaning lost as part of the wing-like extensions used in the women's dances which took place in large outdoor spaces, but they have lost their practical value associated with the hard labor that the village women regularly performed. In an air-conditioned environment, the cooling volume of the gowns is only cumbersome and the strictures of modesty, although still observed, have been modified in their western environment. More tight-fitting gowns with set-in sleeves which would easily tear under conditions of field work have also been adopted in this effort to pare down excess bulk. But since the women are not meant to engage in field work while wearing these garments, any practical argument for retaining them is moot.

Furthermore, Palestinian women and expatriates in the United States are not confined to the use of the basic *thob* in their daily lives, of course. Instead they maintain a "wardrobe" of clothing rather than one basic item which was adapted to different social and practical needs. Therefore, the ceremonial transition in meaning of the everyday *thob* from a hardy field dress to a statement of celebration has been lost. The dress has changed form as the village festival customs have been likewise displaced. What many women do not realize is that the parts which they now consider superfluous formerly embodied many of the traditions which they seek to recapture. Their own re-creations, however, are more suited to their new environments with which they are most familiar. The garments, as originally worn, were not symbolic manifestations of nationalism as they have now become but, like many symbols, in their present reclaimed form they are removed from the everyday life with which they are associated.

Given that the basic form of the garments has changed and the garment has been adapted to a new set of cultural influences, it must be asked what elements about the dress still allow it to be considered "traditional." On one level, the answer lies in the embroidery of the garments, but on another the answer refers to the symbolic associations evoked by both the garment and the wedding ceremony. The basic unit of what is considered to be traditional or Palestinian is not the form of the dress itself, a form which also comprises the basic dress unit of women throughout North Africa and Arabia, but the distinctive embroidery and motifs on the garment. Additional evidence of the connection between embroidery and Palestinian values is seen in the production of embroidery pieces and facsimile reproduction on greeting cards sold to raise funds for Palestinian causes.

Although the motifs may have become standardized, the decoration of the garments has not become static. Like subtle changes in the shape of the garment, the embroidery and its execution have also undergone several changes. In general, the surface of the present garments is neither as highly decorated as was the Hebron garment, nor are there the variations in materials that typified the Bethlehem garment. The embroidery on the new garments is often noticeably larger in stitch size and more sparse. Although fewer motifs are used on each new garment, there is a continuity in the motifs: several motifs which were used on the Bethlehem and Hebron garments are still applied to the more contemporary *thob*. These include the moon (*qamr*), cypress (*saru*), and rose (*wadr*) motifs and their variations. Whereas the embroidered chest panel (*qabbeh*) has been retained and still contains an often vivid use of embroidery, the embroidered sleeve and side panels are usually replaced by several rows of monochromatic isolated motifs. The extensive embroidery of the lower back panel of the *thob*, once a focal point during the women's dances, is either replaced by token horizontal bands of embroidery or is left plain. Embroidery also substitutes for the glittering metallic back hem section woven into the fabric of the Bethlehem garments. Furthermore, a few rows of standardized motifs continue as remnants of the multiple panels of embroidered designs on earlier garments.

Informants were not concerned with the lack of symmetry, skewed grain, or gross construction techniques which would be judged by western consumers as obvious flaws in workmanship. Rather, they spoke of "creative" re-combination of motifs, colors, and materials as indicators of skill, and the most skillfully executed or "creative" garment epitomized the wedding costume. It is noteworthy that this process of re-combination of selected elements and their acceptance by their "audience" is similar to that for storytelling. In response to enquiries about specific meaning of the motifs, many of the women believed that the designs once had a symbolic meaning, but did not know what that meaning was.

This change in the form of the garments and their decoration may be related to the way they are produced. At the beginning of the century, the festival or wedding dress was the culmination of many years of embroidery practiced both by the individual and by the community. These skills were not always retained by women when they moved away from the villages into towns or migrated further abroad. According to middle-age informants, their contemporaries learned to embroider while in school but did not seem to practice this skill as a social pastime; nor did they learn patterns from their family members. The craft became just another skill taught as part of formal education.

In the last thirty years, a conscious revival in the aesthetic and technical traditions of embroidery among Palestinian women has gained momentum. Embroidery cooperatives have been established, using a system similar to the cottage industry which existed in the early decades of the century. Village women are supplied with materials and are paid for each completed piece of embroidery. Such cooperatives include the Ramallah Handicraft Cooperative and the Society of In'ash Al Usra (Steadfastness) at el-Bireh. Both of these organizations produce embroidered household linens in addition to the updated traditional dresses which are in demand by Palestinian women, both locally and abroad.

Several informants had purchased their gowns from these types of cooperatives or from similar workshops attached to tailors' shops in the market places. The placement of garment production in the hands of the cooperative or workshop, rather than the close circle of friends and relatives, is another factor contributing to the change in the garments. Whereas previously designs were memorized by the embroiderer, whose production should show personal innovation, pattern books are now provided for the customer to order a particular design or to create her own design. A dress now takes approximately ten days to embroider, whereas at the beginning of the century a traditional village dress took one and one-half years to complete. The garments reportedly cost between $30 and $1,500 (in 1994) depending upon the amount of labor and materials used.

To keep costs down and to fill the orders as quickly as possible, designs appear to have become standardized with few variations, less surface area is embroidered, and stitch size has been enlarged. These changes in the execution of the embroidery may be a factor in the purchasing woman's desire to retain the most familiar motifs which she considers to be traditional (as indicated by the informants), while incorporating or introducing others which have little or no meaning for the embroiderer. It may also indicate the limited level of skill and repertoire of women who have only recently learned to embroider in the cooperatives, or acceptance of lower standards for workmanship on garments made for strangers. As the workshops mature, and as more young women are initiated into the craft, embellishment and creativity may again increase.

Some of the embroidery cooperatives are affiliated with political and social groups. The Ramallah Handicraft Cooperative, for example, was originally affiliated with Christian missionary organizations, whereas the more recent el-Bireh cooperative uses funds from the sale of the embroidery for the education of Arab-Palestinian children, the vocational training of women, and several related social programs. In this way, the leisure-time skills of refugee *fellaha* women who were displaced from the land are being used not only to provide income for their families but to promote nationalistic sentiment. The garments are no longer the direct product of the agricultural communities made to be worn within their own communities, but are now produced by large groups of fairly anonymous women for an unknown customer, a woman who is now part of another culture. Unlike production for the tourist trade, however, the two groups, producer and consumer, villager and expatriate, are linked through a common binding heritage which the dress has now come to symbolize.

The association of the wedding costume and ritual with the concept of homeland is not confined to the group of women interviewed, but has more universal appeal. Among Palestinian immigrants and refugees, the wedding continues to be an event central to reaffirming communal values, of building on the past while emphasizing the future. The value of community and the focus on future generation continues to be recognized and celebrated, and it is through a language of motifs cultivated by women that these values are promoted. Whether re-invented in new form, modified to better suit new surroundings, or imbued with new meaning, the wedding outfit remains the focus of this celebration. The "embroidering" of the bride's body with henna and the moral tales transmitted primarily by women in their houses are part of the continuum of communication to which embroidery belongs. Although most of the married informants had married since their residence in the U.S., many had attempted to observe some wedding customs of their homeland.

Furthermore, according to two women, a form of the traditional wedding as observed by Granqvist (1931) and others at the beginning of the century has been revived among Palestinians who presently reside on the West Bank. One woman had attended a marriage of two members of a nationalistic organization in which the couple wore village dress which she believed dated from the beginning of the century. Other rituals have also been revived in the diaspora. The hands of the bride in the West Bank had been coated with henna; so too three of the women interviewed had unobtrusive parts of their bodies (heels, little fingers, and toes) stained with henna on the eve of their weddings, and had participated in similar events at weddings of other women. This practice was no longer undertaken as a tradition, but instead as a clear indication of political beliefs. Several informants, for example, knew of women with strong political motivations who had their bodies stained with henna on their wedding eves. Finally, in the above-mentioned wedding as in others in the U.S., the instructional songs which usually accompanied the village wedding had become a public affirmation of common belief. The congratulations which the guests customarily gave to the couple were now phrased in terms not used when the dress was originally worn, terms referring to the common political cause, that of regaining the land.

Conclusions

Just as the traditional dress has undergone revival as part of the cultural heritage of the Palestinian people, so also has the traditional wedding and rituals associated with it. The application of henna to parts of the body of the bride (and her guests if they wish) by a special artist who draws motifs similar to those incorporated into the wedding dresses has regained popularity, for example; the "embroidering" of the body with henna and the moral tales transmitted primarily by women in their houses are part of the continuum of communication to which the wedding costume belongs.

Traditions associated with the wedding and the wedding dress are not only revived and renewed, but consciously created and invented as indicated by several of the younger, more politically-active women interviewed. Just as earlier village women had allowed for creativity in embroidery motifs representative of their communities, the younger women were highly selective as to which elements of village life they chose as "traditional." For instance, proof of virginity of the bride was still required, if no longer by public exhibition of a bloodied undergown following successful consummation, then by a more private display of a large kerchief. Yet many of the women decried proof of virginity as "coarse;" that is, the custom has a negative association with village life and village mentality which the urban women could not accommodate into their present lives. Similarly, embroidery was considered an "essential element" of the traditional Palestinian dress, whereas the cheap, brightly-colored, printed cottons currently favored by rural women for everyday dress were dismissed with the term "gypsy." These cottons, although decorative, contain neither the historical associations of the land nor the cultural associations of the wedding.

Among Palestinian immigrants and refugees, the wedding continues to be an event central to reaffirming communal values and ties to a homeland, of building on the past while emphasizing the future. The value of community and the focus of future generations continues to be recognized and celebrated, and it is through a language of motifs cultivated by women that these values are promoted.

Whether re-invented in new form, modified to better suit new surroundings, or imbued with new meaning, the wedding outfit remains the focus of this celebration.

References

Antran, S. (1989), "The Surrogate Colonization of Palestine, 1917–1939," *American Ethnologist*, vol. 16, pp. 719–44.

Baizerman, S. (1990). "Trade in Hispanic Weavings of Northern New Mexico and the Social Construction of Tradition," in *Textiles in Trade*, Washington, D.C.: Proceedings of The Textile Society of America, Biennial Symposium.

Baldensperger, P.J. (1893), "Peasant Folklore of Palestine," *Palestine Exploration Fund*, pp. 203–19.

—— (1894), "Birth, Marriage and Death among the Fellahin of Palestine," *Palestine Exploration Fund*, pp. 127–44.

—— (1899), "Women in the East," *Palestine Exploration Fund*, pp. 132–60.

—— (1900), "Women in the East," *Palestine Exploration Fund*, pp. 171–90.

—— (1901), "Women in the East," *Palestine Exploration Fund*, pp. 66–90; 167–84.

—— (1903), "The Immovable East," *Palestine Exploration Fund*, pp. 163–70.

—— (1904), "The Immovable East," *Palestine Exploration Fund*, pp. 49–57; 258–64.

Clifford, J. (ed.) (1988), *The Predicament of Culture*, Cambridge, MA: Harvard University Press.

Crowfoot, G. (1936), "Embroidery of Bethlehem," *Embroidery*, vol. 5, pp. 9–14.

Crowfoot, G., and Sutton, P.M. (1935), "Ramallah Embroidery," *Embroidery*, vol. 3, pp. 25–39.

Csikszentmihalyi, M., and Rochberg-Halton, E. (1981), *The Meaning of Things: Domestic Symbols of Self*, Cambridge: Cambridge University Press.

Dominguez, V. (1986), "The Marketing of Heritage," *American Ethnologist*, vol. 13, pp. 546–55.

Eisenstadt, S. (1973), *Tradition, Change, and Modernity*, New York: John Wiley and Sons.

Firth, R. (1988), "Fact and Fiction in Ethnography," in E. Tonkin, M. McDonald, and M. Chapman (eds), *History and Ethnicity*, New York: Routledge.

Geertz, C. (1983), *Local Knowledge: Further Essays in Interpretative Anthropology*, New York: Basic Books.

Granqvist, H. (1931), *Marriage Conditions in a Palestinian Village, I*, Helsinki: Societas Scientarium Fennica.

—— (1935), *Marriage Conditions in a Palestinian Village, II*, Helsinki: Societas Scientarium Fennica.

Handler, R., and Linnekin, J. (1984), "Tradition, Genuine or Spurious," *Journal of American Folklore*, vol. 97, pp. 273–90.

Hobsbawn, E., and Ranger, T. (eds) (1983), *The Invention of Tradition*, Cambridge: Cambridge University Press.

Jones, C. (1962), *The Ramallah Handicraft Cooperative*, Jerusalem: The Commercial Press.

Kawar, W. (1982), *Costumes Dyed by the Sun: Palestinian Arab National Costumes*, Tokyo.

Kligman, G. (1984), "Oral Poetry, Ideology, and the Socialization of Peasant Women in Contemporary Romania," *Journal of American Folklore*, vol. 97, pp. 167–88.

Lewis, B. (1988), *The Political Language of Islam*, Chicago: University of Chicago Press.

Macdonald, J. (1951), "Palestinian Dress," *Palestine Exploration Quarterly*, Jan.–Apr., pp. 55–65.

Muhawi, I., and Kanaana, S. (1989), *Speak, Bird, Speak Again: Palestinian Arab Folktales*, Berkeley: University of California Press.

Peterson, S. (1988), "Translating Experience and Reading a Story Cloth," *Journal of American Folklore*, vol. 101, pp. 6–22.

Rajab, J. (1989), *Palestinian Costume*, London: Kegan Paul.

Shils, E. (1981), *Tradition*, Chicago: University of Chicago Press.

Stillman, Y.K. (1979), *Palestinian Costume and Jewelry*, Albuquerque: University of New Mexico Press.

Trevor-Roper, H. (1983), "The Invention of Tradition: The Highland Tradition of Scotland," in Hobsbawm and Ranger (eds), *The Invention of Tradition*.

Turner, V. (ed.) (1982), *Celebration: Studies in Festivity and Ritual*, Washington, D.C.: Smithsonian Institution Press.

—— (1980), "Liminality and Morality," Firestone Lecture, delivered at the University of Southern California.

Volger, G., Welk, K. van, and Hackstein, K. (1987), *Pract und Geheimnis: Kleidung und Schmuck aus Palastina und Jordanien*, new series, band 13, Ethnologia, Kon: Rutenstrauch-Joest-Museum.

Weir, S. (1969). "The Traditional Costumes of the Arab Women of Palestine," *Costume*, vol. 3, pp. 44–54.

—— (1973), *Palestinian Embroidery*, London: The British Museum.

—— (1973), "A Bridal Headdress from Southern Palestine," *Palestine Exploration Quarterly*, Jan.–June, pp. 100–9.

—— (1989), *Palestinian Costume*, Austin: University of Texas Press.

—— and Kawar, W. (1975), "Costumes and Wedding Customs in Beit Dajan," *Palestine Exploration Quarterly*, Jan.–June, pp. 39–51.

Weir, S., and Shahid, S. (1988), *Palestinian Embroidery: Cross-Stitch Patterns from the Traditional Costumes of the Village Women of Palestine*, London: The British Museum.

13

Hmong American New Year's Dress: The Display of Ethnicity

Annette Lynch

Hmong Americans are refugees from Laos who settled in the United States as a result of the Vietnam conflict. The Lao Hmong living in the United States originally migrated out of China in the early nineteenth century into northern Lao hill country. During the Vietnam War, Hmong were recruited by the American forces to fight against the Laotian communists. Immigration to the United States began in 1975 after the withdrawal of the American army and the assumption of political power by the Laotian communists. Fieldwork (Lynch 1992) supporting this article was conducted in St. Paul and Minneapolis, Minnesota in a community of approximately 18,000 Hmong Americans (Map 13.1).

Within the Hmong American community, textile arts and dress have continued to play a traditional role in structuring social life and marking significance. *Paj ntaub* (flower cloth) is the general term used to refer to all the varied textile arts created by Hmong women. Techniques used include embroidery, applique', reverse applique' and batik as well as the additive arts of assemblage. These arts, like other *kev cai* (customs) discussed by Tapp (1988), have been self-consciously practiced by Hmong Americans as they have used the customs of the past to fashion meaningful lives in the diaspora.

Drawing generally from the academic literature on the expression of cultural difference within modern nation states (Moerman 1964; Barth 1969; Cohen 1973; Glazer and Moynihan 1975; Epstein 1978; Roosens 1989 and Glick-Schiller and Fouron 1990) and specifically upon the work of Sarna (1978) and Comaroff (1987), I will focus upon Hmong American use of New Year's dress as a marker of ethnic

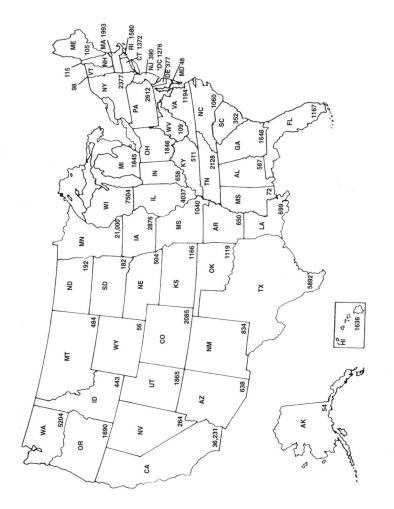
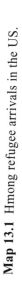

Map 13.1 Hmong refugee arrivals in the US.

identity and pride. I present this Hmong American case study as an argument for a definition of ethnic dress based on its descriptive role in identifying conceptually distinct types of social boundaries marked by the dressed body.

The Concept of Ethnicity

Sarna (1978), writing on the American immigrant experience, argued that American immigrant groups identify themselves by region, village, or family when they enter the United States but are labeled and treated as a homogenous ethnic group by American institutions and power structures. He goes on to argue that ethnic groups use cultural content to construct symbols of cohesiveness and pride as a defensive response to discrimination based on ethnic identity. In this way fragmented clusters of immigrants become cohesive ethnic groups by accepting and eventually symbolizing externally drawn ethnic boundary lines. Cultural content, which is often an eclectic mix of cultural elements drawn from throughout the ethnic group membership, is used both to accommodate and resist dominant American power structures.

Comaroff (1987) posited that the "marking of contrasting identities – of the opposition of self and other, we and they – is 'primordial'" (p. 306). He argues that, despite social and cultural differences, all human groups classify themselves in relationship to others. His argument offers a conceptually distinct definition of ethnicity premised on the fact that the substance underlying boundary lines between groups differs depending upon social and cultural circumstances. Using Comaroff's distinctions, totemic (as opposed to ethnic) boundary lines are established between equally powerful and structurally similar groups. In contrast ethnic boundaries are asymmetrical power-based relationships between structurally dissimilar groups.

In the following analysis I will show that as the Hmong people experienced social and cultural upheaval, they moved from using dress to mark totemic boundaries to using dress to display ethnic identity.

Lao Hmong Dress

Different Hmong dress styles were historically associated with different regions of Laos and Thailand and with different linguistic sub-groups of Hmong. The clearest distinctions existed between the two broad categories of Green and White Hmong dress, which in turn corresponded to two major linguistic sub-groups. Green Hmong handwork can be most simply identified by the use of blue batik to produce pattern. White Hmong handwork used the reverse appliqué' technique to produce intricate white patterns.

The dress of White Hmong women included a white pleated skirt with black leggings worn with a black shirt with blue cuffs and front edging. A rectangular collar at the back of the shirt was heavily decorated with handwork. The ensemble included a black apron and was worn with belts adorned with silver coins. In contrast, the dress of a Green Hmong woman customarily included a pleated skirt dominated visually by a wide central panel of blue batik work and decorated with appliqué' and embroidery. They wore dark shirts similar to the White Hmong women, but their collars were worn face down. Both groups of women wore a version of a dark wrapped turban form, which generally featured a black and white striped turban tie.

White Hmong men wore black shirts with blue cuffs and black flared pants. Accessories included a dramatic pink or red waist sash, narrow coined belts and black skullcaps with red topknots. Green Hmong men's pants were also black but were cut large with a low crotch and fitted ankles. They also wore dark cuffed shirts and black skullcaps (Cubbs 1986).

Scholars trace the roots of the Lao Hmong sub-groups which are marked by corresponding differences in dress styles to China where the Han Chinese ascribed separate status to various sub-categories of Miao (Geddes 1976; Dewhurst and MacDowell 1983; Cubbs 1986). Sub-styles of dress in the Lao context were internally perceived and understood categories. Peterson (1990) pointed out the extensive information that was carried by dress in Lao Hmong communities:

> the individual is recognized as Hmong by other Hmong, who with a glance will know if the stranger they meet shares their dialect, marriage customs, house style, spiritual offerings, standards of beauty in clothing and song, and other cultural facets that distinguish one subgroup from another. They mutually recognize, in a twinkling, what kinds of limits might structure their future relationship. (p. 118)

Dress thus immediately set up a relationship between the Hmong individual wearing the dress and the Hmong individual perceiving the dress. The two individuals knew how to respond socially to one another and what relationships were possible based upon internally understood visual cues.

Lao Hmong dress marked what Comaroff (1987) would call a totemic boundary between the related subgroups. The bounded groups were structurally similar and had roughly the same amount of power. The subgroups of Lao Hmong spoke different versions of the same language and tended to perform rituals in slightly different ways. These cultural differences, while internally perceived, were often not externally appreciated. Dress as a visible sign was more often noticed and commented upon by outsiders, thus perhaps accounting for the use of dress by the outside world to label the differing subgroups.

Hmong American New Year

Hmong-style dress, worn on an everyday basis in Laos, is reserved for special occasions in the United States. Hmong American women are typically married in Hmong-style dress and families dress up for family photographs in the summer. The largest public display of Hmong American dress is the annual public celebration of New Year, generally held in St. Paul over the Thanksgiving weekend. My research focused specifically upon the meaning of dress worn within the context of the public celebration of the New Year.

Hmong New Year as celebrated in the Lao village context was the single annual holiday celebrated at the close of a busy agricultural season. It was an opportunity for families and friends to gather and renew the bonds tying the community and family together. Clan leaders and shamans performed rituals of renewal to usher in the New Year, banish the cares of the old year, and make peace with the spirit world in order to safeguard the community for the coming year. Women sewed throughout the year to prepare new clothing to be worn first for the New Year celebration and subsequently throughout the year for everyday attire. Treasured and costly clothing not worn on a daily basis was taken out of the storage baskets to add additional pomp to the newly sewn ensembles. A ball toss courtship ritual was played throughout the holiday season and provided an opportunity for young Hmong men and women to meet and get to know each other. Many marriages followed the holiday season.

The New Year as celebrated in the United States is a rare opportunity for public display of ethnic pride. While for much of the year community members try hard to fit into American culture, the New Year is an opportunity to be Hmong again in a supportive environment. Lao Hmong who relocated to the United States arrived relatively unprepared for life in the industrialized West. Most (92%)

came from rural backgrounds and many (72%) were not able to read or write in their native language (Mallinson, Donnelly, and Hang 1988: 21). Resulting high rates of welfare dependency have made it difficult for youth to be proud of their heritage and families. Teenagers enrolled in public schools are particularly sensitive to the judgments of their peers. For example, one young man attempted to mask his ethnic identity by claiming to be a member of the more culturally assimilated Vietnamese community. For these teenagers and for the community at large, the New Year provides an arena in which ethnic identity is affirmed and displayed.

The public celebrations of Hmong New Year held in St. Paul in the late 1980s, like comparable nineteenth century immigrant celebrations discussed by Bodnar (1985), drew upon long-standing practices yet were adapted to the new American context. Focusing primarily on youth, the public celebrations in St. Paul juxtaposed ancient Hmong ritual and American popular culture. The auditorium floor was dominated by a ball toss courtship ritual by day and a rock and roll dance by night. The stage featured spectacles ranging from shamanistic rituals to heavy metal rock and roll performed by punk Hmong teenagers. The conflicts inherent in the position of Hmong teens as the generation between Hmong and American cultures were acted out in plays written in local schools, in speeches delivered by Hmong teenage leaders, and in the structure of the celebration, which in 1989 moved from an opening day focused on the Hmong past to a closing day focused on the Hmong future in America.

Dress styles derived from Lao Hmong prototypes were worn to the public celebration by many Hmong American teenagers and some Hmong American children and adults (see Figure 13.1). Hmong American teenagers used dress throughout the two-day festival to mark movement from one cultural world into the other. One Hmong teenager explained the use of clothing by saying that "at the New Year if we do something Hmong we wear Hmong clothes, and if we do something American we wear American clothes"(AL-F-03),[1] thereby indicating a conscious association of dress with cultural identity.

While Hmong style dress was most typically worn by youth at the New Year celebration, it was generally designed by older women in the community. Older styles of Lao Hmong dress were transformed

---

1. Interview data is coded according to the author's initials and subject number through the manuscript.

Figure 13.1 New Year's dress. Photograph by Annette Lynch.

through the process of cultural authentication[2] to reflect American as well as Hmong culture. Teenagers and the older women who sewed the garments drew inspiration from the range of cloth and trims available in American fabric stores to create ensembles that, while rooted in Lao Hmong prototypes, were a creative blend of both Hmong and American influences. As will be outlined, the transformation of Lao Hmong dress marking sub-group membership into Hmong American dress marking cohesive group identity is an apt illustration of Sarna's concept of ethnic group formation and Comaroff's distinction between totemic and ethnic boundary lines.

Dress: The Display of Ethnicity

At my first Hmong American New Year in November of 1988, I naively assumed that teenagers were wearing distinct sub-styles of

---

2. Cultural authentication is a process by which a borrowed cultural element works its way into the culture through language (being assigned a specific name), patterns of significant use, and aesthetic transformation (Erekosima and Eicher 1981).

dress associated with their family and region of origin. I was therefore surprised when a girl told me to be sure to watch for her the next day as she would be wearing a costume associated with different subgroup. Teenage girls typically owned and wore a variety of sub-styles of dress. When I interviewed the winner of the 1989 Teen of the Year contest, she proudly showed me photographs of her taken in four different sub-styles of dress.

Teenagers were perplexed when I asked them why they wore the sub-styles of other groups' and generally attributed little meaning to the practice. Most teenagers simply told me it was the new style, the American way. But importantly, being a Hmong American rather than a Lao Hmong was often associated with the freedom to wear other sub-groups' styles. For example, the following is drawn from an interview with a Hmong American female Teen of the Year contestant:

> See, that is the change now. Now we can wear any one – any kind. I could be a Green Hmong, I could wear White Hmong clothes, it doesn't really matter. It doesn't really matter in Laos too, but in Laos you wear what you are. But now it is the style – if you like it you wear it. We are becoming more Americanized in that way. (AL-F-01)

It was typical that the teenagers discussed the impulse to wear the other styles or to mix the styles as a fashion impulse or as an aesthetic choice. "It looks good" and "it is the new style" were often the words used by the teenagers. The following response concerns the practice of mixing the different sub-styles within a single ensemble: "I usually mix them up. I wear the hat with the White, and the hat doesn't go with the White dress. It doesn't really matter but it surely looks good so why not?" (AL- F-05).

The practice of mixing the sub-styles together and wearing those of groups other than one's own was documented throughout the United States. Sally Peterson (1990) commented that "there are not many Green Hmong families in Philadelphia, but almost every family with daughters owns a Green Hmong skirt – particularly if it is made in the new style"[3] (p. 94). In Missoula, Montana, Susan Lindbergh's (1990) research compared how Hmong American teenage girls dressed for the New Year with the way their mothers dressed in Laos:

---

3. New style Green Hmong skirts are more heavily embroidered and appliqued than the older style skirts – the more heavily embellished the better is an underlying aesthetic criteria of the new style.

Transition is evident in the costumes that the girls wear. Whereas their mothers dressed for the New Year's in Sam Neua [White Hmong sub-style] or Xieng Khouang costumes, depending on the subgroup into which they were born, the young women in this study each own costumes representative of at least two, if not three, different subgroups from which they select one to wear, depending upon personal preference. Wealthy girls may wear a different costume for each night of the New Year celebration to display their riches. Frequently subgroup garments are mixed, creating a hybrid costume. (p. 45)

In a similar vein, Joanne Cubbs (1986) reported that new style ensembles worn by teenagers at the New Year in Sheboygan, Wisconsin combined elements of White Hmong and Green Hmong dress (p. 71). The pattern of mixing sub-styles I discovered at the New Year in St. Paul was thus a national trend moving toward the use of dress to express shared group (ethnic) identity rather than distinct sub-group (totemic) identity.

Lindbergh (1990) discussed the possibility of the above interpretation, but in the end dismissed it as an outsider's perception without internal validity. She provided an example of a response she received when she asked a young woman about the meaning of the blurring of the lines between the sub-group styles:

When asked whether the blurring of lines between costume subgroups meant that the Hmong were beginning to identify with all Hmong rather than with their individual subgroups, a conclusion an outsider might draw, one young woman seemed confused by the question. Ties with her family, her husband's family, their places of origin and shared experiences within their lineages are still more important to her than any general sense of being Hmong. She feels tremendous loyalty to being from Sam Neua (a White Hmong subgroup), even though in the United States as a teenager she chose to wear a variety of different costumes, and though as an adult she continues to collect them for herself and for her daughters. (p. 50)

In contradiction to Lindbergh, I hold that the outsider sometimes sees the bigger picture missed by insiders who tend to offer more personalized interpretations centered upon their own individual experiences rather than the ethnic group as a whole. The fact that the woman quoted above both values her own sub-style of dress and collects a variety of other sub-styles likely indicates that Hmong style dress has a myriad of meanings to her, some of which are perhaps more easily articulated than others. The nationwide trend to mix the sub-styles together into hybrid ensembles and to wear the sub-styles of other groups indicates that Hmong-style dress had group as well as individual significance, an insight that is perhaps more easily perceived by a more objective outsider's eye.

While most forms of new style dress worn to the New Year were tied by their wearers to Lao Hmong prototypes, the popular rooster style women's New Year hat (see figure 13.2), a highly decorated cloth hat topped with a dramatic coxcomb, was consistently classified as Hmong American despite evidence that similar hat styles did exist in historical Green Hmong dress (Cubbs 1986; Peterson 1990; AL-F-03; Lynch, Detzner, and Eicher, 1995). Early versions of the American-style New Year hat combined White Hmong handwork with a Green Hmong children's hat style. The dramatic mixing of the two major sub-styles of dress within a single form makes the hat a prime example of dress expressive of cohesive ethnic identity. The more contemporary versions of the hat integrated elements of American material culture into the design (see figure 13.3). Sequins, lace, and American trims were borrowed and creatively integrated through the process of cultural authentication into striking symbols of Hmong American identity.

Figure 13.2 Rooster style hat. Photograph by Annette Lynch.

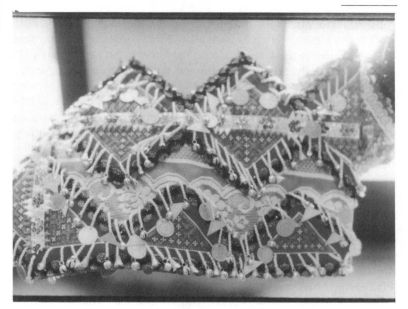

Figure 13.3 Rooster style hat (detail). Photograph by Annette Lynch.

Summary and Conclusions

Hmong Americans entered the Thai refugee camps and later the United States in fragmented groups and continued to categorize themselves by what I would label a totemic classification. However as the integrity of their world was threatened by outside forces they became defensive and thus more conscious of their ethnic as opposed to totemic identity. While allegiance to the White or Green Hmong sub-group or to a specific clan was of fundamental importance in the Lao village context, it became progressively less important as the Hmong were threatened and discriminated against on the basis of their more inclusive ethnic identity.

Sarna posits that as ethnic groups endure discrimination based upon an externally ascribed ethnic boundary line, that line becomes important internally as well. When the Lao Hmong were targeted for extermination by the communists based upon their ethnic identity, the Hmong themselves began to assign more salience to their ethnic as opposed to totemic identity. Allegiances to totemic classifications became less important as the once separate Hmong sub-groups became vulnerable to outsiders based upon their more inclusive ethnic identity. As Hmong refugees were moved into camps in Thailand and later relocated to the United States, they continued to be treated as a cohesive ethnic group and received both positive and negative treatment based upon that identity.

The transformation of regional sub-styles of Lao Hmong dress into a cohesive Hmong American style can be interpreted as symbolic of Hmong American ethnicity. As the generation most acutely experiencing discrimination based on their ascribed ethnic identity, teenagers wear dress which expresses Hmong cohesiveness and pride. By wearing a mix of Hmong sub-styles teenagers visibly accept and celebrate their ascribed ethnic identity both as individuals and as corporate representatives of their families and community.

In conclusion, I propose a classification system for dress that marks opposing cultural identities. My classification system differentiates between dress expressing symmetrical totemic relationships between structurally similar groups, and dress expressing asymmetrical ethnic relationships between structurally dissimilar groups. I propose that regionally distinct Hmong dress styles worn in Lao villages marked totemic differences between similar and equally powerful Hmong sub-groups. In contrast, Hmong American style dress worn at New Year marks an ethnic boundary between the Hmong and what they perceive to be more politically and economically powerful groups.

The term ethnic is often used as a convenient substitute for academically dated terms such as tribal and primitive (see Chapman, McDonald and Tonkin 1989: 14). Because of this convenient quality, ethnicity (and the related term, ethnic dress) is a slippery concept that has been used in many different ways in many different places. The use of the term "ethnic dress" to refer to defined characteristics of a specific type of social boundary, as suggested in this chapter, transforms it from a convenient label into a useful concept. Further, it begins to build necessary linkages between academic literature focused upon defining ethnic identity and research on dress.

References

Barth, F. (1969), *Ethnic Groups and Boundaries: The Social Organization of Cultural Difference*, Boston: Little Brown.

Bodnar, J. (1985), *The Transplanted*, Bloomington: Indiana University Press.

Chapman, M., McDonald, M., and Tonkin, E. (1989), "Introduction" in *History and Ethnicity*, London and New York: Routledge.

Cohen, A. (1973), *Urban Ethnicity*, London: Tavistock Publications.

Comaroff, J.L. (1987), "Of Totemism and Ethnicity: Consciousness, Practice and the Signs of Inequality," *Ethnos*, vol. 52, nos. 3–4, pp. 301–23.

Cubbs, J. (1986), "Hmong Art: Tradition and Change," in *Hmong Art: Tradition and Change*, Sheboygan, WI: John Michael Kohler Arts Center.

Dewhurst, C.K., and MacDowell, M. (1983), "Michigan Hmong Arts," *Publications of the Museum, Michigan State University, Folk Culture Series*, vol. 3, no. 2.

Epstein, A.L. (1978), *Ethos and Identity*, London: Tavistock.

Erekosima, T., and Eicher, J. (1981), "Kalabari Cut-thread and Pulled-thread Cloth," *African Arts*, vol. 14, no. 2, pp 48–51, 87.

Geddes, W.P. (1976), *Migrants of the Mountains: The Cultural Ecology of the Blue Miao of Thailand*, Oxford: Clarendon Press.

Glazer, N., and Moynihan, D.P. (1975), *Ethnicity, Theory and Experience*, Cambridge, MA: Harvard University Press.

Glick-Schiller, N., and Fouron, G. (1990), "Everywhere We Go, We are in Danger: Ti Manno and the Emergence of a Haitian Transnational Identity," *American Ethnologist*, vol. 17, no. 2, pp. 329–46.

Lindbergh, S.M. (1988), "Traditional Costumes of Lao Hmong Refugees in Montana: A Study of Cultural Continuity and Change," unpublished Master's thesis, Minneapolis, MN: University of Montana.

Lynch, A. (1992), "Hmong American New Year's Dress: A Material Culture Approach," unpublished Ph.D. dissertation, Minneapolis, MN University of Minnesota (*Dissertation Abstracts International*, 53, 228B).

Lynch, A., Detzer, D., and Eicher J. (1995), "Hmong American New Year Rituals: Generational Bonds through Dress," in *Clothing and Textiles Research Journal*, vol. 13, no. 2, pp. 111–20.

Mallinson, J., Donnelly, N., and Hang L. (1988), *Hmong Batik: A Textile Technique from Laos*, Seattle, WA: Mallison/Information Services.

Moerman, M. (1964), "Ethnic Identification in a Complex Society: Who Are the Lue?" *American Anthropologist*, vol. 67, pp. 1215–30.

Peterson, S.N. (1990), "From the Heart and the Mind: Creating *paj ntaub* in the Context of Community," unpublished Ph.D. dissertation, University of Pennsylvania (*Dissertation Abstracts International*, 51, 1724A).

Roosens, E.E. (1989), *Creating Ethnicity: The Process of Ethnogenesis*, Newbury Park: Sage.

Sarna, J. (1978), "From Immigrants to Ethnics: Towards a New Theory of 'Ethnicization'," *Ethnicity*, vol. 5, pp. 370–8.

Tapp, N. (1988), "The Reformation of Culture: Hmong Refugees from Laos," *Journal of Refugee Studies*, vol. 1, no. 1, pp. 20–37.

14

Ethnic Conflict and Changing Dress Codes: A Case Study of an Indian Migrant Village in Highland Ecuador

*Carola Lentz**

In Ecuador, dress plays an important role in the construction of ethnic identity and in dealing with ethnic boundaries. It can represent a form of silent rebellion against ethnic stereotypes. In the *mestizo* market towns in the highland, successful Indian migrants deliberately wear the clothing once reserved for *mestizos*, unequivocally demonstrating that they no longer tolerate the image thrust on them of the dirty, primitive, and rustic Indio. By adapting their dress to that of the urban lower classes when on the coast, these same migrant peddlers attempt to hide their ethnic origins. Conversely, at festivals, in music ensembles, or at political meetings, certain articles of clothing such as the poncho are considered symbols of belonging to the Indian community, and are used by returned migrants and other villagers alike to demonstrate cultural difference and a new ethnic consciousness.

Changes in conventions of dress also reflect the transformation of survival strategies of the small-scale Indian farmers as a result of labor migration and increasing scarcity of land. Clothing used to be made by hand; now it is bought at the market. New modes of dress, and shifts in patterns of consumption in general, are results of and at the same time an impetus for a comprehensive process which integrates the

* Translated from German by Allison Brown

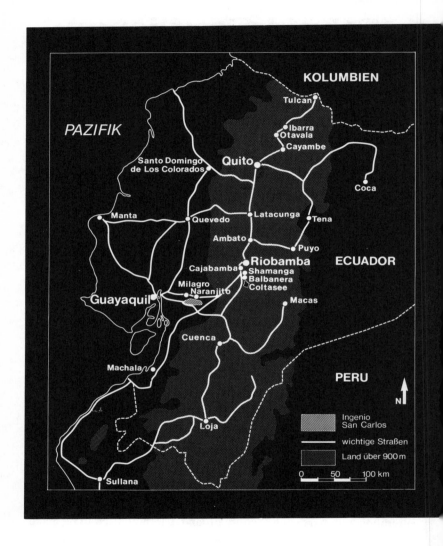

Map 14.1 Ecuador

Indians to a greater and greater extent with the market and the state, thus changing their relationship to the ruling *mestizos* and whites.[1] As a material object, clothing is thus an integral part of the economic transformations that lay the basis for a redefinition of the inter-ethnic relations in the Ecuadorian highland and on the coast. At the same time, dress becomes a symbol in the very struggle over this redefinition.

Dress, however, is not merely a form of non-verbal communication, but is repeatedly the subject of commentary and discourse. Biting remarks by urban *mestizos* clearly show that they understand the message of the Indian fashion rebels, who in fact use clothing to protest against the ethnic status quo. *Mestizos* have voiced complaints regarding the lack of respect they experience, the rebelliousness of the young Indians, and the decline of the "Indian culture" as expressed by the shift in clothing trends. *Indio revestido*, or disguised Indians, is the disparaging expression used for so-called assimilated Indian migrants who dare to deny their background. Young Indian girls sneer at older (and poorer) women who still wear the once common, loosely woven shawls of coarse wool; in the eyes of the young, these woolen shawls are a sign of rural backwardness. As my hosts dressed me in their typical village dress for the Carneval celebration, when everything is turned topsy-turvy, there was much laughter, though it would have been considered presumptuous and an encroachment of ethnic boundaries for me to wear Indian dress in everyday life. As a going-away present, my *compadre* — my host in the village and the father of my godchild — gave me the poncho he had worn at his wedding and told me that I should wear it when I arrived at the airport in Frankfurt, so that my German family and all my friends would see how "we *runas* [Quichua for "people"] live here, what our culture is like . . .".

1. Indians, *mestizos*, and whites are social categories relevant to Ecuadorian society whose definition has experienced significant transformation in the course of history, from a strictly legal interpretation in colonial times to socio-biological and cultural understandings in the post-colony. Current popular usage would define Indians as "pure" descendants of the autochthonous inhabitants, whites as similarly "pure" offsprings of the Spanish conquerors and later immigrants, and finally *mestizos* as persons of mixed Spanish and Indian origins. Of course, this is far from being a factual account of the composition of Ecuadorian society, but it represents a powerful ideology ordering the much more complex social universe. Most of the conflicts referred to in this article are between *mestizos* and Indians, but whites generally discriminate against Indians in a quite similar fashion. Differences between *mestizos* and whites who usually regard themselves as socially superior to the "half-breeds" are beyond the scope of this paper and will be only occasionally referred to.

The elements with which Indians in Ecuador today characterize their cultural difference are often part of the repertoire of the dominant *mestizo* and white cultures. The ethnic identity associated with a particular way of dress is subject to changes and shifts in the course of history; that which is now vehemently referred to as Indian was originally introduced by the Spaniards and later worn by the *mestizos*. Some of the changes in dress which will be discussed here have come as a result of major changes in economic survival strategies; others follow urban fashion trends. The definitive point, however, is that an ethnic boundary is drawn over and over again, both by the *mestizos* and the Indians. Articles of clothing – as well as other consumer goods – designate affiliation to one or the other side.[2] The focus on change with respect to conventions of dress, as suggested by this case study, prevents an excessively rigid structuralistic view with a one-sided interpretation of the dress code as a semiotic system.[3] Instead, it forces a study of the complex interaction of economic, political, and cultural factors concerning dress codes by taking into particular account the structural constraints, and the scope of the actors and the situation-dependent strategic use of dress.

Ethnicity represents the model according to which Indian migrants gauge their many experiences of foreignness, exploitation, and isolation. It stakes out the social sphere within which solidarity can be expected in strange surroundings. As a result, a new imagined community of Indians and a new ethnic consciousness emerge, which extend far beyond village borders. "Traditional" and "modern" elements are integrated in this consciousness, which rejects *mestizo* stigmatization of the Indians as "uncivilized," thus transforming the

2. Ethnicity and "culture" are referred to here in a theoretical framework that stresses the historical construction of social identities; no substantial cultural (or otherwise primordial) differences distinguish Indians from *mestizos* or whites. There is, however, a definite ethnic boundary which has been established by both sides and which is continually justified on the basis of alleged cultural differences. See Barth (1969) for general comments, Cohen (1985) on the symbolic construction of community, and Hobsbawm and Ranger (1983), on the "invention of tradition." With respect to the creation of Indian ethnicity in the Andes, see Rasnake (1982), Stern (1987), Hill (1988), and Jackson (1991).
3. See Cordwell and Schwarz (1979), Schneider (1987), and Weiner and Schneider (1989) for an overview of recent anthropological research on dress. Drucker (1963) is one of the few early examples of the fruitfulness of examining dress codes in a study on social change. See also Douglas and Isherwood (1979) and Appadurai (1986) for a general discussion on the sociology and anthropology of consumer goods.

inter-ethnic relations in the highlands as well.[4] In 1990, this transformed everyday ethnicity also took on collective, political dimensions which came to a peak in a *levantamiento indígena*, an Indian rebellion.[5] Clothing represents a significant field in which inter-ethnic relations are fought out and redefined.

In this chapter, I will first discuss two popular explanations for the shift in patterns of consumption, outlining the perspective found to be most appropriate by this study. This will be followed by some background information on the history of the case study village[6] and the ethnic dress code which influenced highland Ecuador up to the 1950s. I will then show how and why the male migrant workers on the coast have appropriated new articles of clothing. After that, we will return to the village with the migrants and their new dress, and observe the changes in the dress code in the highlands. The last section is devoted to Indian women; since their economic and social roles differ from those of the men, they also deal very differently with ethnicity and dress.

Two Explanations for the Shift in Patterns of Consumption

New goods offered by an expanding capitalistic market are fascinating to residents of "traditional" village communities; at least, that is a common finding of many studies on social modernization processes in the so-called Third World. Acquisition of consumer goods presupposes the earning of money. The felt need for these goods is therefore considered one of the most decisive levers for the growing market integration of households which previously produced mostly for their own consumption. What has rarely been the subject of study,

4. See Lentz (1986, 1991, 1988a, b, and c) for an extensive discussion of changes in the village as a result of migrant labor, survival strategies of migrants away from home, and the emerging new Indian consciousness.

5. See Sanchez-Parga (1984), CONAIE (1988, 1990), as well as Frank (1991).

6. The case study is based on field research that I conducted from 1983 to 1985, also including a shorter visit in 1989, in the Ecuadorian highlands, on a sugar cane plantation, and in various coastal cities having a large number of Indian migrant workers from the province of Chimborazo. In particular, I got to know one village, Shamanga, very intensively, though my observations regarding dress apply to many neighboring villages and other highland provinces in Ecuador as well. The main goal of the project, which can only be described here briefly, was to study the tension between continuity of older social forms and their transformation through labor migration. In particular, the study dealt with the crystalization of new forms of Indian identity.

however, is how and why such new desires develop and spread, and whether and to what extent traditional applications are maintained in the use of new goods, or whether new forms of use emerge.

Two main explanations exist for the shift in patterns of consumption. The first assumes a relatively stable need structure. Since goods produced within a capitalistic system can be less expensive or better in quality, according to this theory, these goods would replace merchandise that was previously produced by the farmers themselves or by craftspeople in a local subsistence economy. With cash income obtained through migration or agricultural production for the market, and through the purchase of the desired goods, small-scale farmers could thus satisfy their needs better and more completely than by direct production for their own consumption. It is not that the needs are new, but society's development of a division of labor which explains the changes in consumer behavior. According to this hypothesis, the residents of a village would replace their self-made wool ponchos with synthetic jackets and scarves that are bought with their migration income, because in this way they can better and more optimally satisfy their clothing needs.

This division of labor theory overlooks the fact that these new patterns of consumption are rarely simple substitutions for the goods no longer used. Many of the bought objects are used alongside home-manufactured goods and satisfy needs which previously did not exist at all. Aside from that, the new merchandise is not necessarily longer-lasting, better-tasting, more nutritious, warmer, more beautiful or even less expensive than the goods formerly used. The supposed advantages of the substitution process are not always apparent.[7]

The second widely expounded theory regarding the change in patterns of consumption attempts to analyze the shift in needs, which the division of labor thesis fails to do satisfactorily. Based on the idea of rising expectations, this theory assumes that members of "traditional" societies have a limited level of need only because they lack information about the options available. Their needs are basically alterable and unlimited. As soon as village residents learn of additional goods through schooling, mass communication, or their work in the city, they become aware of what they lack. Consequently, they desire these goods and spread this desire – via demonstration/imitation – throughout their group. In fact, however, contrary to this theory, acceptance of new consumer goods does not occur automatically as a

7. See Spittler (1982: 93ff).

result of contact and information. Not all new offers are actually taken advantage of and, as with the Tuareg nomads in the Niger, there are cases in which traditionally used foods, cooking utensils, and clothing are tenaciously retained, despite long-term knowledge of modern consumer goods. The use and apparent superiority of the modern goods are often not as evident to the potential consumers as the producers would like. General distribution of new consumer goods almost always seems to be preceded by far-reaching changes in the economic conditions of reproduction of the buyer group. This is a factor which the rising expectations thesis fails to consider, as it instead assumes a kind of automatic force of attraction which guides the influx of modern goods.

Dress is one of the domains of consumption that appears to be particularly prone to change, much more than, for instance, food or housing. The acquisition of new clothing is often regarded as one of the most important levers for the cultural and economic incorporation of villagers into the capitalist labor market.[8] It thus makes an especially worthwhile field for the refutation of the explanations outlined above. The following example that describes changes in the dress code in an Indian village in the Ecuadorian highlands will demonstrate how a very complex process is concealed behind what on the surface seems to be the uncritical acceptance of new consumer goods. Economic and also ideological and ethnic factors play important roles in this process.

It will be shown, at least in the initial phase of adoption of these goods, that the new goods by no means completely replace older ones, nor are they less expensive. On the contrary, the acquisition of these goods, which is actually quite costly, is much more due to the ethnic discrimination on the coast experienced by village migrants. In the subsequent phase, acquiring the goods is closely related to changes in village survival strategies. Not until one confronts the interplay of changes in the economic subsistence foundation of the village and the family division of labor and allocation of time, as well as changes in the measure of social status in the village and ethnic conflicts, is it

8. In particular, studies on migrant labor in Africa describe the substitution of compulsory wage labor on the basis of a motivation to acquire new goods and through a monetization of social relations; see for example Skinner (1965), Habermeier (1982), Franke (1982), and Lentz and Erlmann (1989). Douglas and Isherwood (1979: 15–24) and Spittler (1991) contain a summary and criticism of common explanations for the adoption of new consumer goods; Kaschuba (1988) includes a discussion of historical consumer research.

possible to understand why only certain articles of clothing of all those offered on the market are sought, or why women and men have altered their "traditional" dress in different ways. The one-sidedness of the explanations outlined can only be eliminated if – as is attempted here – the people involved are taken seriously as actors and not seen merely as victims of advertising strategies and external influences.

A Village of Migrant Workers

Shamanga is an Indian village of barely fifty households in the highland Ecuadorian province of Chimborazo. The small, often sloping fields of the village residents, which lie at an altitude of 10,200–11,160 ft and cover a total area of slightly over 40 hectares (approximately 100 acres), are not enough to guarantee survival. Older households rarely have more than one hectare (2½ acres). Younger couples often own only a very small piece of land with a house and a few rows of potatoes, beans and barley; some continue to live with their parents. Almost all of the men in the village – and some of the younger women as well – work on the coast most of the year as street traders in the cities or as seasonal workers on a sugar cane plantation.

Until well into the 1940s, and for some households even up until the 1960s, daily survival of the families was still primarily based on the ties of the village community to the *hacienda* of a local large landowner. Most of the food and a major portion of the clothing was prepared by hand. In exchange for unpaid labor in the fields and residence of the landowner, the Shamangeños were allowed to cultivate parcels of land for their own use and they could use the pastures, water, straw, wood and roads of the *hacienda*.

In the 1930s, the first Shamangeños worked sporadically as wage laborers on the growing coastal plantations. The money they brought back to the village served primarily to finance village festivals, to get through periods of financial crisis due to crop failure or sickness, and – as land sometimes came up for sale in the 1920s and after – to purchase small plots. When in the 1940s a new landlord limited the rights of the tenant farmers with respect to use of *hacienda* resources, finally dissolving the tenure system in the early 1960s and driving the Shamangeños from the *hacienda* land, migration assumed a steadily growing level and significance. The majority of the village households were not able to buy enough land in the highlands to satisfy even their most basic nutritional needs. As a result, for many, income from migrant labor became the greatest financial resource for the family.

Nevertheless, up to now hardly any families have moved to the coast permanently. The ties of the migrants to family and the village community in the highlands have not weakened. Even a small piece of land in the village and the assurance of family solidarity offers security in the case of sickness or unemployment, and in old age. The village community is also the most important point of reference as regards the migrants' sense of social belonging. Baptisms, marriages, funerals, and family and village festivals are still tied to the highland village. Since Indians experience discrimination and isolation on the plantations and in the cities, the migrants receive social recognition only in the village. Migration is a way out for them, which they only take in order to survive at home.

At the same time, this constant confrontation with life outside the village has led to the development in Shamanga of new experiences, knowledge and standards for measuring social status. Everyday family life and the social relationships and political organization in the village have fundamentally changed as a result. "We used to live so backward; but now we're civilized:" such remarks are often made by Shamangeños to summarize the obvious changes in their lifestyle since their dependence on the *hacienda* came to an end. "Civilization" is generally used to refer to the lifestyles of the *mestizos* and the whites in the cities, or rather, to what the Indians consider urban. For them, "being civilized" is using new, manufactured consumer goods, building homes in the village modelled after city houses, celebrating festivals differently from before, adopting new ideas and new ways of doing things, and speaking Spanish.

In the last two decades, more and more goods have indeed made their way into everyday village life. Today almost all of the clothing is industrially produced, and much of the food eaten daily is no longer produced by the village residents themselves. Plastic and enamel bowls have long since replaced the locally-crafted clay and wooden ones; concrete has substituted adobe bricks, and corrugated iron has replaced the thatched roofs. There have been major changes in what is considered necessary for survival in the village, which have incorporated goods to a greater and greater extent, thereby making migrant labor increasingly indispensible.

An Ethnic Dress Code

Clothing was one of the first areas of consumerism in which the Shamangeños introduced change. "They dress *amulaya* [Quichua for

Figure 14.1 The *mestizo* poncho with collar. Photograph by
Carola Lentz.

"just like White men"]!" is how the older villagers criticized the first younger migrants who returned to the village from the plantations in the 1950s, dressed in styles of clothing which were previously reserved for *mestizos*. Up to that time, the Indian men normally wore wide, calf-length pants without a fly, held up at the waist with a colorful woven belt, and a loosely-fitted, simple shirt without buttons or a collar. Both were usually hand-sewn out of light cotton. The *cushma*, a relatively short, small poncho, was worn over this, as it provided some warmth as well as the freedom of movement necessary for work in the fields. Outside work, one or more larger ponchos were worn over the *cushma* for additional warmth and decoration. On their heads, Indian men wore a white wool hat, often dirty from wear, with a cornmeal-stiffened brim, and on their feet they wore hemp sandals or went barefoot. The ponchos, without collars or fringes, were woven from coarsely spun sheepswool. They had colors and stripes that, like their hatbands, varied from village to village and denoted the marital status and background of the wearer.[9]

The local *mestizos*, on the other hand, wore narrower long pants and buttoned shirts, made of flannel, gabardine, or even synthetics. They wore either shoes or leather boots, a felt hat and, most important, a more finely woven poncho with a collar and fringes over a simple suit jacket. As money-lenders, store owners, buyers of Indian products, and local political authorities, the *mestizos* controlled the Indian tenant farmer families economically and politically, and justified their rule on the basis of ethnic discrimination. They labeled the Indians as "uncivilized animals" and "the inferior race," and the ethnic boundary was clearly expressed through dress.[10]

What the *mestizos* considered "traditional Indian" dress, against which the younger migrants were starting to dare to rebel, had of course long since been influenced by colonial Spanish clothing. In a study evaluating archeological and iconographic finds, colonial sources, and early travel reports, Bollinger (1983: 135ff) shows how dress codes were already a means of designating social and regional affiliation during the Incan empire. The authorities of conquered peoples presented the Inca rulers with splendid articles of clothing in order symbolically to integrate themselves into the empire. At the same

9. See Costales (1957: 164ff), Mencias (1962: 29ff), and Barba (1968: 65ff) on Indian dress in the province of Chimborazo in the 1950s and 1960s.
10. Burgos (1977) offers an analysis of the interaction between ethnic discrimination and economic exploitation in the province of Chimborazo; see also Sylva (1986). On the province of Imbabura, see Ramón (1987) and Guerrero (1991).

time, fabric and clothing played an important role in the tribute paid by the conquered regions.[11]

The Spanish adopted this form of politics through clothing after their conquest of the Andean states in the sixteenth century. At first, only the Indian nobility were allowed to wear Spanish clothing – that is, those who held important functions in the colonial ruling order. This external equality with the Spaniards was intended to raise the esteem and authority of the Indian government officials and tax collectors in the eyes of the village population. This was later extended to allow members of the village council and wealthier farmers interested in assimilating themselves to wear certain articles of traditional Spanish clothing, such as a felt hat, shoes, a sleeveless coat, short pants gathered at the knee, and a collared shirt. The number of articles of Spanish clothing and the quality of the fabric designated the social status of a person. Only the Indian upper class was permitted to dress exclusively in Spanish clothing; any Indian of lower status was required to continue to wear items of what was considered traditional Indian dress. Generally, the lower class was only allowed to wear a Spanish hat.

In the second half of the eighteenth century, however, the Spanish colonialists attempted to push through a new, largely Hispanicized dress code for the Indian population, which consisted of baggy pants, jacket, shirt, hat, and the poncho, which had only been introduced during the colonial period. The differences among the various Indian classes were to be levelled out in order to disempower the Indian authorities who had played a leading role in the anti-colonial rebellions which flared up at the time. A fossilized form of the city dress became commonly regarded as the Indian costume in various Andean regions, and lasted until long into the twentieth century. After independence, in the early nineteenth century, though varying from region to region, the farming Indian population had been economically forced into the defensive. They had less and less chance of bettering their positions socially and, no longer participating in the shift in fashion that other social groups experienced, isolated themselves culturally.

The *mestizos*, on the other hand, maintained political and economic power as the rural and small town upper class. Not until much later did they have to give up this power to the "white" city bourgeoisie;

11. See Salomon (1980: 137ff), Moya (1988), and Murra (1989) on Incan and Spanish politics through clothing.

thus they continued to experience the European changes in fashion much longer than the Indians.[12] The *mestizos* were interested in maintaining the differences between their dress and that of the Indians, as this made it easier immediately to recognize the ethnic affiliation of a person and treat them according to their status. When the first Shamangeño labor migrants not only bought a new type of hat, shoes, pants and shirts to use on the plantations, but also in the 1950s started wearing a mestizo-style poncho, the *mestizos* considered their behavior to be a presumptuous encroachment of their once uncontested superiority.

A New Mode of Dress on the Coast

As in the highlands, Indians were also considered an "inferior race" on the coast. The first migrants who arrived on the plantations in "traditional" Indian dress, which was and is considered a sign of backwardness, were mocked by *mestizo* foremen and co-workers. This is why the first purchases of the Shamangeños were often new pants tailored in the style common on the coast, colorful nylon shirts, shoes or at least rubber sandals, and a different type of hat, in order to discourage ethnic discrimination as much as possible. Showing up in new, clean clothes in the small plantation towns also demonstrated that they had enough money to match the *mestizos* and earn a certain respectability. On the other hand, for the Indian traders in the cities, modern clothing such as jeans or synthetic pants, tennis shoes, a nylon shirt, and a sport jacket was virtually indispensible as a work tool; they assumed that no one would want to buy from traditionally dressed Indians who were considered to be "dirty."

In trying to adapt to urban fashions, the migrant workers have selected only a few particularly obvious aspects from the wide variety of contrasts between the foreign dress and their own. That which they have taken on from urban dress is more often characterized by its great distinction from what used to be commonly seen in the village, as by the fact that it is considered a central piece of clothing among the city dwellers.[13] Everything "modern" is crystalized, in the view of the

---

12. See Lindig and Münzel (1976: 349ff).

13. See Bourdieu (1982) on the relevance of "difference" in consumerism for the expression of social affiliation. For Ecuador, the theory can be put forward that different social (ethnic) groups have each developed their own respective reference system for the definition of "difference," and that perception criteria are not shared among all members of society.

Figure 14.2 Young migrants back in the village. Photograph by Carola Lentz.

Indian migrant workers, in such details, which are quickly adopted by the less innovative imitators in the village peer group. Such "modern" items and details often develop a remarkable resistance to subsequent shifts in urban fashions, a fact that leads to the rural Indian origins' easy identification, in spite of the migrants' original intention of making ethnic differences unrecognizable.

For example, one of the favorite articles of clothing of younger Indian migrants is a plastic baseball cap. This was apparently "in" among lower class adolescents in the city at one time, though this is no longer the case; usually they do not wear any hat at all. Most Indians might feel uncomfortable and naked without anything at all on their heads, since in the highlands, both women and men always wear a hat. A plastic baseball cap, compared to the common wool or felt hats, is a considerable concession to the urban pattern and certainly a suitable compromise between feeling naked and appearing "traditional."

The young migrants like to wear this cap not only on the coast, but, to impress their peers, in the highlands as well. Young Indians who have not yet become migrant laborers consider these migrants as role models. Before ever setting foot in the city, they already have the idea that this is "the" way to dress there and that wearing such a cap is a way to avoid ridicule. Although unintentional, this cap has become a signal identifying Indian migrants on the coast. Other articles of clothing or other objects which are very popular among Shamangeños have a similar effect. The bell-bottom pants, nylon shirts with large floral patterns or old-fashioned plastic travel bags from airlines, for example, that are so popular with Indian migrants have little in common with the tastes of lower class *mestizos* in the cities.

A New Mode of Dress "At Home"

Wearing a new style of clothing on the coast had, above all, the goal of concealing one's ethnic background. In the highlands, however, it served primarily as a silent form of protest against the unwritten ethnic dress code. It was an affront to *mestizos* and a way in which Indians could oppose their stigmatization as uncivilized, dirty, dumb peasants. But even in their own village, "modern" dress and a conspicuous wristwatch were symbols of opposition, often provoking criticism from the older generation. In the village hierarchy, young migrants did not enjoy especially high status. They were unmarried or recently married, and still lived in the parents' household; they owned very little or no land at all and had not yet organized a village festival. In short, they were not yet considered full members of the community according to rural standards. Their dress, as well as the consumption of alcohol or new foods, became a means of demonstrating their success as wage laborers and their newly achieved access to cash. Differences in price and quality between traditional and modern clothing played only a secondary role in deciding on a new wardrobe. Wool spun by women in the village was used for the common Indian collarless ponchos. They were woven either by male family members or by local specialists who were paid with food, liquor, or other services. The finely woven and carefully dyed *mestizo* ponchos worn by returning migrant workers were only made in certain locations and sold at the market. They had to be bought with cash, and even after common ponchos were available at the market, the finely woven ponchos with a collar were considerably more expensive. Buying a *mestizo* poncho instead of trading for an ordinary collarless one or wearing a self-made one, was primarily a matter of prestige.

Not until the late 1960s did it become an absolute economic necessity to buy certain articles of clothing. After the *hacienda* was dissolved, the Shamangeños lost their access to pastureland and consequently had to reduce drastically the size of their sheep herds. Today, no family in the village has access to enough wool to produce all of its own clothes. Buying additional raw wool to spin, weave and dye would be more expensive than purchasing the finished synthetic products that are increasingly available at the market. Further, it is not only a shortage of raw materials that leads to decreased demand for the old, self-made ponchos and shawls, and makes room for bought synthetic products; changes in the allocation of time in daily life also contribute to this shift. Women have less and less time to spin, since they are responsible for all the farming tasks while their migrating husbands are absent. Children, who used to help with sheep tending, spinning, and weaving, now attend school during the day. And only the older men know anything of the art of weaving, while the younger ones spend most of the year on the coast. Whereas thirty years ago modern clothing was considerably more expensive than "traditional" clothes, exactly the opposite is true today.

Since modern clothing bought at the market has become more widely used, it has lost some of its significance as a demonstration of ethnic consciousness. Even so, dress patterns remain a sphere in which a silent battle for status and prestige is fought out. While most of the young migrant workers tailor their own pants and shirts out of synthetic fabrics or buy the least expensive goods on the market, some

Figure 14.3 Female dress: "traditional" of wool (right) and "modern" of synthetics (center). Photograph by Carola Lentz.

– especially high school students in the village – wear much more expensive, tightly fitting jeans. Anyone taking pride in himself wears a two-sided poncho of the finest wool made in Otavalo, a region famous for its weaving, even though these cost many times over the price of synthetic ponchos or the lined nylon blousons that have recently gained popularity. Although returning seasonal workers appear in the fields wearing rubber boots, young migrant traders, who often own hardly any land, demonstrate their distance to farming tasks by wearing clean, delicate leather shoes.

The "Conservatism" of the Women

While the men took on the role of the "money maker" very early on, until only a few years ago the women were tied almost exclusively to the sphere of subsistence production in the village. Recently, many young women have started accompanying their husbands as small traders in the coastal cities and some young girls travel to the city to assist relatives at home and with the shopping. Their contacts to the world outside the village are much more closely associated with the family and other village residents than those of the men, however, and Shamanga women are generally more "conservative" than the men in terms of accepting new consumer goods. However, especially since clothing can no longer be made by hand, the typical dress of the women has also changed in the last fifteen or twenty years. In contrast to changes in the men's dress, the women almost never use modern articles of clothing to replace the conventional dress; instead, colorful synthetic fabrics are used in old applications.

The *anacu*, a large rectangular piece of fabric which is wrapped around the hips and held at the waist with a woven belt, is worn like a long skirt. Even Indian women traders in the city have maintained it in their dress. They have also refused to do without elaborate jewelry – numerous necklaces and bracelets, and large earrings – and colorful woven bands tied around long ponytails hanging down their backs. Only the *bayeta*, a rectangular shawl that is held together around the shoulders by a large pin in the front, is sometimes left at home by women in the city if it is too hot, though it is always worn in the highlands. Coarse woolen cloth undershirts have been largely replaced by synthetic sweaters or embroidered blouses. Very few younger women now go barefoot. Women normally do not respond to discrimination by the *costeños*, or coastal residents, with attempts to fit in as the men do; rather, they tend to retreat to their own Indian groups.

Verguenza, or shame, is the expression often used by Shamanga women with respect to issues of dress. For example, a young migrant man wanted to convince his wife, who accompanied him to the plantation to work as a cook, to wear a simple dress like the *mestizo* women on the coast and to wear her hair down, since it was embarrassing to him to have a woman in Indian dress at his side. She refused adamantly, saying that she would be ashamed in front of her mother and the whole world to cast off the traditional Indian dress. Young Shamanga girls are ashamed to wear the conventional coarsely-woven dark woolen fabrics, and they tease girls from other regions of the province who still do. Their first self-earned money is inevitably spent on jewelry, new fabrics and plastic sandals, and they rival in their efforts to get dressed up lavishly. The two daughters of a successful Shamanga potato trader in Machala, who go to high school on the coast in simple *mestizo* dress and with their hair down, would be ashamed to dress that way in their highland village; they would be sure to receive criticism from other Indian women for acting like *mestizos* and whites.

The following story of a young Indian woman plainly shows that women's dress takes on strategic significance regarding ethnic identification and isolation. She initially dresses like a *mestizo* while working in the capital city as a maid. Later on, when she returns to the province of Chimborazo, she wears Indian dress again.

I came back to Riobamba three years ago and when I saw so many Indian women and girls here in the city wearing *anacus* and *bayetas*, I wanted to dress that way again, too. Especially for my mother's sake, I can't wear *mestizo* clothes anymore. She would be ashamed if she visited me in Riobamba and I was wearing different clothes than hers. She would feel like a villager compared to me, since I would be denying my background. When my mother comes to the city, then I just take care that she wears clean and especially beautiful *bayetas* and *anacus*, but I would never want her to change her clothes for my sake . . .

Now there are more and more Indian girls from other villages who go to high school in Riobamba who no longer wear the Indian dress. They are ashamed of their heritage and don't want to be treated like Indians anymore. They think they can better themselves socially by wearing other clothes and rejecting their parents, but they're fooling themselves. Classmates and others notice right away that they're Indians. They aren't accepted as real *mestizos*, but they do think that they're better than their parents. When relatives from the village visit them, they act as though they don't know them. They don't say hello, or they even claim to their *mestizo* schoolmates that they're their servants from the country! You can't imagine what that means to parents who are paying for their education in the sweat of their brow.

When these girls then go back to their villages with their *mestizo* clothing, of course the people talk. First they just laugh and make their jokes, but when the girls don't put the *anacu* back on, then the comments get meaner and they're accused of thinking they're something better, acting like whites. And if it goes that far, then it gets harder and harder to be re-integrated into the village. It's just that in the city, they aren't taken all that seriously either . . . (Excerpted from an interview with Mercedes Tenelema of Licto, held in Riobamba on May 24, 1984)

Despite all permissable and desirable variations in materials and colors, the break with "traditional" dress represents a rejection of the village heritage and ethnic affiliation for the women, as this story clearly shows. For the women much more than for the men, clothing is not just a material possession selected on the basis of price, durability or comfort. Instead, it is a symbol of belonging to a particular social group. Whether made of loosely woven coarse wool, as used to be the norm and is nowadays only common for the older women in Shamanga, or synthetics, even the most economical version of Indian women's clothing was and is more expensive than that of the poorer *mestizos*. That the women have tenaciously held on to elements of "traditional" dress conventions more than the men is primarily due to the fact that they entered into the migration process much later, and even today women only work in the cities for several years before and after getting married, then quickly return to the village.

In the end it is the women who are the small farmers in Shamanga and the ones who maintain the village support network and the local, rural knowledge base and behavior norms, while the men are responsible for earning the money and maintaining contact outside the village as migrant workers. Strong ties to the highland village also make the network of social control among the women very close, whether within or between generations. Breaking convention with respect to dress is sanctioned vehemently.[14]

14. See Lentz (1991) for a thorough discussion of Indian women and their attitudes on changes in patterns of consumption and ethnicity; similarly, Weismantel (1988) shows gender-specific behavior with respect to changes in patterns of consumption in the area of food, and Nadig (1986) discusses the role of women as "guardians of ethnicity."

Conclusion

The example of adoption of new forms of dress and new fabrics in Shamanga clearly shows that changes in patterns of consumption take place within a complex arena of conflict and tension which is adequately analyzed neither in the division of labor theory nor the rising expectations theory. It is not because of an inherent attractive force or superiority of these modern goods that new dress codes evolve; rather, it is due to major historical developments in the village reproductive strategies, the growing crisis in the Shamanga agricultural system, and the increasing significance of the migrant workers' income. As a result of raw material scarcity and changes in time allotment in daily life, clothing which used to be produced by hand must now be purchased at the market.

Nevertheless, especially in the earlier phase but also later in the second phase of widening the general sphere of use, it is not exclusively economic constraints which have led to the adoption of new articles of clothing. Ethnic conflicts and striving for social recognition and acceptance in the village play just as important a role. Male migrant workers respond to the discrimination they experience on the coast with attempts to hide their ethnic affiliation by adopting *mestizo* dress. Wearing "modern" clothing upon returning to the highland, however, is also a way for them to display their access to cash and to rebel against the *mestizos* who attempt to stigmatize them as members of an inferior, uncivilized race. Many men use this adoption of *mestizo* dress as a way of emphasizing their raised consciousness. Women, on the other hand, held and hold on to their "traditional" dress – which is very distinct from that of the *mestizos* – though they supplement this dress with new fabrics and colors.

Both innovative strategies – the women's preservation of a "traditional" Indian style of dress with the incorporation of new materials, and the men's adoption of articles of clothing which were once reserved for the *mestizos* – are part of a single process of re-defining Indian culture and re-structuring the Indian-*mestizo* relationship. To some extent these strategies complement each other, though sometimes bitter arguments ensue between husband and wife or parents and children as to the correct path between "one's own culture" and "civilization."

Such conflicts make it evident there is a price to pay for the construction and stabilization of a new Indian consciousness which demands respect for Indians as "civilized", modern people on a par with, though distinct from, the *mestizos*. Those elements of their own lifestyle which might seem to support the old, contended and feared image of a backward Indian tend to be suppressed and denied. This denial is directed first and foremost at their own history, the history of their own way of dress, onto which the negative stereotype of the Indians held by the *mestizos* is projected. Residents of nearby and more distant Indian villages who have not accepted the new patterns of consumption as much as in Shamanga also suffer from this denial when they are ridiculed as "backward" by Shamangeños. And finally, those in the village who correspond least to the image of the "modern" Indian become targets of such denial — that is, the older and above all the poorer villagers who cannot afford the new clothing, and the women who choose to retain their old way of dressing.

Without the "traditional" foundation which is maintained mostly by the rural women, however, the "modern" village would not be able to survive. A more lasting integration into the urban labor force is denied Indian migrant workers because of ethnic discrimination and lack of adequate training and education, and a more far-reaching monetarization of the economics of the home would result in increased insecurity and poverty. There is much discussion as to what is most appropriate, beautiful, durable or economical, what can be tolerated, or what is considered to be going too far regarding dress codes in the village, in the fields, in the market towns, on the coast, in school or in the capital city. This debate represents a central factor in the weighting of city and village life in the survival strategies of the Indians and their struggle for ethnic identity.

References

Appadurai, A. (ed.) (1986), *The Social Life of Things: Commodities in Cultural Perspective*, Cambridge: Cambridge University Press.

Barba, J. (1968), "La comunidad de San Bartolo-Castug de la provincia del Chimborazo," *Atahualpa*, vol. 2, pp. 49–81.

Barth, F. (ed.) (1969), *Ethnic Groups and Boundaries: The Social Organization of Cultural Difference*, London: George Allen & Unwin.

Bollinger, A. (1983), *So kleideten sich die Inka*, Zürich: Schriftenreihe des Instituts für Lateinamerikanistik.

Bourdieu, P. (1982), *Die feinen Unterschiede. Kritik der gesellschaftlichen Urteilskraft*, Frankfurt: Suhrkamp.

Burgos, H. (1977), *Relaciones interétnicas en Riobamba. Dominio y dependencia en una región indígena ecuatoriana*, México: Instituto Indígenista Interamericano.

Cohen, A.P. (1985), *The Symbolic Construction of Community*, London: Tavistock.

CONAIE (1988), *Las nacionalidades indígenas en el Ecuador. Nuestro proceso organizativo*, Quito: Ediciones Tinkui – CONAIE.

CONAIE et al (1990), *Declaración de Quito y resolución del encuentro continental de pueblos indígenas, Quito, 17–21 de Julio 1990*.

Cordwell, J., and Schwarz, R. (eds) (1979), *The Fabrics of Culture: The Anthropology of Clothing and Adornment*, The Hague: Mouton.

Costales, A. y P. (1957), *Katekil o historia cultural del campesinado del Chimborazo*, Quito.

Douglas, M., and Isherwood, B. (1979), *The World of Goods: Towards an Anthropology of Consumption*, London: Allen Lane.

Drucker, S. (1963), *Cambio de la indumentaria. La estructura social y el abondono de la vestimenta indígena en la villa de Santiago Jamiltepe*, México: Instituto Nacional Indígenista.

Elwert, G., and Fett, R. (eds), *Afrika zwischen Subsistenzökonomie und Imperialismus*, Frankfurt: Campus.

Frank, E. (1991), "Movimiento indígena, identidad étnica y el levantamiento," in *Indios*, Quito: Abya Yala, pp. 499–527.

Franke, M. (1982), "Migration in Nord-Ghana. Auswirkungen auf eine Subsistenzwirtschaft und Perzeption durch die Bauern," in G. Elwert and R. Fett (eds), *Afrika zwischen . . .*, pp. 157–74.

Guerrero, A. (1991), *La semántica de la dominación: el concertaje de indios*, Quito: Ediciones Libri Mundi.

Habermeier, K. (1982), "Selbstversorgende bäuerliche Gemeinschaften, kapitalistische Domination und Migration zwischen Volta-Niger-Raum und Süd-Ghana," in G. Elwert and R. Fett (eds), *Afrika zwischen . . .*, pp. 141–56.

Hill, J. (ed.) (1988), *Rethinking History and Myth: Indigenous South American Perspectives on the Past*, Urbana: University of Illinois Press.

Hobsbawm, E., and Ranger, T. (eds) (1983), *The Invention of Tradition*, Cambridge: Cambridge University Press.

Jackson, J. (1991), "Being and Becoming an Indian in the Vaupés," in G. Urban, and J. Sherzer (eds), *Nation States and Indians in Latin America*, Austin: University of Texas Press, pp. 133–55.

Kaschuba, W. (1988), "Konsum – Lebensstil – Bedürfnis. Zum Problem materieller Indikatoren in der Kultur- und Mentalitätsgeschichte," *Sozialwissenschaftliche Informationen*, vol. 3, pp. 133–8.

Lentz, C. (1986), *Saisonarbeiter auf einer Zuckerrohrplantage in Ecuador. "Buscando la vida" – Auf der Suche nach dem Leben*, Aachen: Herodot. (Spanish edition (1991), *"Buscando la vida." Trabajadores temporales en una plantación de azúcar*, Quito: Abya Yala).

—— (1988a), "Zwischen 'Zivilisation' und 'eigener Kultur'. Neue Funktionen ethnischer Identität bei indianischen Arbeitsmigranten in

Ecuador", *Zeitschrift für Soziologie*, 17, pp. 34–46.

—— (1988b), *"Von seiner Heimat kann man nicht lassen"* – *Migration in einer Dorfgemeinde in Ecuador*, Frankfurt: Campus.

—— (1988c), "Why the Most Incompetent are on the Village Council – Development Projects in an Indian Village in Ecuador", *Sociologia Ruralis*, vol. XXVIII, pp. 199-215.

—— (1991), "Traditionelles Selbstbewußtsein: der 'Konservatismus' der Indio-Frauen in Ecuador," in M. Kampmann and Y. Koller-Tejeiro (eds), *Madre Mia! Kontinent der Machos? Frauen in Lateinamerika*, Berlin: Elefanten Press, pp. 106–25.

—— and Erlmann, V. (1989), "A Working Class in Formation? Economic Crisis and Strategies of Survival among Dagara Mine Workers in Ghana," *Cahiers d'Études Africaines*, 113, pp. 69–111.

Lindig, W., and Münzel, M. (1978), *Die Indianer. Kulturen und Geschichte der Indianer Nord-, Mittel- und Südamerikas*, München: Deutscher Taschenbuch Verlag.

Mencias, J. (1962), *Riobamba: Estudio de la elevación socio-cultural y religiosa del indio*, Bogotá.

Moya, R. (1988), *Los tejidos y el poder y el poder de los tejidos*, Quito: CEDIME.

Murra, J. (1989), "Cloth and Its Functions in the Inka State," in A. Weiner and J. Schneider (eds), *Cloth and Human Experience*, pp. 275–302.

Nadig, M. (1986), *Die verborgene Kultur der Frau. Ethnopsychoanalytische Gespräche mit Bäuerinnen in Mexiko. Subjektivität und Gesellschaft im Alltag von Otomi-Frauen*, Frankfurt: Fischer.

Ramón, G. (1987), *La resistencia andina. Cayambe 1500–1800*, Quito: Centro Andino de Acción Popular.

Rasnake, R.N. (1982), *Domination and Cultural Resistance: Authority and Power among an Andean People*, Durham: Duke University Press.

Salomon, F. (1980), *Los señores étnicos de Quito en la época de los Incas*, Otavalo: Instituto Otavaleño de Antropología.

Sanchez-Parga, J. (1984), "La cuestión étnica: realidades y discursos," in J. Mora Domo et al., *Etnia en el Ecuador: Situaciones y analisis*, Quito: Centro Andino de Acción Popular, pp. 145–82.

Schneider, J. (1987), "The Anthropology of Cloth," *Annual Review of Anthropology*, vol. 16, pp 409–48.

Skinner, E. (1965), "Labor Migration among the Mossi of the Upper Volta," in H. Kuper (ed.), *Urbanization and Migration in West Africa*, Berkeley: University of California Press, pp. 60–84.

Spittler, G. (1982), "Kleidung statt Essen. Der Übergang von der Subsistenz- zur Marktproduktion bei den Hausa (Niger)," in G. Elwert and R. Fett (eds), *Afrika zwischen . . .*, pp. 93–105.

—— (1991), "Armut, Mangel und einfache Bedürfnisse", *Zeitschrift für Ethnologie*, vol. 116, pp. 65–89.

Stern, S.J. (ed.) (1987), *Resistance, Rebellion, and Consciousness in the Andean Peasant World, 18th to 20th Centuries*, Madison: University of Wisconsin Press.

Sylva, P. (1986), *Gamonalismo y lucha campesina*, Quito: Abya Yala.

Weiner, A., and Schneider, J. (eds) (1989), *Cloth and Human Experience*, Washington, D.C.: Smithsonian Institution Press.

Weismantel, M.J. (1988), *Food, Gender and Poverty in the Ecuadorian Andes*, Philadelphia: University of Pennsylvania Press.

15

World Fashion, Ethnic, and National Dress[1]

Joanne B. Eicher and Barbara Sumberg

Ethnicity and ethnic group, like so many less scholarly terms of human identification, occupy one side of a duality, tacit or otherwise of familiarity and strangeness. It is, therefore, unsurprising that their appropriate application would vary very much from one context to another. Even given an agreement about the meaning of the adjective (which is not to be taken for granted), those groupings that look 'ethnic' from south-east England are not those that look 'ethnic' from California, Moscow, or Peking (Chapman, McDonald, and Tonkin 1989: 16).

Introduction

The phenomenon of change in the twentieth century is captured by Appadurai's (1991) concept of a global ethnoscape where human beings move quickly and easily from one part of the globe to another. Appadurai contends that as many people travel from one country to another, they gain access to information about the world beyond their home community, places that are often seen from the outside as ethnic communities. However, the influence and availability of international media in the form of movies, television, and print are pervasive, and are also influential on many people in such ethnic communities who never travel beyond their national or even regional boundaries. The

1. Eicher first presented some of these ideas in papers given in Shanghai and Seoul, for the Symposium on Modern Chinese Attire, January, 1992, and for the annual meeting of the Korean Society of Clothing and Textiles, October, 1992, respectively. She and Sumberg collaborated in revising the latter paper after exchanging observations about fieldwork and travel in Nigeria and India in the 1990s.

media portray people wearing what has been commonly called western dress, especially when the media sources emanate from western countries. Although a wide variety of tailored garments, as well as certain haircuts, cosmetics, and accessories, are often referred to as western, many people in both eastern and western hemispheres wear such items of apparel. Designating items as western for people who wear them in other areas of the world, such as Asia and Africa, is inaccurate. Instead, the terms "world fashion" or "cosmopolitan fashion" are more apt. The anthropologist Ernest Crawley used the latter term in 1912 in an essay on dress, when he commented: "A remarkable tendency is observable at the present day, which is due to increased facilities of travel and inter-communication, towards a cosmopolitan type of dress, European in form" (p. 68).

Such cosmopolitan dress for women can easily be viewed in the pages of *Cosmopolitan* magazine and its wide dispersion understood when we learn from an advertisement that it is printed in twenty-eight editions, in twelve languages, and in more than eighty countries (1993). A prime example of a specific world fashion is that of the ubiquitous blue jeans worn by both males and females on many continents and in many countries (Hofmeister 1994). Similarly, the decision of MTV to begin retailing items of dress to its audience by using its own brand of humor and communication style is intended to have world-wide consumer appeal (Shaw 1994).

Although this volume focuses on dress and ethnicity, ethnic dress in the late twentieth century cannot be analyzed without acknowledging the phenomenon of world fashion, for ethnic dress and world fashion are inter-related. Factors encouraging rapid change in the dress of many people, including the adoption of non-indigenous items, occur along with factors encouraging continued adherence to indigenous forms and styles of dress. Awareness of group affiliation and the power of identification with a group can mobilize actions and emotions of group members in order to identify with a group through dress. The complexities of ethnic identity are acknowledged by de Vos and Romanucci (1982: xi). They define ethnicity on four levels of analysis: "first, in respect to a social structural level; second, as a pattern of social interaction; third, as a subjective experience of identity; and fourth, as expressed in relatively fixed patterns of behavior and expressive emotional style." These patterns of behavior and expressive emotional style include styles of dress and the meanings associated with them.

In a world of shifting identities, dress often indicates an aspect of

Figure 15.1 Young Kalabari man on Bugoma Island, Nigeria. (Photograph by Carolyn Nqozi Eicher, 1991.)

identity, for both group exclusion and inclusion are made apparent through the processes of modifying and supplementing the body. Exclusion and inclusion may be viewed from either an outsider's or insider's perspective. For example, adoption of the seemingly universal or ethnically neutral style of the tailored suit for both males and females in a business setting may communicate willingness and ability to operate in international corporate and political worlds. Leaders of independence movements in Africa were often educated in Europe or the United States and consequently adopted Euroamerican styles of dress while abroad and even later while negotiating or fighting with colonial governments to achieve independence. However, in the flush of independence in the 1960s, many African leaders such as Nkrumah in Ghana and Azikwe in Nigeria reinforced the newly won political sovereignty of their countries by appearing at the United Nations in the attire of their indigenous culture.

An issue that arises in the analysis of ethnic dress is its apparent disappearance and replacement by world fashion as everyday dress around the world. Sometimes ethnic dress is retained solely as display for ceremonial and ritual occasions; often males abandon indigenous styles while females continue to wear them. The wearing of world fashion often appears closely linked to urban living. However, these phenomena are not limited to a division between urban and rural dwellers, for people in non-urban areas are also influenced by world fashion. A review of photographs in newspapers, magazines, and television news images reveals that not only urban dwellers but many others in fairly remote geographical locations wear dress similar in form and style.

Terms and Definitions

The definition of dress as an assemblage of modifications of the body and/or supplements to the body (Roach-Higgins and Eicher 1992; Eicher and Roach-Higgins 1992) includes obvious items placed on the body (the supplements) such as garments, jewelry, and accessories, and also changes in color, texture, smell, and shape made to the body directly. The visual aspect of dress is primary in most face-to-face interaction,[2] but dressing the body can involve all five senses. Fabric

---

2. Gregory Stone (1962), a symbolic interactionist, asserted that appraisal of dress precedes and sets the stage for face-to-face verbal exchange.

textures, lipstick or lip pomade taste, perfume or shaving lotion fragrance, and the sounds made by wearing some jewelry stimulate the senses of touch, taste, smell, and hearing.

Although some scholars use clothing, dress, and fashion interchangeably,[3] these terms are not synonymous (Roach-Higgins 1981). First, clothing and dress are not synonyms because a focus on clothing ignores body modifications as a part of dress. As an example, both temporary and permanent tattoos are popular among young adults and teenagers in the United States and Britain in the 1990s. As part of dressing the body, tattoos, as a body modification, demand as much attention as the study of body supplements or clothing styles in order to understand dress in these countries among this age group. Second, fashion and dress are not synonyms because fashion can be found in many arenas of life, not just in clothing and body adornment.[4] Third, clothing and fashion are not synonyms because not all clothing is fashionable dress.

Ethnic dress is best understood as those items, ensembles and modifications of the body that capture the past of the members of a group, the items of tradition that are worn and displayed to signify cultural heritage. With the introduction of the word "tradition," we must reckon with the phenomenon of change or its apparent lack (Shils 1981).

World Fashion

Most authors agree that fashion is a process involving change, from the introduction of a variation of a cultural form to its acceptance, discarding, and replacement by another cultural form.[5] Roach-Higgins (1981) declares that in addition, awareness of change within one's lifetime is a requisite aspect of fashion:

> One means for determining if fashion in dress exists as a concept among a group of people is to consider fashion in relation to the life span. If people in a society are generally not aware of change in form of dress during their lifetimes, fashion does not exist in that society. Awareness of change is a necessary condition for fashion to exist; the retrospective view of the historian does not produce fashion. (128)

---

3. For a recent example of ignoring the difference between these terms see Davis (1992).

4. See Blumer (1969) for a discussion of this point.

5. A variety of definitions exist. See Sproles (1979) for a useful review.

Many fashions in dress exist simultaneously in complex industrial societies where heterogeneity, rather than homogeneity, of the population is found (Roach-Higgins 1981; Kaiser 1990; Davis 1992). However, simultaneous variations in fashion are not always acknowledged. Frequently the word fashion, when referring to dress, implies styles emanating from an acknowledged fashion center such as Paris,[6] where designers launch new lines each season. This concept suggests a dominant or monolithic fashion with exclusive, custom-made creations found in designer salons. Ensembles, coiffure, and make-up created by *haute couture* designers are presented by world-renowned models on runways and in press releases, fashion magazines, and newspaper articles.

In contrast, daily dress can easily be distinguished from high fashion or *haute couture*; we refer to ordinary dress as world fashion or cosmopolitan fashion. These fashions are the apparel, coiffure, and cosmetics of males and females, adults and children: the dress of ordinary people. Clothing examples of world fashion include jeans, sweatshirts, T-shirts, trench coats, parkas, trousers, skirts, blouses, shirts, blazers, business suits, school uniforms, and athletic shoes. The same process of acceptance, rejection, and replacement of form is found in both high fashion and world fashion whether local or global, for daily dress exhibits change from year to year or season to season just as *haute couture* does.[7]

Ethnic Dress

Ethnic dress is the opposite of world fashion. The former is worn by members of one group to distinguish themselves from members of another by focusing on differentiation. Ethnic dress visually separates one group from another, and can also involve other sensory aspects of dress. Often known as traditional,[8] ethnic dress brings to mind

6. Today, of course, there is no one center of fashion. Although Paris still captures world attention, well-known designers are located in many major cities of the world: London, Milan, New York, Hong Kong, Tokyo.

7. Daily fashions are often influenced by *haute couture* as indicated by theories of trickle down, but can also influence *haute couture* as noted by the idea of bubble up. Many examples of trickle down can be found, ranging from the influence of Dior's new look in 1947 to the influence of designer wedding gowns for Princess Diana on clothing of the masses. Examples of bubble up include jeans and denim and a wide variety of peasant or commoner shoe styles, such as huaraches, espadrilles, and sandals (Polhemus 1994).

8. There are several other words that fall into this category, such as folk, peasant, tribal. These are discussed by Baizerman, Eicher, and Cerny (1994).

images of coiffure, garments, and jewelry that stereotypically never change. In Roach-Higgins' definition of fashion, the implication is that awareness of change within one's lifetime does not occur in ethnic dress.[9] In other words, when used in such a way, the terms "traditional" and "ethnic" imply non-fashionable dress, dress that reflects the past, with slow change and few modernizing influences.[10]

Ethnic dress is bound closely to concerns relating to ethnicity. Controversies by social scientists about group identities abound, relating to political and social tensions of today's world. Major arguments regarding ethnicity center on whether ethnicity is primordial or circumstantial, and are not central to an analysis of dress. Instead, we argue that dress is often a significant visible mark of ethnicity, used to communicate identity of a group or individual among interacting groups of people.

Ethnicity embraces ideas of group cohesion, of insiders versus outsiders, with boundaries that separate outsiders and insiders and symbols that identify members of a group as being distinct from other groups.[11] This "we-ness" includes a common heritage with shared language, similar dress, manners, and lifestyle.

An orientation to the past is also included in defining ethnicity and ethnic identity. De Vos and Romanucci-Ross (1982) provide a useful definition of ethnic identity as "a past-oriented form of identity, embedded in the cultural heritage of the individual or group . . . [that] contrasts with a sense of belonging linked with citizenship within a political state, or present-oriented affiliations to specific groups demanding professional, occupational or class loyalties" (p. 363).

Some authors see ethnicity as distinguishable from religion, caste, or nationality, for the latter focus on current commitments of the individual or group, even though the organization has a significant and identifiable history. Analytically distinguishing ethnicity from religion, caste, or nationality implies that ethnic dress can also be

---

9. Some publications such as Harold and Legg (1990) typically exhibit stereotypes of ethnic dress.

10. Non-fashion is a category that Davis proposes in his chapter on anti-fashion. He extends Polhemus and Proctor's (1978) idea that fashion and anti-fashion are opposing forces, with non-fashion a category for dress outside either of these categories. Roach-Higgins (1981) proposed that some ways of dressing were not fashionable, but she did not discuss anti-fashion.

11. All aspects of social identity are similar in regard to including aspects of insider and outsider identification of group members (Hyman 1942). Berreman (1982) says these may differ and create cognitive dissonance and an effort to rectify the dissonance (p. 71). For an explanation of the theory of cognitive dissonance, see Festinger (1957).

analytically separated. Ethnic dress indicates common or shared ways of dress that identify a group of people who share a common background and heritage. National dress, linked to the socio-political concept of nation-state and political boundaries, identifies citizens with their country. Sometimes national dress has originated as the dress of one ethnic group within a nation-state composed of many ethnic groups. Confounding the concept of ethnic dress is the fact that the cultural heritage of a group may coincide with or include national, religious, or caste factors, depending on the specific group of people and their socio-cultural history.

A classic example of the mixing of ethnic and religious identities can be found in Berreman's (1982) study of a northern city in India. Examples of dress ranged from the conspicuous, all-concealing *burkha* of traditional Muslim women, to the *sari* of stylish Hindu women that can involve subtle regional and sub-regional differences. Berreman cites a *San Francisco Chronicle* dated October 1, 1969 about a Hindu-Muslim riot in Ahmedabad, India. One thousand were said to have died, because "would-be killers identify their victims through dissimilar Hindu and Moslem ways of dressing, many Ahmedabadis have started wearing western clothes as a measure of safety" (p. 85). In this example, individuals used cosmopolitan fashion as a blocking device to escape violence that could ensue from being identified as a member of a particular group.

In a largely homogenous population like that of contemporary South Korea, national and ethnic backgrounds have been isomorphic for most of Korean history. One exception occurred during occupation by the Japanese, which brought about a decree that Japanese trousers called *mompe* must be worn for work; these were an item of dress that the Koreans did not consider their own. Traditional Korean dress, *hanbok*, however, appears simultaneously as national and ethnic because the ethnic borders and national borders coincide. *Hanbok* is therefore ethnic dress only outside the borders of Korea; within the country it is national dress.

In many places, ethnic dress appears to be daily wear for females. Men seem to replace ethnic garb with trousers and shirts more readily than women replace their ethnic apparel with western alternatives. Perhaps in many situations men are recruited or volunteer earlier than women to participate in wage and migrant labor away from home villages and small towns (see chapter 14). Hay (1992) points to exposure to new ideas and situations, plus the demands of the labor market, as factors in shaping the clothing practice of Kenyans in the early twentieth century. Laborers knew they would receive a higher wage if they applied for work wearing shorts and shirt, and subsequently spent their first paychecks upgrading their wardrobes (p. 16). Christian missionaries also affected the dress patterns of many of the people they came in contact with. In the nineteenth century United States, missionaries worked equally as diligently to convert the Dakota Indians of Minnesota to wearing European-style clothes as they did to convert them to Christian beliefs. Cultural and religious values were seen to walk hand in hand, one changing in conjunction with the other (Trayte 1995).

The wearing of western dress was associated with a society moving from a state of "primitivism" to one of "civilization" (Darwin 1872; Dunlap 1928). Indigenous civil servants of colonial regimes were required to adopt the prescribed dress of their masters. But this uniform dress was not without its ambivalences. It was usually differentiated from the dress of the colonialists to make apparent the relative place of everyone in the administration. African and Indian civil servants were required to wear shorts instead of trousers and remove their shoes in the presence of a white superior (Callaway 1992). Some missionaries in Kenya saw Africans in western clothing as a direct threat to the kind of church they wanted to create, and tried to forbid the wearing of trousers and shoes by mission residents and employees (Hay 1992: 10–11).

Ethnic dress often differs from the national dress associated with citizens of a country when several or many ethnic groups exist within the country's boundaries. In Nigeria, what has often become identified as national dress is a composite of the garb of the two largest ethnic groups, the Yoruba and Hausa, giving groups like the Kalabari a reason to wear and flaunt their Kalabari dress as highly distinct. The Kalabari example also illustrates additional points. First, ethnic dress may include borrowed items from other cultures that result in a distinctly identifiable ethnic ensemble because the new outfit is culturally authenticated. Second, ethnic dress is not usually static over time.[12] Although change may not be obvious unless carefully researched, it does occur and needs investigating through oral history, photographs,[13] sketches or drawings, as well as documents. Third,

12. This idea has been developed in Baizerman, Eicher, and Cerny (1994).
13. We refer to the last 150 years that photography has been in existence. Sometimes visual evidence exists, but has not been consulted or recognized even if available.

variety in dress can also be found within a group at any one point in time as creativity and individuality are common human expressions. Some individuals enjoy and practice the art of dress more than others, with the result that not all ethnic dress examples are duplicates of one another. Finally, ethnic dress may not always be worn daily but may constitute dress for a special occasion or for a special location. Thus an individual's wardrobe may contain both ethnic dress and world fashion, to be worn as appropriate to time and place.

Conclusions

World, ethnic, and national dress are inter-related in today's global community. Not everyone living in urban areas wears world fashion, nor does everyone living in non-urban areas wear ethnic dress. Not everyone wants to wear world fashion, for many people prize the distinction offered by wearing ethnic dress. However, people in urban areas may be influenced by ethnic dress when designers use examples as inspiration and when travelers bring back items that become fashionable. A case in point is the *danshiki*, a West African shirt popular with Peace Corps volunteers from the United States that later became adopted widely as fashion among African-Americans.

On the one hand similar dress, as in world fashion, can lower barriers of perceived difference, in contrast to ethnic dress that emphasizes, by means of similar dress, the homogeneity of one group in contrast to members of another. The similarity of world fashion garments, hairstyles, and cosmetics allows individuals to convey to others that they are not members of an esoteric group and consequently open to communication with others. An example in a Hyatt Regency lobby in Atlanta in 1989 of young Japanese businessmen, all dressed in navy blue suits with white shirts and sedate neckties, serves as an illustration. How differently might they have been perceived by others if they had worn *kimonos*, whether or not they spoke English?

On the other hand, world fashion in certain circumstances may invite tension among people if associated with secular values and unseemly behavior. At times, world fashion represents opposition to traditional values and ways of behaving. For example in the case of Iran, after the coming to power of the Ayatollah Khomeini, the veil was encouraged or even required for women to wear. Cosmopolitan dress as street dress for women was banned as a negative symbol of an undesirable world. In such a case, some groups may insist on differentiating themselves visually through dress in order to communicate their actual or desired autonomy.[14] Expecting people to confine themselves to wearing only one type of dress, ethnic dress, is not realistic. Instead, individuals' wardrobes in many places contain both cosmopolitan and ethnic dress ensembles, allowing them to adapt with ease to communicate effectively with others and establish their desired image as any given situation demands.

References

Appadurai, A. (1991), "Global Ethnoscapes: Notes and Queries for Transnational Anthropology," in R. Fox (ed.), *Recapturing Anthropology: Working in the Present*, Sante Fe.

Baizerman, S., Eicher, J.B., and Cerny, C. (1993), "Eurocentrism in the Study of Ethnic Dress," *Dress*, vol. 20, pp. 19–32.

Berreman, G. (1982), "Bazaar Behavior: Social Identity and Social Interaction in Urban Media," in G. de Vos and Romanucci-Ross (eds), *Ethnic Identity: Cultural Continuities and Change*, Chicago: University of Chicago Press.

Blumer, H. (1969), "Fashion: From Class Differentiation to Collective Selection," *The Sociological Quarterly*, vol. 10, no. 3, pp. 275–91.

Callaway, H. (1992), "Dressing for Dinner in the Bush," in R. Barnes and J.B. Eicher (eds), *Dress and Gender: Making and Meaning in Cultural Context*, Oxford: Berg Publishers.

Chapman, M., Tonkin, E., and McDonald, M. (1989), Introduction: *History and Ethnicity*, London: Routledge.

Crawley, E. (1931), *Dress, Drinks, and Drums: Further Studies of Savages and Sex*, London: Methven & Co.

Darwin, G. (1872), "Development in Dress," *Macmillan's Magazine*, vol. 26, pp. 410–16.

Davis, F. (1992), *Fashion, Culture, and Identity*, Chicago: University of Chicago Press.

de Vos, G., and Romanucci-Ross, L. (eds), *Ethnic Identity: Cultural Continuities and Change*, Chicago: University of Chicago Press.

Dunlap, K. (1928), "The Development and Function of Clothing," *Journal of General Psychology*, vol. 1, pp. 64–78.

Eicher, J.B., and Roach-Higgins, M.E. (1992), "Describing and Classifying Dress: Implications for the Study of Gender," in R. Barnes and J.B.

---

14. The example of the veil raises another question about whether or not it symbolizes ethnic dress, national dress, religious dress, or a combination of all three. A recent book by MacLeod (1991) raises this issue and indicates multiplicity of meaning in the act of wearing the veil in Cairo.

Eicher (eds), *Dress and Gender: Making and Meaning* in Cultural Context, Oxford: Berg Publishers.

Festinger, L. (1957), *A Theory of Cognitive Dissonance*, Evanston: Row Peterson.

Harrold, R., and Legg, P. (1990), *Folk Costumes of the World*, London: Blandford.

Hay, M.J. (1992), "Constructing a Modern Identity: Christian Missions, the Labor Market, and Clothing in Colonial Western Kenya," paper presented at conference on Cloth, the World Economy, and the Artisan, Dartmouth College.

Hofmeister, S. (1994), "Used American Jeans Power a Thriving Industry Abroad," *New York Times*, August 22.

Hyman, H. (1942), *The Psychology of Status*, New York.

Kaiser, S. (1990), *The Social Psychology of Clothing: Symbolic Appearances in Context*, New York: Macmillan.

MacLeod, A.E. (1991), *Accommodating Protest: Working Women and the New Veiling in Cairo*, New York: Columbia University Press.

New York Times (1993), January 4.

Polhemous, T. (1994), *Street Style from Sidewalk to Catwalk*, New York: Thames and Hudson.

———, and Proctor, L. (1978), *Fashion and Anti-fashion: Anthropology of Clothing and Adornment*, London: Thames and Hudson.

Roach-Higgins, M.E. (1981), "Fashion," in G. Sproles (ed.), *Perspectives of Fashion*, Minneapolis: Burgess Publishing Co.

Roach-Higgins, M.E., and Eicher, J.B. (1992), "Dress and Identity," *Clothing and Textile Research Journal*, vol. 10, no. 4, pp. 1–10.

Shaw, D. (1994), "On MTV, Home Shopping to a New Beat," *New York Times*, August 22.

Shils, E. (1981), *Tradition*, Chicago: University of Chicago Press.

Sproles, G. (1979), *Fashion, Consumer Behavior Toward Dress*, Minneapolis: Burgess Publishing Co.

Stone, G. (1962),"Appearance and the Self," in A.M. Rose (ed.), *Human Behavior and the Social Processes: An Interactionist Approach*, New York: Routledge and Kegan Paul.

Trayte, D.J. (1995), "Nineteenth Century Missionary Views of the Hygine and Dress of the Eastern Dakota" in M.E. Roach-Higgins, J.B. Eicher, and K.K.P. Johnson (eds), *Dress and Identity*, New York: Fairchild Publications.

Index

(ethnicity)
see also Japanese (ethnicity)
see also Kalabari (ethnicity)
see also Swaziland
   (ethnicity)
exotic, 95, 98, 101–2, 110, 112,
   114, 144, 202

family solidarity, 277
fashion, 29, 191, 202, 299
   cosmopolitan, 296, 302, 304
   Euro-American styles of, 298
   European, 72, 192
      style suits, 74
   definition of, 301
   dominant or monolithic, 300
   glamour and, 198
   high, 300
   in dress, 299–300
   international, 189
   sign system, as a, 29
   uniform, 97
   urban, 281, 283, 304
   Victorian–era, 185
   western, 97
   world, 296–304 *passim*
feminism, 49
figural sculpture, 218
folkloric ornament, 25
funerals
   Botswana, 186, 188, 190
   Kalabari, 153–6, 160

gender, 30–1, 48, 199
   and ethnicity, 195–7
   dual gender systems, 195–
      206 *passim*
   gendered identity, 197
   gender relations, 29
   femininity, 35, 40
   honor-shame societies, 29

identity, 200, 206
namus, 34
shame, 34
shame syndrome, 29
systems of gender relations,
   199
see also women's
girls(')
   dress, 31
   Hmong teenage, 260–64
   single, 39
   Turkish Cypriot, 48
   young Indian, 271
   young Shamanga, 287
global
   community, 304
   ethnoscape, 295
Greek, 53–76 *passim*
   Albanian, 58–61, 75
   costume, 54, 56, 61, 67, 75
   dress, 54–5, 62, 65, 68
      court, 61
      duluma (sleeveless dark
         woolen coat), 67–8
      ethnic, 62, 65, 68, 76
      foundi, 68
      foustanella (outfit with
         short full skirt), 59,
         60f3.1, 61, 63, 67–8, 75
      foustani (outer dress with
         full skirt), 53, 63, 70,
         72, 75
      gouna (sleeveless
         overgarment), 69
      kavadi (open coat with
         sleeves), 53
      national, 54, 61, 75
      panovraki (trousers), 63
      regional, 53–5, 62, 68–9,
         75–6
      sigouni (sleeveless coat),

314 **Index**

Kalabari, 139–61 *passim*, 165–
79 *passim*
ceremony
iria, 172–4, 176
iriabo, 172
cloth, 144, 156
injiri (Indian madras), 151,
172, 176
pelete bite (cut-thread
cloth), 146
dress, 143, 151–2, 155–6,
172
female, 170
iriabo, 176
pelete bite, 146, 170
male, 170, 170n8
attigra, 172
doni (chief's dress),
147–9, 156, 159, 170
ebu, 172
etibo (young men's
shirt), 147–9, 154,
170, 176
injiri wrapper, 176
woko (gentlemen's
dress), 147–9, 154,
156, 170
traditional, 154–6, 159
ethnicity, 143, 147, 152–3,
160–1
funeral, 174, 176–7, 178
identity, 139, 142–44, 152–3,
155–6, 159–61, 167–8

levels of the social formation,
theory of, 29

marriage,
civil, 198
customary, 198–9
inter-marriage, 58, 80,

90n15, 169, 186
also see Bunu (marriage)
also see Greek (marriage)
also see Japanese (marriage)
*also see Turkish Cypriot
(marriage)*
material culture, 207, 210, 216,
222, 264
missionaries, 303
migration
income, 274
Indian culture, 271
Koreans in Japan, 80–92
passim
Pakistani and Sikh, 30
seasonal workers, 276
Tuareg nomads in Niger, 275
Turkish Cypriots in London,
31–49 *passim*
modern, 74, 152
capitalist labor market, 275
changes in dress code, 273
clothing, 281–4
dress styles, 191–2
goods, 275
identity, 16–20
traditional and, 202
urban, 277
modernity, 27, 37, 48, 188–9,
191
modesty, 37, 42–3, 45, 186,
245–6
dress, 29, 30, 35

national heritage, 54
nationalism, 230
Palestinian, 243, 246
nationality, 65

Palestinian, 227–52 *passim*
costume, 231